Teaching Modern Languages

An essential resource for trainee teachers and graduate students, this textbook presents strategies and practical advice for preparing and planning lessons in a clear, step-by-step way and demonstrates how to inspire confidence and competence in language learners. Chapters cover many important aspects of initial teacher training including skills development, modes of teaching, unit and lesson planning, assessment, remote learning, digital literacy, and student and teacher well-being. Packed with pedagogical value, each chapter includes clear learning objectives, concise chapter summaries, defined key terms, interactive box features, reflective questions and further reading recommendations. Supplementary resources include templates for planning and assessment, feedforward and feedback forms, extra tasks and activities, and sample answers. By connecting theory and practice, this authoritative guide provides trainee teachers with the necessary tools to develop the knowledge, skills and methods required to become an effective modern languages teacher in the contemporary world.

Michael Lynch is Senior Lecturer in Language Studies at the University of Edinburgh and a principal fellow of the Higher Education Academy. He has been a teacher educator for several decades, is fluent in four languages, and regularly serves as an external examiner for initial teacher education programmes. He has contributed to the development of a national resource for languages through his work as a founder member of the Scottish Council of Deans of Education Languages Group and co-creator of the National Framework for Languages.

'*Teaching Modern Languages* is an essential read for student teachers, in-service teachers and teacher trainers alike. Michael Lynch's elegant and lively style helps to explain the intricacies of foreign language teaching, providing ample food for thought and a myriad of very practical examples that unlock a treasure trove of linguistic and didactic insights.'

Markus Wiesinger, Linz Private University of Education, Austria

'This groundbreaking book is an indispensable companion for educators at all stages of their careers. It masterfully bridges theory and practice, offering a comprehensive framework for effective teaching. A must-read that will inspire and empower teachers to create engaging, impactful learning environments. This resource is set to become a cornerstone in teacher education and professional development.'

Patricia Arnáiz Castro, University of Las Palmas de Gran Canaria, Spain

'This valuable book offers a comprehensive and practical guide for language educators. It bridges theory and classroom practice, equipping instructors with essential strategies for effective modern language teaching. Its structured approach, with a variety of useful supplementary resources, ensures accessibility for both new and experienced teachers, as well as teacher-trainers, making it a valuable resource for building linguistic proficiency and pedagogical excellence.'

Karen Ludke, Edge Hill University, UK

Teaching Modern Languages

Knowledge, Skills and Methods

Michael Lynch

University of Edinburgh

CAMBRIDGE
UNIVERSITY PRESS

Shaftesbury Road, Cambridge CB2 8EA, United Kingdom

One Liberty Plaza, 20th Floor, New York, NY 10006, USA

477 Williamstown Road, Port Melbourne, VIC 3207, Australia

314–321, 3rd Floor, Plot 3, Splendor Forum, Jasola District Centre,
New Delhi – 110025, India

103 Penang Road, #05–06/07, Visioncrest Commercial, Singapore 238467

Cambridge University Press is part of Cambridge University Press & Assessment,
a department of the University of Cambridge.

We share the University's mission to contribute to society through the pursuit of
education, learning and research at the highest international levels of excellence.

www.cambridge.org
Information on this title: www.cambridge.org/highereducation/isbn/9781009385190

DOI: 10.1017/9781009385183

First published 2025

Cover image: Javier Zayas Photography / Moment / Getty Images.

A catalogue record for this publication is available from the British Library

A Cataloging-in-Publication data record for this book is available from the Library of Congress

ISBN 978-1-009-38519-0 Hardback
ISBN 978-1-009-38516-9 Paperback

Additional resources for this publication at www.cambridge.org/lynch

Cambridge University Press & Assessment has no responsibility for the persistence
or accuracy of URLs for external or third-party internet websites referred to in this
publication and does not guarantee that any content on such websites is, or will remain,
accurate or appropriate.

To my wife, Rafaela, and to my children, Katharina, Michael and Philomena, who have always supported and encouraged me in all that I do. My grateful thanks for keeping me motivated while writing this book, and all my love.

Contents

List of Figures   *page* xv
List of Tables   xvi

1   Introduction   1
  1.1   Target Audiences   1
    1.1.1   Student Teachers   1
    1.1.2   Experienced Teachers   2
    1.1.3   Teacher Educators   2
  1.2   Why a Handbook for Student Teachers?   2
  1.3   The Structure of This Book   3
  1.4   How to Use This Book   6
    1.4.1   Read, Reflect and Discuss   7
    1.4.2   Approaching Notetaking   7
    1.4.3   Further Reading and Online Resources   8

2   Approaches to Language Teaching and Target Language Use   10
  Introduction   10
  Overview   10
  A Note on Terminology   10
  2.1   Approaches to the Learning and Teaching of Foreign Languages   11
    2.1.1   Grammar–Translation Approach   11
    2.1.2   Audio-lingual and Audiovisual Methods   12
    2.1.3   A Communicative Approach to Language Teaching   12
    2.1.4   Task-Based Language Teaching   17
    2.1.5   Content and Language Integrated Learning   17
    2.1.6   A Pluriliteracies Approach to Teaching for Learning (PTL)   18
    2.1.7   Common European Framework of Reference for Languages   19
  2.2   Cognitivism and Other Socially Oriented Approaches to Second
  Language Acquisition   19
  2.3   Post-Method Condition   20
  2.4   Purposes of Learning Foreign Languages   21
  2.5   How to Increase Exposure to the Target Language   22
    2.5.1   Issues to Consider in the Teaching of L2 Grammar   23
    2.5.2   Comparison of Two Different Approaches to the Teaching
    of Grammar   24
  2.6   Use of the Target Language, Code-Switching and Translanguaging   28
    2.6.1   Issues Surrounding the Use of the Target Language   28
    2.6.2   Code-Switching   29

2.7   Strategies to Support Teachers in Using the Target Language   31
    2.7.1 Perceived Problems in Using the Target Language in Class   31
    2.7.2 Strategies to Support the Use of the Target Language in Class   31
Summary   33
Reflective Questions   34
Key Terms   34
Further Reading   34

3   Skills Development   36
Introduction   36
Overview   36
3.1   Developing Skills in L2   37
    3.1.1 Developing Skills in Reading   37
    3.1.2 Developing Skills in Listening and Viewing   37
    3.1.3 Developing Skills in Speaking   38
    3.1.4 Developing Skills in Writing   39
3.2   Strategies for Developing Different Skills in the L2 Classroom   39
    3.2.1 Developing Listening Skills   39
    3.2.2 Developing Speaking Skills   42
    3.2.3 Developing Writing Skills   45
3.3   Developing Reading Skills   47
    3.3.1 The Sound–Symbol Relationship   48
    3.3.2 Problems in Developing Reading Skills in L2   48
    3.3.3 Development of Reading Strategies in L1   49
    3.3.4 Application of L1 Reading Strategies to Developing Reading
          Skills in L2   51
    3.3.5 Suggestions for Simple Reading Activities in L2   53
    3.3.6 Some Useful Apps and Sites for Online Games to Develop
          Reading   54
    3.3.7 Using Literary Texts in the Classroom   54
3.4   Multi-Skill and Multi-Task Activities   56
Summary   57
Reflective Questions   57
Key Terms   57
Further Reading   58

4   Modes of Teaching   59
Introduction   59
Overview   59
4.1   Exploration of Educational Theories   60
    4.1.1 Behaviourism   60
    4.1.2 Constructivism   60
    4.1.3 Social Constructivism   60
    4.1.4 Cognitive Apprenticeship   61

4.2	Modes of Teaching	61
	4.2.1 Features of Different Modes of Teaching	62
4.3	Using the Different Modes of Teaching in Class	65
	4.3.1 Issues to Consider in the Choice of Mode(s) of Teaching	65
	4.3.2 Influences on Teacher Choice of Approach or Teacher Cognition	66
	4.3.3 Modes of Teaching That Encourage Communication	67
4.4	Other Approaches to the Learning and Teaching of L2 That Promote Communication	71
	4.4.1 Resource-Based Learning	71
	4.4.2 Task-Based Language Teaching	71
	Summary	73
	Reflective Questions	74
	Key Terms	74
	Further Reading	75

5   Unit Planning   76

	Introduction	76
	Overview	76
5.1	Long-Term Planning	77
5.2	Rationale for Creating a Unit of Work	78
5.3	Developing a Unit of Work	79
	5.3.1 Needs Analysis	80
	5.3.2 The Title	80
	5.3.3 Aims of the Unit	80
	5.3.4 Functions	81
	5.3.5 Language Area	81
	5.3.6 Lexicon	81
	5.3.7 Grammar	82
	5.3.8 Activities and Games	83
	5.3.9 Keeping the Learner at the Centre	83
	5.3.10 Review and Revise	84
5.4	Use of Commercial Textbooks in Unit Planning	84
5.5	Ways of Approaching the Planning Process	85
5.6	Short-Term Planning	87
5.7	Progression and Coherence in Planning	91
	Summary	93
	Reflective Questions	93
	Key Terms	93
	Further Reading	94

6   Lesson Planning   95

	Introduction	95
	Overview	95

6.1   Principles of Successful Lesson Planning   96
    6.1.1   Promoting Self-Esteem   96
    6.1.2   Building on Prior Knowledge   97
    6.1.3   Making the Purpose of the Lesson Clear   97
    6.1.4   Supporting Learning   97
    6.1.5   Planning for Mixed Ability and Mixed Needs   98
    6.1.6   Assessment and Feedback   98
    6.1.7   Knowledge of Pedagogy   99
6.2   How to Plan Your Lesson   100
    6.2.1   Setting Objectives for Language Learning   101
    6.2.2   Writing Your Lesson Plan   101
6.3   Ways to Obtain Evaluative Feedback and Support Both before
      and after Your Lesson(s)   106
Summary   115
Reflective Questions   116
Key Terms   116
Further Reading   116

7   **Differentiation and Responding to Pupils' Needs**   117
Introduction   117
Overview   117
7.1   Why Differentiate?   118
7.2   Differentiation Strategies   119
    7.2.1   Differentiation by Length, Presentation and Density of Text   120
    7.2.2   Differentiation by Support   120
    7.2.3   Differentiation by Outcome   121
    7.2.4   Differentiation by Task   121
    7.2.5   Differentiation by Questioning   122
    7.2.6   Learning Styles   123
    7.2.7   Some Useful Online Sites and Digital Tools   124
7.3   Additional Support Needs and How to Respond to Them   125
    7.3.1   Dyslexia   126
    7.3.2   Dyscalculia   126
    7.3.3   Visual Impairment   127
    7.3.4   Hearing Impairment   128
    7.3.5   Mobility Issues   128
    7.3.6   Emotional Issues   129
    7.3.7   Mode of Teaching   129
    7.3.8   An Inclusive Approach   130
7.4   Information and Communications Technology and Digital Tools
      to Support Learners with Additional Support Needs   130
    7.4.1   Vision   131
    7.4.2   Hearing   131
    7.4.3   Neurodiversity   131

       7.4.4 Mobility   131
       7.4.5 Mental Health   131
   7.5 Overarching Teacher Skills for Effective Differentiation   132
   Summary   133
   Reflective Questions   133
   Key Terms   133
   Further Reading   133

8 Assessment *of*, *for* and *as* Learning in Modern Foreign Languages   135
   Introduction   135
   Overview   135
   8.1 Connection between Learning and Assessment   136
   8.2 Choosing between Summative and Formative Assessment   136
       8.2.1 Features and Use of Summative Assessment Strategies   139
       8.2.2 Features and Use of Formative Assessment Strategies   140
   8.3 Relationship between Assessment *of*, *for* and *as* Learning in Modern Foreign Languages   146
       8.3.1 Assessment *of* Learning   146
       8.3.2 Assessment *for* Learning   146
       8.3.3 Assessment *as* Learning   146
   8.4 Developing Metacognitive Strategies in Assessment   147
       8.4.1 Role of the Learner in Developing Metacognitive Strategies   147
       8.4.2 Role of the Teacher in Developing Metacognitive Strategies in Learners   147
   8.5 Providing Learners with Feedback on Their Learning and Recording Their Progress   148
       8.5.1 Giving Feedback on Learning   148
       8.5.2 Record Keeping   149
   Summary   150
   Reflective Questions   151
   Further Reading   151

9 Digital Literacy   152
   Introduction   152
   Overview   152
   9.1 Importance of Digital Literacy   152
       9.1.1 Digital Literacy: A Definition   153
       9.1.2 Types of Online Sources   153
   9.2 Safety Online   155
       9.2.1 Use of Social Media   156
   9.3 Digital Literacy Issues for Modern Foreign Languages Teachers   156
       9.3.1 Respecting Owners' Rights   157
       9.3.2 Appropriateness of Content   157

9.4   Developing Knowledge and Skills in Digital Literacy   160
9.5   What Is Useful and How and When to Use It   161
Summary   162
Reflective Questions   162
Key Terms   162
Further Reading   162

10   Remote Learning, Teaching and Assessment   163
Introduction   163
Overview   163
10.1   Models of Remote Delivery   164
    10.1.1   Synchronous Learning and Teaching   164
    10.1.2   Asynchronous Learning and Teaching   165
    10.1.3   Hybrid Learning and Teaching   165
    10.1.4   Virtual Learning Environments (VLEs)   166
10.2   Advice for Remote Learning, Teaching and Assessment   167
    10.2.1   Advice for Synchronous Teaching   167
    10.2.2   Advice for Asynchronous Teaching   169
10.3   Choosing between Synchronous and Asynchronous Modes
    of Learning and Teaching   171
10.4   Practical Considerations for Schools on Remote Learning,
    Teaching and Assessment   172
10.5   Points to Note in Planning Lessons Involving Remote
    Learning, Teaching and Assessment   172
    10.5.1   Inclusion of Remote Learning, Teaching and Assessment
        for Pedagogical Reasons   174
    10.5.2   Inclusion of Remote Learning, Teaching and Assessment
        Due to External Factors   175
Summary   176
Reflective Questions   176
Further Reading   176

11   Drama, Music and Games   177
Introduction   177
Overview   177
11.1   Drama as a Tool in L2 Learning and Teaching   178
    11.1.1   Why Drama Is Useful in L2 Learning   178
    11.1.2   Drama Techniques for the L2 Classroom   179
11.2   Music and Song in L2 Learning and Teaching   181
    11.2.1   Ways in Which Music and Song Can Aid L2 Learning   181
    11.2.2   Contribution of Music and Song to Aspects of L2 Learning   181
11.3   Place of Games in L2 Learning and Teaching   182
    11.3.1   Why Games Are Useful in L2 Learning   183

	11.3.2 Games and Activities for the L2 Classroom	183
	11.3.3 Issues to Consider When Using Games in Class	185
Summary		186
Reflective Questions		187
Key Terms		187
Further Reading		187

12 Organisation and Management   189
Introduction   189
Overview   189
12.1 Effective Classroom Organisation and Management   190
  12.1.1 Creating Effective Learning Opportunities   190
12.2 Benefits of Carousel GroupWork   193
  12.2.1 Skills Practice   193
  12.2.2 Differentiation   193
  12.2.3 Teaching of Grammar   194
  12.2.4 Assessment   194
  12.2.5 Classroom Management   194
  12.2.6 Behaviour Management   194
12.3 Working Collaboratively with Colleagues   195
12.4 An Examination of Behaviour Management, What Causes
    Disruption and How to Prevent It   196
  12.4.1 Causes of Disruption   196
  12.4.2 Preventing Disruption   197
  12.4.3 What to Do When Disruption Occurs   198
12.5 A Restorative Approach to Behaviour Management   199
  12.5.1 Features of Restorative Practice   200
Summary   200
Reflective Questions   201
Further Reading   201

13 Collaboration and Professional Development   202
Introduction   202
Overview   202
13.1 The Importance of Continuing Professional Development   203
13.2 Maintaining Knowledge and Skills   203
  13.2.1 Keeping Abreast of Current Research   206
  13.2.2 Keeping Abreast of Curriculum Developments   207
  13.2.3 Examples of Professional Learning   207
13.3 Collaborative Networks and Opportunities for Networking   209
  13.3.1 Local Networks   209
  13.3.2 National Networks   210
  13.3.3 International Networks and Programmes   210

13.4　The Importance of Teacher Well-Being   212
　　13.4.1　Factors That Contribute to Poor Self-Efficacy   212
　　13.4.2　Building Emotional Resilience   213
　　13.4.3　How and Where to Find Support   214
Summary   215
Reflective Questions   215
Key Terms   216
Further Reading   216
Appendix 13.1   217

References   218
Index   229

Figures

1.1	An example of how OneNote can be set up as an electronic PDP	*page* 9
2.1	A child communicating through making discomfort sounds	13
2.2	A child communicating through making pleasure sounds	14
2.3	A child babbling	14
2.4	A child at the holophrastic stage	14
2.5	A child at the two-word stage	15
2.6	A child displaying evidence of the telegraphic stage	15
2.7	A child displaying speech beyond the telegraphic stage	15
2.8	A diary page in French of the current week	26
2.9	A diary page in French of the previous week	27
5.1	An example of a spider diagram approach to unit planning	86
5.2	An alternative layout for planning a unit of work	86
5.3	An approach to unit planning using step boxes as a unit planning template	87
6.1	A suggested lesson planning cycle	100
6.2	An extract from the start of a lesson plan	103
6.3	An extract from the middle of a lesson plan	104
6.4	An at-a-glance summary of the main steps in lesson planning	107
6.5	Sources of evaluative feedback	108
10.1	An example of a launch page for an online language learning course	166
12.1	A graphical representation of what a carousel group work setting in an L2 class might look like	195
13.1	A graphical representation of how multiple support networks relate to each other	211
13.2	A tired and stressed teacher at a desk	212

Tables

1.1	An example of a weekly development sheet to record action points and reflections on progress	*page* 8
2.1	Socially oriented approaches to SLA	20
2.2	An example of a note consolidating structures in the past tense in French	28
4.1	A summary of the features of Direct Teaching	62
4.2	A summary of the features of Discussion	63
4.3	A summary of the features of Activity Learning	63
4.4	A summary of the features of Enquiry	64
5.1	An example long-term plan for a first year language class at a secondary school	78
5.2	An example of using a grid planning template to design a unit of work	87
5.3	A tabular approach to planning a unit of work	88
5.4	An example of a first short-term plan for a unit of work in a sequence of short-term plans	89
5.5	An example of a second short-term plan for a unit of work in a sequence of short-term plans	90
6.1	An example of learning intentions and corresponding success criteria	99
6.2	An at-a-glance checklist of things to consider when planning your lessons	109
6.3	A checklist for writing draft lesson plans	110
6.4	A suggested lesson plan template	112
6.5	A feedforward sheet for mentors	113
6.6	A lesson feedback sheet	114
6.7	A self-evaluation sheet	115
7.1	Different task types and examples	122
7.2	Different question types and examples	123
8.1	An example of typical mark ranges for summative assessments	137
8.2	Extract from the modern foreign languages experiences and outcomes in the Scottish Curriculum for Excellence	138
8.3	Formative assessment techniques for the modern foreign languages classroom	142
8.4	Self-assessment strategies for pupils	144
8.5	Peer-assessment strategies	145
8.6	An example of a Pupil Record Sheet	149
10.1	Giving feedback on image files or PDFs	170
10.2	Giving oral feedback to pupils	170

10.3 Potential benefits of different models of remote learning, teaching   173
and assessment (LTA)
10.4 Factors influencing choice of different models of remote learning,   173
teaching and assessment (LTA)
13.1 Steps in the professional learning process   204
13.2 An at-a-glance audit of areas of strength and areas of concern   205
13.3 An example of a planning and review sheet to record professional   206
learning

1 Introduction

1.1 Target Audiences

This textbook is primarily aimed at student teachers of modern foreign languages (MFL), to provide them with the advice and strategies they need for each step of their initial teacher education. It is hoped that the book will also be of interest to serving teachers and teacher educators.

1.1.1 Student Teachers

There are many programmes and courses of initial teacher education (ITE) for modern foreign languages (MFL), and these vary in scope and length from country to country and indeed sometimes within a country. In the UK, the most widely offered courses are the Professional Graduate Diploma in Education in Scotland (PGDE) and the Postgraduate Certificate in Education in England, Wales and Northern Ireland (PGCE), which last typically for one academic year, that is, two university semesters. There are other variations, for example Teach First, offered in England and Wales, where teachers enter the classroom after a six-week summer camp. In addition, some universities offer ITE courses across a four-year undergraduate BA degree programme, where subject knowledge and content are studied together with education courses across the four-year programme.

Each of these ITE courses seeks to provide student teachers with a grounding in basic pedagogy for the subject area and to explore educational topics. In addition, these ITE courses try to give strategies for management of the classroom, developing resources and activities, as well as looking at how to respond to a wide range of abilities and educational needs. Within a typical one-year 36-week PGDE or PGCE programme, student teachers will have eighteen weeks of contact time at university, with the other eighteen weeks being spent trying out their craft in different placement schools.

As a result, there is often limited time to spend on each section of the course before student teachers go out on placement and try to put ideas and advice into practice. This means there is little opportunity in a busy academic year to revisit areas and to reflect upon progress. What this book provides is advice and guidance on many important aspects of language teaching to accompany student teachers of modern languages during their initial teacher education, which they can return to time and again as they seek to develop their craft.

1.1.2   Experienced Teachers

This book, however, is not only for student teachers. Teachers in post will find this book a valuable resource and source of reference to review and refresh their knowledge and skills, whether this is to look at particular parts of MFL pedagogy, part of a programme of professional update of particular or specialised areas, or a general revision of their craft.

1.1.3   Teacher Educators

By bringing together in one volume the knowledge, skills and pedagogy for each important stage of development for student teachers of MFL, this book may be useful as a resource for teacher educators of MFL upon which to base or supplement their programmes of initial teacher education for modern foreign languages.

1.2   Why a Handbook for Student Teachers?

Whichever route students have chosen to become modern foreign languages teachers, the majority will have completed an undergraduate language degree at university focusing for the most part on the language, literature and culture of the country or countries where this language is spoken. Some students may have observed or helped out in school settings or have been involved in some youth work during their studies. This is useful preparation, as it demonstrates a commitment to working with young people. However, unless the undergraduate degree has included courses in educational topics, most students will start their course of teacher education with little knowledge of educational theories and approaches.

In this digital age where access to information is readily available via a simple mouse click, it is easy to find advice from online sources throughout the world on how to teach languages. There are websites with information on every aspect of language teaching, such as vocabulary, grammar, classroom management, assessment, or where to find ready-made resources for the classroom. However, a lot of this is often offered in a bite-sized 'tips for teachers' format, sometimes without examining why a particular approach may be useful.

Having used a variety of resources, some commercial, some my own, I have not come across a textbook specifically designed with the *practical needs* of student teachers in mind. Many books will study approaches to the learning and teaching of modern languages in great detail, which is useful, but often this is explored at a deep theoretical level, and is more suited to thesis writing for a Master's or higher degree. I have tried with this book, therefore, to offer a guide that will accompany student teachers throughout their course(s) of initial teacher education in modern languages and hopefully into their early years as language teachers. As such, this book focuses on the practical aspects of the job of a language teacher. The chapters in this book will provide an introduction to different aspects of a language teacher's role, with advice and guidance for further development while working in the foreign language classroom. The areas explored in each chapter are the areas I have observed over the years and consider to be the most relevant to modern foreign languages teachers. At the same time, the advice and guidance are based on research-informed theory and practice and referenced where appropriate, while still remaining accessible.

The major focus of this book is to help beginning teachers master the craft of teaching modern languages in schools and gain a better understanding of what they are doing and why they are doing it. This is intended to aid them in giving their pupils the confidence and competence in learning and using the language studied to find joy in becoming effective and successful communicators in the language.

Although this book concentrates on the teaching of modern languages for students who typically teach in contexts where English is the national or home language, it is hoped that the advice will also be useful for teachers training to teach English as a Foreign Language (EFL) in other countries, for example in Europe, Asia and anywhere that English is taught as a foreign language in schools. Indeed, it is hoped that the advice contained in this book will help modern foreign languages teachers anywhere, regardless of the home language or the modern language taught.

What the chapters in this book do *not* do is provide a comprehensive examination of the multitude of theories of language learning and teaching that abound (Second Language Acquisition [SLA], Complexity theory, Sociolinguistic approaches to SLA, etc.). To do so would require a much lengthier text that is not within the scope of this book. Instead, advice will be given for follow-up reading and deeper study of the chapter content at the end of each chapter.

1.3   The Structure of This Book

The choice of the order of the chapters has been based on a perception of what student teachers may find most useful. That said, depending on the structure of ITE courses that students follow at their ITE institutions or providers, students may find it more useful to look at a particular chapter or chapters out of this order if it suits the focus of their study. Depending on the topics covered, some chapters may be longer than others.

Chapter 2: Approaches to Language Teaching and Target Language Use

Chapter 2 examines a range of approaches in foreign language learning and teaching and the features of each one. The chapter provides an analysis of common perceived problems in language teaching, notably in using the target language, and explores strategies to help teachers in their use of the target language in class.

Chapter 3: Skills Development

Chapter 3 looks at how to develop the individual skills of listening, speaking, reading and writing in the MFL classroom, as well as how and when to use multi-skill and multi-task activities with learners.

Chapter 4: Modes of Teaching

Chapter 4 provides an examination of the range of teaching modes: the direct, discursive, individual, pair, collaborative and group approaches used in MFL learning and teaching and when it may be appropriate to use each of these.

Chapter 5: Unit Planning

A necessary pre-cursor to planning lessons is knowing how to develop an appropriate learning programme. Chapter 5 therefore provides advice and guidance on how to develop age- and stage-appropriate schemes of work and unit plans aimed at providing progression for specific groups of learners.

Chapter 6: Lesson Planning

Building on the preceding four chapters, Chapter 6 covers in detail all aspects of lesson planning, including vital pre-planning stages, core elements of planning and important post-lesson aspects.

Chapter 7: Differentiation and Responding to Pupils' Needs

Having looked at theories of language learning and modes of teaching in Chapters 2 and 4 and unit and lesson planning in Chapters 5 and 6, Chapter 7 takes a detailed look at how to plan for and manage differentiation in the language class and why this is so important. This chapter also gives valuable advice on responding to pupils' additional support needs and collaborative working with other experts in that field.

Chapter 8: Assessment *of, for* and *as* Learning in Modern Foreign Languages

The connection between learning and assessment is examined in Chapter 8, which includes approaches and strategies for using both formative and summative assessment. How to plan for and manage assessment *of* learners' progress is examined in detail with practical advice on how to do this in a structured way appropriate to the needs of different groups of learners across a range of classes and year groups.

Chapter 9: Digital Literacy

Chapter 9 explores the subject of digital literacy, what this means for the student teacher in a MFL classroom, and how the student teacher can best develop their knowledge and skills in this area. The chapter looks at the benefits and usefulness of technology in modern foreign language learning and teaching, discusses how and when to use it, and highlights important caveats and common pitfalls.

Chapter 10: Remote Learning, Teaching and Assessment

Chapter 10 looks in detail at remote learning, teaching and assessment. Developing these skills has become particularly important in recent years due to the Covid-19 pandemic, when teachers and pupils had to adapt to new ways of learning brought about by lockdowns and school closures. This chapter examines different models of remote delivery – synchronous, asynchronous and hybrid – in terms of pedagogical principles, and looks at the benefits and drawbacks of each approach in the learning, teaching and assessment of modern foreign languages. Practical steps and advice on how to prepare for remote learning, teaching and assessment are given. It has proven vital for teachers to be ready for possible future interruptions to learning and teaching programmes and these approaches can be valuable alternatives to conventional teaching. In addition, this chapter looks at how to use a number of the digital tools and platforms currently available to teachers and learners.

Chapter 11: Drama, Music and Games

Modern foreign languages have always been known for their interdisciplinary nature. The typical MFL curriculum in any school encompasses a wide range of topics and lends itself to embedding other subject disciplines in modern foreign language learning. It is not surprising, therefore, that drama and music are used widely in MFL teaching. Chapter 11 focuses on how the skills and competencies necessary for successful language learning can be developed in the language classroom through the use of drama, music and games.

Chapter 12: Organisation and Management

For student teachers, developing good classroom organisation and management skills is essential, as well as understanding how to maintain a safe, positive and interactive ethos in class. Chapter 12 looks at the importance of classroom organisation and management in terms of resources, materials and equipment, and how to maintain a safe and orderly environment in the MFL class that is conducive to successful learning. This chapter also looks at how to create and maintain a restorative approach to behaviour management in the classroom, while promoting successful student–teacher relationships and academic engagement.

Chapter 13: Collaboration, Professional Development and Teacher Well-Being

The final chapter of this book emphasises the importance for student teachers, and for all involved in education, of maintaining one's teaching skills and of keeping abreast of current research and curriculum developments in the learning and teaching of modern foreign languages. Chapter 13 looks at sources of development available to student teachers, as well as giving advice on how to work collaboratively with colleagues locally, nationally and internationally to enhance learning and teaching. Links are given to sources of further information and advice on a range of opportunities available to teachers to help them with their career-long professional learning (CLPL). This chapter will also examine the important area of teacher well-being: guidance and advice are provided on how students can build their own emotional resilience, preparing them for a career in the classroom with details of how and where to find support for their own mental health and well-being.

1.4 How to Use This Book

To help students get the most out of this book, I have adopted a standard approach across each of the chapters. At the beginning of each chapter, there are learning objectives, each being the subject of a different section within the chapter. A short overview of the chapter follows the list of learning objectives, and each chapter ends with a short summary of the main points examined in the chapter. Key terms are highlighted in **bold** and *italic* is used for emphasis. Within each chapter there are two types of boxed activities. The features of these boxed activities are as follows:

FOOD FOR THOUGHT

As the name implies, this type of activity asks students to reflect on an aspect, or aspects, of the topic of a particular section(s) of the chapter.

TRY THIS OUT

This type of box invites students to carry out a task or activity introduced in a particular section(s) of the chapter.

These two types of interactive tasks encourage students to engage with the subject matter more critically – 'to think outside the box' – and to enhance their knowledge and skills.

As the term 'teacher education' implies, courses of ITE are not about 'training' students to learn from an 'expert' and then apply this knowledge and these skills as best they can in the classroom. It is rather about introducing students to ideas and theories and encouraging them to take a critical, analytical stance vis-à-vis what they are exposed to. Students should be reflective and inquiring with regards to what they encounter on courses, and the same applies to this book. The goal of courses of ITE should be to help students to develop and become reflective practitioners, since in this way they will become transformative teachers. To this end, each chapter poses reflective questions designed to make students think more deeply and critically about pedagogy.

1.4.1   Read, Reflect and Discuss

To aid the process of reflection and critical analysis expected of them, student teachers are advised to allocate time to reading each chapter regularly. This may coincide with areas being looked at as part of the ITE programme on which they are studying, or as part of a mentoring programme in a school where they are undertaking a placement, or where they may be employed as part of a non-university-based programme of initial teacher education or teacher training.

While reading chapters, or sections within chapters, student teachers are advised to take notes of the main points and write down questions they may have, or general comments and reflections. These notes will be very useful when discussing with ITE tutors, teacher mentors or other student teachers any areas that they find difficult or confusing. Discussion of points, comments and reflections they have made will not only help individual students or novice teachers in developing their *own* understanding and skills, but will also help *other* student teachers with whom they discuss these issues, since they may be struggling with the same areas too.

1.4.2   Approaching Notetaking

There are a number of ways in which student teachers can organise and structure their thoughts and writings on sections and chapters. Here are a number of ways in which to go about this.

1.4.2.1   Professional Development Portfolios

Many ITE providers require student teachers to maintain a *Professional Development Portfolio* (*PDP*), sometimes called a *Teaching File*, in which they ask students to collate notes on areas studied, lesson plans, feedback on classes taught on placement and weekly reflections or diaries on their progress. A PDP is an excellent way to organise your studies, experiences and reflections in a coherent and cohesive manner, since it can be shared with other students, tutors and mentors whether this is required by tutors or not. Table 1.1 is an example of how student teachers can design a template to set themselves action points and to record their weekly reflections and progress to include in their PDP. Some action points may be general, applying to all classes, and some points may be specific to a certain class or classes. Some italicised sections in Table 1.1 have been filled in as an illustration.

1.4.2.2   Digital Solutions

Universities and educational bodies are increasingly adopting a digital approach to maintaining a PDP, using digital tools and applications that enable easy collaboration. This makes the process of asking for and receiving feedforward advice and feedback on work straightforward and user-friendly. Applications and services such

Table 1.1 An example of a weekly development sheet to record action points and reflections on progress

Modern Foreign Language:	e.g. *Italian*	Weekly development sheet	Week no:
Student Name:		Date (w/b):	School Name:
Target (You may add your own titles to this column)	Target influence	Action required	Progress and development
Learning and Teaching	*Presenting aims clearly*	*Write aims on board/ slide/worksheet and draw pupils' attention to these*	*Achieved a measure of success with most classes, who found this useful in focusing their attention*
	Develop differentiation strategies	*Provide tasks at different levels of ability for 3rd year class*	*Pupils found it helpful having tasks at their level*
		Develop reading texts for 1st year at different levels (less/more dense text; change language used depending on group)	*Worked well with class*
Assessment			
Class organisation and management			
Whole school			

You can view and download this table at www.cambridge.org/lynch.

as Microsoft OneNote, Padlet, Wakelet, Evernote, Zoho Notebook, Microsoft Teams, WikidPad and OpenNote all provide opportunities to create, store and share information. For a number of these services, the user must grant access to people with whom they wish to share information. Some of these applications and services require each person requiring access to install the app on their device(s) or to create an account, whilst others do not. Figure 1.1 is an example of how OneNote, or similar tools, can be set up as an electronic PDP with different tabs for different sections of the PDP.

1.4.3   Further Reading and Online Resources

At the end of each chapter, I have made suggestions for further reading on the relevant topics covered within the chapter. This is sometimes to give students more practice in certain areas introduced in the chapter, or to indicate useful texts or articles that explore ideas, concepts and approaches from the chapter in greater

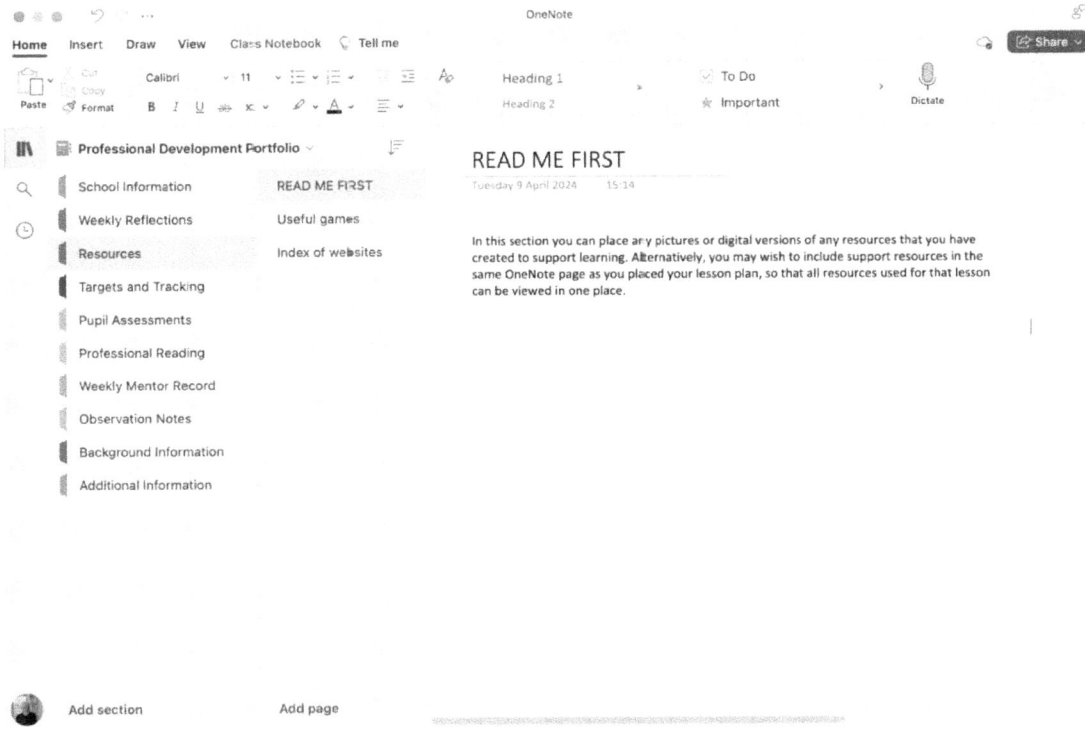

Figure 1.1 An example of how OneNote can be set up as an electronic PDP

depth. The website which accompanies this book offers additional materials and resources to supplement this book, for example:

- additional examples of lessons or parts of lessons;
- additional tasks and activities to try out;
- possible responses to questions asked in the chapters;
- templates for lesson plans, reflection, observation, feedback.

The supplementary resources for this book can be found at: www.cambridge.org/lynch

2 Approaches to Language Teaching and Target Language Use

Introduction

In this chapter we will look at several approaches to language learning and teaching with a view to establishing which may be effective. The importance of the use of the target language in class will be explored, as well as code-switching and translanguaging.

The learning objectives for this chapter are, therefore, as follows:

1. Examine and evaluate approaches to the learning and teaching of foreign languages.
2. Consider the difference between cognitive and socially oriented approaches to Second Language Acquisition.
3. Determine whether language teaching is post-method.
4. Consider the purposes of learning foreign languages.
5. Determine how to increase exposure to the target language for learners.
6. Examine the use of the target language in class, code-switching and translanguaging.
7. Consider strategies to support teachers in using the target language.

Overview

This chapter examines historical and current approaches to the learning and teaching of foreign languages and considers the features of each approach. The meaning of the term 'post-method' and whether we are now in a period that can be regarded as such will also be examined. This leads on to a consideration of why we learn foreign languages. A very important aspect of foreign language learning and teaching is how to increase exposure to the target language and how to promote its use amongst pupils. Through analysis of common perceived problems associated with language teaching, advice will be given to help teachers develop strategies to stay in, or increase their use of, the target language.

A Note on Terminology

Although there is debate amongst teachers and researchers regarding the terminology to use when discussing languages, I have chosen to use the terms student teachers will come across most frequently in literature around modern languages teaching, namely *L1, L2, target language, own* or *home language*, often using these interchangeably. The meaning each time will be clear from the context.

2.1 Approaches to the Learning and Teaching of Foreign Languages

In this section I shall introduce some influential approaches used to teach foreign languages over the years to try to give an overview of the pedagogical landscape that has been the background to the learning and teaching of modern languages in schools, particularly with reference to the use of the foreign language in class. There is, of course, a volume of literature on different approaches to the learning and teaching of modern languages, indeed whole books have been dedicated to individual approaches. This chapter does not seek to replace these books or studies, but to highlight key points and areas that student teachers will hopefully find useful and practical in their teaching.

2.1.1 Grammar–Translation Approach

The **Grammar–Translation (GT) Approach** (or **Method**) has been very popular in language classes over many years. This method consists of giving learners an understanding of how a foreign language system works rather than how to use it for communicative purposes (Richards & Rodgers, 2001). The method focuses a lot on learning grammatical rules and vocabulary and using the metalanguage to describe the language rather than facilitate communicative learning (Natsir & Sanjaya, 2014). Although classroom activities, grammar drills and translation exercises are conducted in the foreign language, speaking is disregarded in the Grammar–Translation Approach as the emphasis is on reading and writing. Teaching and learning focus on individual language points and accuracy and 'grammar itself becomes the purpose of learning' (Hall, 2011: 82). As such this approach does not meet the needs of the majority of learners in schools (Omaggio, 1990).

The Grammar–Translation Approach is favoured by some researchers as the structure of the language in L2 can be compared with that of L1 (Butzkamm, 2003; Cook, 2001; Pachler & Field, 2001). However, although this method may help the learners understand how a foreign language works, they are not using it for real communication (Richards & Rodgers, 2001), so are not involved in using the L2 actively for any communicative purpose. Teachers using this method often believe it is quicker to use L1 to explain grammar and that this ensures comprehension. The 'explanatory' approach is very traditional with the result that teachers just give declarative knowledge of grammar rules, rather than approach the teaching of grammar in a communicative manner that would foster learners' procedural L2 knowledge (Lynch, 2015). This emphasis on grammar explanations leaves the learners with a bank of grammatical rules, but without any context. Learners taught in this manner need to decide what they want to say, think of the rules, and apply them to their situation. This usually produces stilted and hesitant speech and is counter-productive to developing communicative ability and fluency. Despite being overtaken by other approaches, features of the Grammar–Translation Approach can still be seen in many L2 classrooms (Matamoros-González et al., 2017).

2.1.2 Audio-lingual and Audiovisual Methods

Audio-lingualism, which gave birth to the audio-lingual method, originates from research on learning concerned with behaviourist psychology and was popular in the 1970s and early 1980s. In accordance with behaviourism, this method considers learning as a process of habit formation and students learn by drills and memorisation of the target language patterns (Chang, 2011). In the audio-lingual classroom dialogues and drills form the basic practices. In a word, this method promotes the principle of 'practice makes perfect'. The audio-lingual method was actually a reaction against the traditional Grammar–Translation Approach in that it prioritises the skills of listening and speaking rather than reading and writing. The audio-lingual method subsequently gave rise to the audiovisual method, in which film strips and tape-recorded dialogues were used as a basis for drills to practise structures. A problem with this method is that students are not encouraged to initiate the interaction. What they are required to do in the class is respond to the stimuli given by the instructor, in a habit-forming manner, which means students are put in a passive position that may in turn be demotivating. There is criticism that the habit formation does not happen as fast through a series of mere drills (Krashen & Terrell, 1988). Another criticism is that drilling leads students simply to memorise patterns in short-term memory without internalising knowledge.

2.1.3 A Communicative Approach to Language Teaching

Perhaps the most discussed approach to modern language teaching is Communicative Language Teaching (CLT). Sometimes also termed the **communicative approach** (CA), CLT aims to use the **target language** (TL) as much as possible as the means of communication in the classroom, while also addressing the need to understand the grammar of the language (Lightbown & Spada, 2006; Matamoros-González et al., 2017). Generally, researchers divide CLT into two versions: a 'strong' version where language is learned through extensive use, with grammar being learnt inductively, and a 'weak' version that provides opportunities for using language for communicative purposes and includes a focus on grammar. Long (1991) refers to this difference as 'focus on form' (strong version) and 'focus on forms' (weak version).

If we want the pupils in our schools to be successful foreign language learners, then we need to look at how children acquire their first language and what we can emulate from that. After all, this process has shown itself to be very successful in helping us *all* to master our first language. CLT borrows a lot from what we know about how learners acquire their first language, so it follows that an understanding of this process will be of value to modern foreign languages teachers.

2.1.3.1   Stages of L1 Acquisition

It is helpful to look at this in stages. Although there is no such thing as 'an average child', each child can be said to go through the same stages of language learning, although the times at which the various stages happen may vary slightly. The process is a progression the child goes through from a baby to a toddler. There is debate as to the age and range attributed to these stages: those outlined below are a broad approximation of what happens in the different phases and at what times in the infant's linguistic development.

The Pre-Language Phase The first three stages are what is known as the pre-language phase. This is where children do not have developed language skills, communicating instead with sounds. The first stage of pre-language is often characterised by discomfort sounds and typically occurs between the ages of 0–2 months, as in Figure 2.1 below.

This is followed by the second stage where the baby, in addition to making discomfort sounds when in pain, adds pleasure sounds, usually at age 2–4 months (see Figure 2.2).

After this, the third stage is babbling, where the child thinks they are saying something intelligible, but it is really a stream of sounds, as in Figure 2.3. This occurs usually between 4 and 9 months.

The Language Stages Later, at age 9–18 months, comes the holophrastic, or one-word stage, where the child is starting to build a phoneme system (see Figure 2.4).

Then comes the two-word (or two-phrase) stage, usually when the child is between 18 months and two and a half years (see Figure 2.5).

Typically, at the age of two and a half years to four years old, the child is acquiring patterns of speech, or grammar, expanding their vocabulary and completing the phoneme system. This is known as the telegraphic stage (see Figure 2.6).

Beyond the telegraphic stage, at approximately four to six years, the child acquires a much better knowledge of adult grammar and syntax (see Figure 2.7) and is basically fluent in their mother tongue, at least in terms of listening and speaking, before they go to school, or even nursery school.

Figure 2.1 A child communicating through making discomfort sounds

Figure 2.2 A child communicating through making pleasure sounds

Figure 2.3 A child babbling

Figure 2.4 A child at the holophrastic stage

Caretaker Speech Now this is all pretty wonderful, but it is not happening in a vacuum. The person taking care of the child (the caretaker or the caregiver) plays a very important role. As the child moves through these stages, the caretaker (usually the mother, father or guardian) is providing invaluable stimulus and input to the child. This takes many forms; for example, the caretaker will ask frequent questions ('Do you want some soup? Do you want to go for a walk?') often using very exaggerated intonation, gesticulation to help convey the meaning, and lots of repetition. In

Figure 2.5 A child at the two-word stage

Figure 2.6 A child displaying evidence of the telegraphic stage

Figure 2.7 A child displaying speech beyond the telegraphic stage

addition, instead of using normal words, they will often use special forms, what we call 'baby talk', for example 'tummy' instead of 'stomach' and 'walkies' instead of 'walk'. Caretakers will also use simple sounds for objects, for example 'choo choo' for a train, and sentence structures are kept very simple, for example 'You want to go walkies? You want some soup?' Along with these simple questions, caretakers are also answering for the child, for example 'You want to go walkies? Yes Mummy, I want to go walkies! You want some soup? Yes Daddy, I want some soup!', thereby modelling the answers for the child, even though the caretaker will not expect the child to answer at this stage. What the caretaker has done is to assign an interactive role to the child before they have become a speaking participant. From birth onwards, the child is being showered with input, as those nearest to the child continually interact with the child in the ways I have described above. This input is made comprehensible for the child, for example the caretaker may hold up objects in front of the child – a soup dish or a cup – when asking 'Do you want some soup/tea?' and make gestures to accompany what they are saying. What is more, the child does not need to speak until they are ready, which is known as the 'right to be silent'. Parents often get worried if their child does not seem to be speaking, when their friends' children are doing so already. I always reassure parents that this is normal, that their son or daughter will speak when they are ready. When they do begin to speak, this is not the beginning of their language learning, it is testimony to all the language they have acquired up to that point.

And if the child makes a mistake when speaking (and children appear to do this a lot when they speak), parents do not scold the child. Instead, they use praise, happy that the child is speaking, and model the correct answer. For example, if a child says 'Mummy, I rided my bike', the mother will typically reply 'Well done, I rode my bike, too!' In this way, the mother has modelled the correct answer without any disapproval of the mistake the child has made. The child may continue to make this mistake for some time to come, but due to continually hearing the right version, the child will soon acquire this correct form and use it appropriately. You could say that all parents (caregivers) are latent language teachers, without having done any form of teacher training. They do this instinctively and it all feels natural.

2.1.3.2 Features of L1 Acquisition used in CLT

In CLT, we replicate a number of features of first language acquisition. Teachers using CLT employ gesture, mime, images and props to convey meaning, as well as *Total Physical Response* techniques (encourages physical movement as reaction to verbal phrases or instructions). Language is made understandable to the learner through these techniques, which provide large amounts of comprehensible input (Krashen, 1985). Teachers also use frequent repetition: they employ simple phrases that progressively move to more complex phrases and structures as learners develop their competence and confidence in the new language. This language is set in authentic contexts with realistic tasks requiring real language to be used. In addition, teachers maintain a sympathetic attitude to error, confident that errors will eventually be replaced by accurate usage.

When teaching using a communicative approach, it is helpful to examine Ellis's ten principles of instructed language learning (Ellis, 2005). Ellis proposes a model for reconciling sociolinguistic and psycholinguistic factors, where learners feel free to express themselves in the foreign language at the same time as becoming aware of the language's structure. An adaptation of the ten principles is given in Box 2.1.

> **Box 2.1** An adaptation of Ellis's ten principles of instructed language learning
>
> 1. Instruction needs to ensure that learners develop both a rich repertoire of formulaic expressions and a rule-based competence.
> 2. Instruction needs to ensure that learners also focus on form.
> 3. Instruction needs to be predominantly directed at developing implicit knowledge of the L2 while not neglecting explicit knowledge.
> 4. Instruction needs to take into account the learner's 'built-in syllabus'.
> 5. Successful instructed language learning requires extensive L2 input.
> 6. Successful instructed language learning also requires opportunities for output.
> 7. The opportunity to interact in the L2 is central to developing L2 proficiency.
> 8. Instruction needs to take account of individual differences in learners.
> 9. In assessing learners' L2 proficiency, it is important to examine free as well as controlled production.
> 10. Instruction needs to ensure that learners focus predominantly on meaning.
>
> Source: *Lynch, M. (2015)*.

2.1.4   Task-Based Language Teaching

Task-Based Language Teaching (TBLT) has received much attention from education communities, which have witnessed its development and implementation in the field of second language (L2) learning (Long, 2014; Robinson & Robinson, 2001; Sun, 2008). TBLT, attributed by many to Willis (Willis, 1996), focuses on purposeful communication and functional language use (Ellis, 2009) where a 'communicative outcome is achieved' (Ellis, 2019: 10), facilitates L2 learning (Kim, 2012) and improves learning outcomes (Lou & Noels, 2016). There has been much discussion as to what constitutes a task. One way of thinking of this is to consider the goal of a task. According to Nunan (2004), a task goal refers to 'the vague and general intentions behind any learning task' (Nunan, 2004: 41). In other words, task goals indicate the general purpose and aim set by teachers to be achieved by learners in a learning task. Some complex tasks, including a series of sub-tasks, often have several goals.

2.1.5   Content and Language Integrated Learning

An approach that has become increasingly popular in a number of countries is **Content and Language Integrated Learning (CLIL)**. Often thought of as belonging to the domain of bilingual education and plurilingual education (Coyle & Meyer, 2021), CLIL brings together language teachers and subject teachers, where subject matter is taught through the medium of the foreign language (Marsh, 2012). For instance, in a country where English is the official national language, there may be a Geography class taught via German or a Physics class taught via French. There are different models of how this takes place. One model is where language and subject teachers work together; the language teachers thereby acquire subject knowledge, while the subject teachers develop expertise in combining language development with the teaching of subject matter. Another model is where the subject teacher has a high level of the foreign language and uses the foreign language to deliver the subject, as opposed to the traditional use of L1. Whichever model is used, the benefits for pupils are enormous. First of all, pupils receive huge amounts of foreign language input; second, they receive huge amounts of content matter; and third, they are learning the foreign language *in a relevant context*, instead of learning dry rules about how to use the language. After all, subject teaching, when taught in the foreign language, is also *language teaching*.

A CLIL approach seeks to promote learning through integrating a number of components – content, cognition, communication and culture (the 4Cs Framework) – recognising that deepening a learner's understanding requires a blend of these processes. This approach does not need to be reserved for officially designated 'CLIL' or bilingual schools: 'CLIL relates to any language, age and stage not only in the compulsory education sector but inclusive of kindergarten, vocational and professional learning' (Coyle, 2007: 97). Language teachers in mainstream secondary schools can use a CLIL approach by either working in an interdisciplinary setting with subject colleagues in their school, or by adapting the curriculum so that they are teaching subject matter (science, social subjects, music or indeed any subject) through the medium of the foreign language. This can be part of an interdisciplinary approach to learning and teaching. Teachers in primary or elementary schools can use the foreign language in their teaching of aspects of the curriculum as is appropriate, that is, using the foreign language to teach environmental studies or numeracy. A CLIL approach does not prioritise language learning over content learning, or vice versa. As Marsh states: 'It does not give emphasis to either language teaching or learning, or to content teaching and learning, but sees both as integral parts of the whole' (Marsh, 2002: 59).

2.1.6   A Pluriliteracies Approach to Teaching for Learning (PTL)

Building on the success of a CLIL approach, which brings subject learning and language learning together, focus has shifted to advocating a pluriliteracies approach. In this approach, integration of learning is generally seen as having an impact across languages, be this first, second, foreign or other languages. Learners often find it difficult to understand content or concepts when their language skills are not at a level to facilitate this. A pluriliteracies approach encourages learners to combine familiar and less familiar languages and to use this to understand knowledge and concepts in their learning. To help learners do this, they are encouraged to use appropriate cognitive discourse functions (CDFs). CDFs allow higher-order thinking skills and through these learners build and develop knowledge. Examples of CDFs are classifying, defining, describing, evaluating, explaining, exploring and reporting. These are applied to the learning scenario, for example classifying types of cloud formation in a geography class or reporting on an experiment in a science class. To enable progression, learners need to be supported by having their learning scaffolded, and this involves bringing together their subject literacies with their linguistic skills to evidence their learning. A multinational team of language experts brought together by the European Centre for Modern Languages of the Council of Europe has developed a set of principles and practices with a wealth of learning materials and other resources which is freely downloadable by teachers at https://pluriliteracies.ecml.at.

2.1.7   Common European Framework of Reference for Languages

Many of the approaches outlined above set themselves within the Common European Framework of Reference for Languages (CEFR). The CEFR is a set of specifications of language proficiency levels developed by the Council of Europe to set teaching and certification requirements. Originally produced in 1975 for the English language and a year later for French, it is now used in multiple contexts and has been widely used across the world for all languages. The descriptors used in the CEFR are non-language-specific, which guarantees its applicability and relevance for all languages, and it is a de facto standard used in many national language programmes to define expected levels from beginner to advanced levels. Full details can be found on the Council of Europe website at www.coe.int/en/web/common-european-framework-reference-languages.

2.2   Cognitivism and Other Socially Oriented Approaches to Second Language Acquisition

The approaches listed above, despite sometimes being similar and sometimes totally different, share a *cognitive* approach to explaining Second Language Acquisition (SLA). According to Ortega, these cognitively oriented theories see knowledge as 'residing in the mind, assume that learning is an individual accomplishment, and posit that mind achieves learning through environmental stimuli' (2011: 168). Since the mid-1990s, the cognitive foundations of these theories of SLA have been questioned amid the backdrop of a number of emerging socially oriented reconceptualisations of SLA. These socially oriented approaches are numerous and various as can be seen in Table 2.1, which lists them and highlights the main features of each.

Shared perspectives connecting the socially oriented approaches to SLA examined above are flux, relations and practices, and dynamic interaction. Research into these approaches has emphasised how knowledge and learning are socially intertwined and enmeshed in greater wholes. These studies of socially oriented approaches to SLA have often concentrated on the relationships and power dynamics of SLA involving adults seeking to integrate with new communities where their home language is not the dominant one. An example of this is Norton's Identity Approach to SLA (Norton & Toohey, 2011), where she studied several immigrant women who were eager to learn English as L2, yet under certain social conditions felt uncomfortable and unlikely to speak English. These socially oriented approaches to SLA, I would argue, have less relevance to most modern foreign

Table 2.1 Socially oriented approaches to SLA

Approach	Main features
Sociocultural theory	Emphasises the dialogic processes (such as 'scaffolding') that arise in a task performance and how these shape language use and learning. *L1 can mediate L2 learning.*
Sociolinguistic approach	Focuses on the study of the impact of society, including the impact of social context, on the way language is used. *Code-switching between L1 and L2.*
Complexity theory approach	Language use and its acquisition are mutually constitutive. *Soft-assembly of L1 and L2.*
Identity approach	Social status and power and idea of investment. *L1 or L2 used according to how 'invested' learner feels in talk.*
Language socialisation approach	How participation in talk can be marginal, peripheral or legitimate. *L1 can mediate L2 learning.*
Conversation-analytic approach	Analysis of talk can facilitate orderly interaction. Adoption of different identities. *L1 can mediate L2 learning.*
Sociocognitive approach	Mind, body and world work integratively in SLA. *L1 can mediate L2 learning.*

languages teachers, whose pupils are 'conscripts' based on age and postcode. That being said, it is important for language teachers to recognise the 'predominant Eurocentric knowledge system in language teaching' (Wang, 2024: 1388) and adopt a **decolonial approach** in their teaching to 'enable the harmonious coexistence of different worldviews and bodies of knowledge' (Wang, 2024: 1388) in the curriculum in which they are teaching. This is particularly important to remember when teaching classes where the learners come from a multitude of different countries and cultures. It helps to make visible the recognition and valuing of different cultures and bodies of knowledge, giving voice to all in the class. However, such a decolonial approach should not be reserved only for classes with learners from a mix of cultures. It should be adopted in all classes to promote an inclusive and open classroom ethos and ways of knowing that will help to push back against Western imperialism (Mignolo and Walsh, 2018).

2.3　Post-Method Condition

A number of researchers do not subscribe to the notion of methods and propose that we are in a post-method condition (Kumaravadivelu, 2006). Disillusioned by what they see as failings of CLT, which they feel often clashes with national language policies and learner expectations, they suggest there is no method which caters for all needs and contexts. Instead, they argue, we should seek to adapt existing methodologies to our specific learning environments (Richards & Rodgers, 2001).

Kumaravadivelu proposes his 'macrostrategic framework', which is based on 'particularity, practicality, and possibility' and which he further develops into ten macrostrategies (Kumaravadivelu, 2006), suggesting that teachers build their own pedagogy. However, as CLT itself is often seen as a collection of existing strategies, Kumaravadivelu's proposal could be seen as a redefinition of CLT and not post-method. Didenko & Pichugova (2016: 4) state that 'All methods that have followed CLT, such as Task-Based Language Teaching (TBLT) and content and language integrated learning (CLIL), necessarily highlight the importance of communicativeness for their implementation', arguing that following the principles of CLT is still the most prevalent strategy in classrooms.

Despite the popularity and effectiveness of CLT, it is still common to see grammar-translation techniques being used by languages teachers as their main approach. This is often the result of a number of reasons. Beliefs that learners hold from very early on in life are very hard to change, even when presented with evidence to the contrary. When student teachers (and also experienced teachers) are faced with problems in class, for example difficulty teaching a certain point, explaining what they want pupils to do or dealing with indiscipline, they often switch to how they were taught. If these teachers as young language learners were taught through grammar–translation, then this is the technique they will use in a knee-jerk reaction to get through the 'here and now' of the problem(s) they are facing. This often becomes the default reaction for a number of teachers to dealing with such problems and can quickly become their main teaching approach. This phenomenon is known as **language teacher cognition** and is very useful in helping to examine what teachers think, know and believe, and the relationships of these mental constructs to what teachers do in the language teaching classroom (see Section 4.3.2). Research in this area is helping to shed light on possible decisions made by the teachers vis-à-vis their classroom practice (Borg, 2003; Watzke, 2007; Korthagen. 2010; Lynch, 2020).

2.4 Purposes of Learning Foreign Languages

Thinking about the purpose of language learning helps us to focus on what the primary motivation of the learner is. Is it to pass exams? Is it enjoyment of the language? Is it to be able to communicate in the countries where the second language (L2) is spoken? For most people, it is usually about being able to communicate with speakers of the foreign language. They need to know enough vocabulary to understand speakers of the foreign language and to make themselves understood. They also need to know:

- the basic structure of the foreign language;
- how to express themselves in different situations;
- how to talk about themselves;
- how to ask about others;

- how to access different services;
- generally, how to get by in the country or countries where that language is spoken.

What they do *not* need is to know every grammatical rule or the entire vocabulary of a specific topic. They need, however, linguistic competence, sociolinguistic competence and pragmatic competence (Malovrh & Benati, 2018). Linguistic competence in terms of being able to express themselves; sociolinguistic competence in terms of dealing with the social dimension of language use (including politeness, recognising and acting on sociocultural cues, adopting an appropriate register); pragmatic competence in terms of how the learner organises and arranges messages and how they perform communicative functions.

These competences are intertwined with each other and overlap. They are components of a communicative approach to language learning and teaching which relies on real interaction and real conversations about practical subjects in which interaction is both the means and the ultimate goal of study.

It is about learners using communication to both learn and practise the foreign language at the same time, using authentic materials, *real* language for *real* use, both inside and outside the class.

Typical features of this include learners talking about their own experiences and the situations they find themselves in, as opposed to dry, out-of-context traditional grammar teaching and drilling exercises. Learners use the foreign language to talk about themselves, as well as the foreign language being the vehicle to learn the foreign language itself. Of the methods and approaches outlined in Sections 2.1 and 2.2 above, CLT, TBLT and CLIL are the ones that contain more of these features.

Developing these communicative skills in the learner is the language teacher's job. In an approach to language teaching concentrating on communication, developing these skills is often achieved through a topic-based syllabus where pupils learn the language and skills to communicate in different situations. More information on syllabus construction is provided in Chapter 5.

This section has considered the purposes of learning a foreign language. We will now move on to how to increase exposure to the target language for learners.

2.5 How to Increase Exposure to the Target Language

Considering the purposes of learning foreign languages as outlined above, a basic feature of language lessons is exposure to the foreign or *target* language. Another essential feature is to be given the opportunity to use it. Whether your teaching approach is CLT, TBLT or CLIL, this will involve extensive use of the target language.

Here is a summary of ways in which you can increase your use of the target language in the L2 class:

1. Devise a scheme of work or syllabus which responds to the communicative needs of the learners and contains topics that are useful to the language learner.
2. Decide on the key vocabulary and language structures to include in each lesson.
3. Walk the lesson through in your head in advance and decide how you will manage the activities and tasks in the lesson (see Chapter 6 for advice on lesson planning).
4. Plan what language you are going to use, not just the core language that you are going to teach, but also the target language you will use to manage the classroom (i.e., to give instructions, to explain tasks, etc.).
5. Think about how you can present the language to be learnt in a communicative way, which allows learners to discover for themselves how the language works.
6. Keep the learning manageable. Don't be tempted to teach everything that can possibly be known about the topic, the language structure or the grammatical point.
7. Give plenty of opportunities for output in realistic, authentic scenarios.
8. Maintain a sympathetic attitude to error.

2.5.1 Issues to Consider in the Teaching of L2 Grammar

If we look at schools, the modern foreign languages class is the place where learners gain exposure to the foreign language and it is the place where they have the opportunity to use it. Frequently, however, teachers feel overwhelmed by what they see as the enormity of course content that they feel they must cover. This often results in pushing teachers in the direction of 'presenting' or 'explaining' language, but not giving any opportunity to use the language.

What most student teachers find especially difficult during their teacher education is teaching grammar in the foreign language. Often students give an explanation of a grammatical rule in the learners' first language (L1) and then have the pupils try this out in practice, using the *Presentation, Practice, Production (PPP)* model. Teachers who use this model believe it speeds up the rate of language acquisition (Long, 2001), perhaps, however, at the expense of communication and accuracy (Zhao & Morgan, 2004).

This is different from a more communicative approach to grammar where teachers introduce grammar communicatively in L2 and delay giving a note of the grammatical rule until the pupils can produce the target language structure competently and confidently. The rule or explanation does *not* need to cover everything that is known about this point of grammar (as many teachers end up giving), but enough to draw attention to patterns and structures in the L2. This serves then to underpin the language the pupils have learnt, has a context and is easier to understand. This is a more an inductive approach to language teaching, as well as providing more exposure to L2.

FOOD FOR THOUGHT

Think back to how you were taught grammar points in your modern foreign languages classes at school.

Were you taught in a communicative way or did your teachers use a Grammar–Translation approach?

Has this influenced your ideas on how modern foreign languages should be taught?

2.5.2   Comparison of Two Different Approaches to the Teaching of Grammar

To help student teachers consider how they may approach teaching a grammar point in the target language, there follows an example of a lesson, or rather part of a lesson focusing on learning a new grammar point. The grammar point chosen is one that student teachers often identify as being difficult to teach if they are using the target language, that is the teaching of a new tense, in this case the past tense. The first example is of a Grammar–Translation approach, the second example will look at how this same lesson might be taught using a more communicative approach. The choice of language for these examples has been deliberately chosen as French for the foreign language for native English speakers, due to difficulties presented when moving from the written form to the spoken form in this context.

2.5.2.1   Teaching a Grammar Point Using the Grammar–Translation Approach

This example is looking at using the French verb *jouer* (to play) as the vehicle for teaching the formation of the past tense. Teaching points of grammar using a GT approach typically starts with the teacher giving an explanation to a class in a very expository way. The teacher's explanation will usually be something along the lines of:

1. Take the infinitive of the verb;
2. Remove the *-er* ending from the infinitive to form the stem;
3. Add *é* to the stem to form the past participle of the verb;
4. Use the correct form of the present tense of *avoir* as the auxiliary or helping verb.

This is typically followed by getting pupils to write out the full verb paradigm, such as:

j'ai joué	I have played
tu as joué	you have played
il a joué	he has played
elle a joué	she has played
on a joué	one has played
nous avons joué	we have played
vous avez joué	you have played
ils ont joué	they have played (masculine plural)
elles ont joué	they have played (feminine plural)

This gives the pupils a declarative knowledge of how to form this tense, but at the expense of spontaneity and fluency. Such explanations are often followed by drill-type exercises, where pupils are required to write or say lots of similar sentences to practise the construction (the PPP approach). Having to go through a series of rules in their head before they can speak leads to hesitancy in pupils and faltering speech at best. At worst, it prevents pupils being able to say anything at all as they struggle to remember a long list of rules. One feature of this GT approach is that it is almost always explained using the learner's L1, thereby depriving the learner of valuable L2 input and giving very little scope for them to practise the new language in meaningful ways (L2 output). Another feature of the GT approach is that the new language structures are often introduced out of context in a specially designated 'grammar lesson'.

2.5.2.2   Teaching a Grammar Point Using a Communicative Approach

Compare the Grammar–Translation approach to teaching the past tense in French to teaching the above language using a communicative approach.

The following approach sets the introduction of the past tense within a topic on leisure activities, where learners talk about themselves and the sports they play.

I typically use a diary page (*agenda*) from the current week, as in Figure 2.8.

Through gesture and mime of sports, you reactivate pupils' knowledge of how to say I play certain sports in the present tense using the French construction *Je joue au ...*, for example, *Le lundi, je joue au badminton* (on Mondays, I play badminton); *Le mardi, je joue au football* (on Tuesdays, I play football). Through lots of question and answer with pupils in class, you can revise *Le lundi, je joue au football; Le samedi, tu joues au rugby; Robert, il joue au tennis; Katie, elle joue au golf* (on Mondays, I play football; on Saturdays, you play rugby; Robert, he plays tennis; Katie, she plays golf) and so on. Once pupils are using this language correctly, that is, the language has been suitably revised, you show a diary page of the previous week (Figure 2.9).

In the same way, through gesture and mime, you can introduce *Lundi dernier, j'ai joué au football* (last Monday, I play*ed* football); *Mardi dernier, j'ai joué au rugby* (last Tuesday, I play*ed* rugby). Again, through question and answer, you can bring in *Mercredi dernier, Robert, il a joué au badminton* (last Wednesday, Robert play*ed* badminton); *Jeudi dernier, Sarah, elle a joué au golf* (last Thursday, Sarah play*ed* golf). In this way, with the diary page from last week acting as a clue that we are talking about things that happened in the past, this will introduce the 'structure' for talking in the past. The structure or grammatical rule is relatively easy to work out, as most of the language used is familiar, making it easy to spot the difference in sound, that is, *je joue* to *j'ai joué*; *tu joues* to *tu as joué* and so on. Through this process, the learners are consciously noticing changes (Schmidt, 2001) and thereby converting input into intake as they compare original or previously learned structures with new structures (Sharwood Smith, 1986). This is using prior learning and also mirrors L1 acquisition. This can be followed by tasks where learners use the new language in listening, speaking, reading and writing activities, which can take

Mon agenda

| lundi, 24 mars |
| mardi, 25 mars |
| mercredi, 26 mars |
| jeudi, 27 mars |
| vendredi, 28 mars |
| samedi, 29 mars |
| dimanche, 30 mars |

Figure 2.8 A diary page in French of the current week

place over a number of lessons, giving more familiarity with the language and consolidating the vocabulary and grammatical structures. Do not rush to present to the class all parts of the verb paradigm (i.e., we, you (plural), they) in the past; these can be brought in later. Give practice of this new form with communicative activities, but keep to a few pronouns (i.e., I, you, he and she), and use the form for other high-frequency verbs that follow a similar pattern (e.g., *regarder*, to watch). You can spread this over a number of lessons, eventually bringing in other parts of the verb in a similar communicative and inductive way. This again is more like L1 acquisition. The natural and most effective way to improve a learner's ability to understand and produce L2 constructions is to build up their language resource gradually, following their hierarchy of needs, that is, by helping them to learn what they need to know and to be able to use this in a logical step-by-step manner. The

Mon agenda

| lundi, 17 mars  |
| mardi, 18 mars  |
| mercredi, 19 mars  |
| jeudi, 20 mars |
| vendredi, 21 mars  |
| samedi, 22 mars  |
| dimanche, 23 mars |

Figure 2.9 A diary page in French of the previous week

learners do not need to learn the entire verb paradigm or verb table to be able to talk about themselves and others. Once pupils are familiar with this and using the new language competently and confidently, you could give a note of the structure to help them see the pattern and be able to use this in other contexts with other verbs (although you do not need to use complicated metalanguage, as most grammar books do), for example in Table 2.2.

This is not Grammar–Translation, but it *is still* teaching grammar and helps learners by giving practice of the language in realistic ways and showing how the language works. It also allows the users to use the new language straight away in realistic situations, contributing to a sense of achievement in the learners.

Table 2.2 An example of a note consolidating structures in the past tense in French			
Talking about what you play			
What you play today or normally		What you played yesterday/last week	
Je joue	I play	*J'ai joué*	I have played
Tu joues	You play	*Tu as joué*	You have played
Il joue	He plays	*Il a joué*	He has played
Elle joue	She plays	*Elle a joué*	She has played

With some thought in advance, you can devise similar approaches for other grammar points. It does not need to be done as a descriptive, out-of-context, traditional-style grammar lesson full of metalanguage that is difficult to understand and remember.

⫸ TRY THIS OUT

Think of a grammar point that you have been taught as a learner in a Modern Language class.

Design a lesson where you introduce and practise this grammar point in a communicative manner.

2.6 Use of the Target Language, Code-Switching and Translanguaging

This section will explore the use of the target language in L2 teaching and consider different views of how much of it should be used and when. **Code-switching** (switching from one language to another) and **translanguaging** (using one's linguistic knowledge of more than one language) are also examined.

2.6.1 Issues Surrounding the Use of the Target Language

A review of the literature surrounding target language (TL) use in the classroom reveals that while teachers agree that it is desirable to use L2 in the classroom within an overall communicative approach, a large number do not use it in their own classrooms (Franklin, 1990; Gatbonton & Segalowitz, 2005; Meiring & Norman, 2002; Neil, 1997). The majority of studies support the use of the target language as the main means of communication in the classroom. However, not all researchers agree that total exposure to the TL is the most effective.

Research has suggested various reasons why teachers will frequently use L1 in class. This may be for explicit grammar teaching, instructions for tests and instruction for examination techniques, with teachers claiming that L1 is used to reduce ambiguities. Other reasons for using L1 often include behaviour management (Macaro,

2001), teachers' lack of confidence and class size. Teachers frequently report finding it easier to explain things in L1, that is, for general classroom management and task management, or for social chat with their pupils (Lynch, 2020).

Some teachers see L1 as providing clarity and reassurance for learners, particularly when a complicated item of grammar is being taught, and talk about a 'judicious use' (Butzkamm, 2003) of L1. What is problematic, however, is when too much L1 is used and the learners' valuable exposure to the TL is significantly reduced. The danger here is that the L1 may become *the lingua franca* of the classroom, with learners receiving very little exposure to the TL. If the dominant language in the classroom becomes L1, at what point does the lesson stop being a *language* lesson and become a lesson *about* language?

What it is important to bear in mind is that pupils need to be exposed to a lot more target language than they will initially use. As language classes in most schools are only a few hours at best (often 3 × 50-minute lessons per week), if teachers use L1 for:

- explaining;
- teaching grammar;
- classroom management (organising pupils, materials, equipment);
- behaviour management;
- social chat;
- the general means of communication in the classroom.

then pupils will receive very little exposure to the foreign language indeed. Is the class there to help learners understand and communicate in the target language, or is it a lesson *describing* the language? With the taught language classes often being the only time many learners come into contact with the foreign language, reducing the amount of L2 used in favour of L1 may mean that pupils experience very little of the TL, which will have a direct effect on the ability of pupils to produce anything in it at all.

It is imperative, therefore, that teachers provide learners with as much input as possible and that this input is comprehensible. This *comprehensible input* can be in the form of accompanying gestures used with the TL, or images, demonstrations and the use of cognates, amongst other strategies. Alongside the input that they provide, teachers need to provide lots of opportunities for the learners to use the target language in authentic activities (output).

2.6.2 Code-Switching

Code-switching (Macaro, 2005) is when users change between L1 and L2 and this may be for different reasons. The competence of the language teacher is usually a lot higher than that of their pupils. This is one of the reasons why teachers need to think carefully about the level of language competence of their pupils and plan accordingly. To be able to maximise your use of L2 as a teacher means thinking through not only what you are going to teach (i.e., which language structure, vocabulary, grammar point), but also *how* you are going to teach it. This is important, as this forward planning will enable the teacher to choose language they will use in class that they are confident the learners will understand, be this the topic language to be taught or classroom management language to organise the class. Preparing the target language to be used in advance will prevent teachers using the foreign language spontaneously, since it may otherwise be too difficult for the learners to understand it. Rehearsal will also help keep the teacher in the TL throughout. This will provide much-needed L2 input for the learners, as well as modelling the language structures.

2.6.2.1   Teacher Code-Switching

There may be times, however, when the teacher finds it difficult to say everything in L2. Occasionally, the teacher will use L1 to explain or manage learning in the class. This is not normally regarded as a problem and may help them convey what they want to say. It may be seen as part of the teacher's strategy to maximise, or *optimise* (Macaro, 2005) their use of the target language. This becomes problematic where this strategy is overused. If a teacher does not monitor and reflect on their use of the target language, it can be quite easy to switch more and more to using L1 when communication problems are perceived. Before one notices, a teacher may well be using L1 for the majority of their talk in class, which inevitably reduces the exposure the learners have to L2.

2.6.2.2   Pupil Code-Switching and Translanguaging

It is normally the case that the language teacher's level of competence in the foreign language will be greater than that of the learners, unless you have pupils in your class who are native speakers of that language. As learners start to learn and use the foreign language, they may not be able to express everything they want to say in L2 and there may be many occasions where what they say is a mixture of L2 and L1. This happens quite often and is normal. When it occurs, you as the teacher can, and should, still use L2, as the learners may still understand you; it is just that they may have difficulty saying what they want to say in L2. In other words, their receptive skills are further developed than their productive skills, which is only natural. Indeed, we see the same when children acquire their mother tongue. In combining the new language that they are learning with their mother tongue to convey their meaning, the learners are acting strategically to communicate. This strategy of using all of one's linguistic resources to communicate is called **translanguaging**. It is often seen in dual language, bilingual or multilingual speakers, who use whichever of their languages (or often all in combination) seems the most appropriate or efficient to get their meaning across.

Section 2.6 has looked at issues surrounding the use of the target language, as well as the reasons why teachers and pupils may code-switch or translanguage. Next, we will consider some strategies to support the use of the target language in class.

2.7   Strategies to Support Teachers in Using the Target Language

This section will explore one of the biggest issues in language teaching, namely how to use the target language effectively in class. This section sets out five problems commonly perceived by student teachers and offers solutions and strategies to promote the use of the target language.

2.7.1   Perceived Problems in Using the Target Language in Class

Teachers often say they find it difficult to use the TL as much as they would like. The five areas where teachers seem to find most difficulty in using the TL are explaining things to the class, teaching grammar, classroom management, behaviour management and social chat with pupils. However, there are a number of effective strategies that teachers can use to support themselves in using the TL.

2.7.2   Strategies to Support the Use of the Target Language in Class

The following subsections will now examine the main areas of difficulty in which use of the target language is encountered.

2.7.2.1   Explaining Things to the Class

Perceived problem

What teachers want to tell or explain to pupils is complicated – this may be explaining a task, setting up groups, talking about assessments, giving back homework or something else. Teachers may decide to use L1 for this, as they feel that the language to explain this to learners in L2 is too difficult for the learners to understand, or that it will take too long to explain in L2.

Solution

1. Think about what you want to say in advance. Is there any way you can simplify the L2 so that the pupils understand? For example, using a simple imperative, instead of a complete sentence, will help keep you in L2.
2. Use high-frequency, routine language as regularly as you can. Pupils will pick this up, even if they have not yet learned the grammar behind it.
3. If you have a lot of steps in your explanation, break it down into shorter, discrete steps. Often the pupils can carry out the initial steps of a task, then be given the next steps. This allows the teacher to use shorter, simplified L2, and fewer steps reduces memory load.
4. As well as giving instructions and explanations orally, you can have these explanations on the screen, on the board or on worksheets. These instructions can be in L2 with graphics or icons to depict the task, e.g., for a reading task. You could also have the task explained in L1 alongside the L2. As learners become more familiar with the L2, the L1 scaffolding can gradually be withdrawn in future lessons.
5. Frequently needed language can be displayed on posters on the classroom walls. Pupils will often put up their hand asking for help with a point, then notice the

rule on the poster before the teacher turns to them. These posters can be interchanged with others depending on the current topic and focus of the lesson. This does have implications for storage and retrieval, but should not cause you problems as a teacher. For instance, you can display the language on laminated card, which will last a lot longer than a sheet of ordinary paper. Posters can be stored in a cupboard or drawer, or in the staff base and brought out as needed.

2.7.2.2   Teaching Grammar

Perceived problem

The teacher wants to introduce or explain a grammatical point and, to be sure that the pupils understand this, decides to explain the rule in L1, thereby reducing exposure to L2.

Solution

1. Introduce the grammatical point inductively, as was shown in the French example in Section 2.5.2.1 with the past tense of *jouer*, and let the pupils work out the rule, as opposed to telling them it first and then getting them to use it in practice. If this grammatical point has already been introduced inductively and the pupils then use it competently and confidently, they may only need a few examples of it to copy into their exercise books as a reminder.
2. Think how you can simplify the explanation using language the pupils know. This involves thinking through what you will say in L2 in advance of the lesson.
3. Use a mixture of L2 and images or gestures and mime to convey the meaning.
4. Ask yourself how much of a rule the pupils need to know. Is it enough that they recognise a pattern to use it in appropriate situations? For example, when teaching English as a Foreign Language, providing enough input and practice for pupils to recognise that the 3rd person singular of verbs ends in *s* may be enough explanation.
5. Review Point 5 of Section 2.7.2.1 above.

2.7.2.3   Using the Target Language for Classroom Management

Perceived problem

The teacher wishes to organise the lesson into a number of tasks and use various resources and equipment, which may also involve the pupils moving around the classroom. The teacher finds it difficult to organise this using L2.

Solution

1. The secret here is in the forward planning. Plan in advance what you are going to say in L2 for each step of the lesson, bearing in mind the level of the learners.
2. Have a plan on the screen or board using simple language and images or icons and explain the steps needed for a particular task.
3. Show only the steps needed for the particular stage of the lesson. After each stage of the lesson has been completed, take the learners through the instructions for the next stage of the lesson. Resist the temptation to give a long list of instructions at the beginning of the lesson.

4. Give the learners the task management language they will need to carry out the task in L2, for example 'It's your turn', 'Shall I start?', etc.

5. Review Points 3 and 4 from Section 2.7.2.1 above, which are valid in terms of general classroom management.

2.7.2.4   Using the Target Language for Managing Pupil Behaviour
Perceived problem

A pupil or a group of pupils cause disruption in class, either through not paying attention, talking out of turn or distracting other pupils and the teacher does not feel competent to deal with this in L2.

Solution

1. Could the problem be resolved by other means? (This will be discussed in Chapter 12.)

2. A firm tone of voice while using L2 may often be enough to stop the disruption. For example, in a German foreign language class, a forthright 'Ruhe!' or 'Silence!' in a French class may be all that is needed.

3. Ask yourself if you used language that is beyond their comprehension, thereby causing them to switch off. Review Points 1–5 in Section 2.7.2.1 above.

2.7.2.5   Using the Target Language for Social Chat with Pupils
Perceived problem

You want to ask pupils how they are, what they have been doing or just to chat on a personal level, but feel you need to use L1 in case the learners do not understand.

Solution

1. Think of all the topics and language you know the pupils have already learned and use structures and language with which they are familiar. Use these structures for social chat.

2. Recycling language they already know in authentic social chat is good cumulative revision and keeps this common language active in learners' minds.

3. Sometimes your actual topic will lend itself naturally to social chat, e.g., talking about hobbies, sport, leisure pursuits.

Section 2.7 has looked at perceived problems that modern languages often cite as creating difficulties for using the target language in class and has teachers provided practical strategies to address these problems.

....

SUMMARY

Chapter 2 has examined different approaches to the learning and teaching of modern foreign languages, highlighting the features of each one. This has led to an evaluation of which approaches might best help student teachers to increase communication in their classes. To this end, a comparison of two different methods for teaching a point of grammar was given. The issue of how to increase effective use of the target language in class was explored and five issues seen as problematic for student teachers were examined. Each issue presented was accompanied by a proposed solution or strategies to promote use of the target language.

REFLECTIVE QUESTIONS

1. How do you think grammar should be taught in a modern languages class? Do you think it is better to teach it explicitly in grammar lessons? Or do you think it is better to teach whatever grammar point(s) are needed inductively as they arise in lessons? Give reasons for your answer.
2. Do you think using a learner's L1 to explain things in the L2 classroom is useful, or do you think that it is better to stick to L2 all the time? Why?

KEY TERMS

code-switching Where language users switch between L1 and L2 to communicate.

communicative approach An umbrella term to describe L2 teaching where learners use communication to both learn and practise the foreign language at the same time, using authentic materials, *real* language for *real* use, both inside and outside the class.

Content and Language Integrated Learning (CLIL) An approach to L2 teaching where subject matter is taught through the medium of the foreign language.

decolonial approach A way in which Eurocentric views are challenged and different worldviews and bodies of knowledge are incorporated in the curriculum.

Grammar–Translation (GT) Approach or **Method** A form of L2 teaching where explicit explanation of grammar rules is the main mode of teaching.

language teacher cognition The study of what language teachers think, know and believe about teaching languages.

target language (TL) The foreign language that is to be taught in class.

translanguaging The strategy whereby learners use whichever of their languages (or often all in combination) seems the most appropriate or efficient to convey their meaning.

FURTHER READING

For more information on features of language learning, read Ellis's work:

Ellis, R., 2005. Principles of instructed language learning. *Asian EFL Journal.* Special edition. Conference proceedings, May. Article 1. Online. https://asian-efl-journal.com/journal-2 005/index.htm

For a comprehensive look at issues surrounding use of the target language, see my thesis:

Lynch, M., 2015. Target language use in modern language classrooms: Perception and change among newly qualified teachers in Scotland. PhD thesis. University of Edinburgh.

If you would like to read more about Task-Based Language Teaching, have a look at:

Ellis, Rod, Peter Skehan, Shaofeng Li, Natsuko Shintani & Craig Lambert, 2019. The pedagogic background to task-based language teaching, in R. Ellis, P. Skehan, S. Li, N. Shintani & C. Lambert (eds.), *Task-Based Language Teaching: Theory and practice.* Cambridge: Cambridge University Press, 3–26.

Willis, D. & J. Willis (2007. *Doing Task-Based Teaching.* Oxford: Oxford University Press.

For further information on CLIL:

Coyle, D., 2007. Content and language integrated learning: Towards a connected research agenda for CLIL pedagogies *International Journal of Bilingual Education and Bilingualism*, 10(5): 543–62.

Arnaiz Castro, P. et al., 2022. Deeper learning and assessment in drama-based CLIL learning spaces. *Language Education and Multilingualism – The Langscape Journal.* doi:10.18452/25444

The European Centre for Modern Languages (ECML) provides detailed information on a pluriliteracies approach at:

https://pluriliteracies.ecml.at

If you are interested in socially oriented approaches to SLA, then a good overview is given in:

Atkinson, D., 2011. *Alternative Approaches to Second Language Acquisition.* Abingdon: Routledge.

To learn more about language teacher cognition and how this influences teachers' choice of pedagogy in the classroom, have a look at the following:

Borg, S., 2003. Teacher cognition in language teaching: A review of research on what language teachers think, know, believe, and do. *Language Teaching*, 36(2): 81–109. doi: 10.1017/s0261444803001903

Korthagen, F., 2010. Situated learning theory and the pedagogy of teacher education: Towards an integrative view of teacher behavior and teacher learning. *Teaching and Teacher Education*, 26(1): 98–106. doi: 10.1016/j.tate.2009.05.001

Lynch, M., 2020. Problematising early career teacher cognition and its impact on pedagogic positioning in the teaching and learning of modern foreign languages in secondary schools. *Pädagogische Horizonte*, 4(2): 1–24. https://pedagogical-horizons.org/index.php/ph/article/view/103/65

Watzke, J., 2007. Foreign language pedagogical knowledge: Toward a developmental theory of beginning teacher practices. *The Modern Language Journal*, 91(1): 63–82. doi: 10.1111/j.1540-4781.2007.00510.x

3 | Skills Development

Introduction

Chapter 2 examined different approaches to the learning and teaching of modern languages, as well as the use of the target language. Strategies to overcome commonly perceived problems were explored, particularly with reference to promoting use of the target language.

In Chapter 3, the focus is on how to develop the skills of listening, speaking, reading and writing in L2, examining why skills development is important. Multi-skill and multi-task activities are also examined and how to use these in class.

The learning objectives for this chapter are, therefore, as follows:

1. Examine the importance of developing the skills of listening, speaking, reading and writing in the L2 classroom.
2. Develop strategies for using these skills in class.
3. Explore how an understanding of how reading skills developed in L1 can contribute to developing reading skills in L2 in learners.
4. Look at how skills interact to produce multi-skill and multi-task activities and how to practise these for use in class.

Overview

This chapter explains the importance of developing skills progressively amongst one's pupils throughout language learning and how each skill interlaces with other skills to help overall communicative competence. The different skills of speaking, listening, reading and writing can complement each other and the chapter explores ways in which this can be achieved in lessons, as well as how to maintain an appropriate balance of skills in language learning. Practical advice is also given on how to develop each individual skill, as well as how to create multi-skill and multi-task activities. Tasks included in this chapter are designed to give student teachers practice in developing these individual skills, as well as how to create multi-skill and multi-task activities for use in their modern languages classrooms. The development of reading skills is given particular attention, as this is an area which can affect all other skills if not given due care and consideration. To this end, an examination of how an understanding of learning to read in L1 is given and what we can borrow from this to help develop reading skills in L2.

3.1 Developing Skills in L2

It is fundamental in the learning of a foreign language that the skills of listening, speaking, reading and writing be developed. In any course or lesson, there may be an emphasis on a particular skill, but this should not be at the exclusion of other skills. The importance of these different language skills and how they complement each other cannot be stressed enough in terms of their interconnectedness and reciprocity (Nation, 2009). There should be a balance, of course, between student-led and teacher-led activities that together provide students with the chance to develop the knowledge, understanding and practice of skills that allow these to develop.

Skills are not developed automatically through practice, which is why an approach that merely provides opportunities for skill practice is flawed. Reading, listening, interacting, speaking and writing in the foreign language can and should be taught. For each unit and course, the balance of time spent on each skill may be weighted depending on the emphasis in the unit. At the beginning, the unit may involve more teaching and learning; at the end, more practice and learning.

3.1.1 Developing Skills in Reading

Every student (at whatever level they are operating) must learn *how* to read. Reading in L2 should not be regarded as simply understanding a code. The importance of background and personal experiences in helping to find meaning in the text cannot be overemphasised. Freebody and Luke (2003) maintain that we should be aware of a text's cultural and social purposes so that we better understand it and can recognise any underlying biases.

In reading, there should be occasions when the teacher draws the whole class, or a group of them, together and teaches them the tricks of the trade: how to use grammar to unlock meaning (Where are the verbs? What kind of ending does the verb have? What does that tell you about tense and therefore time?); how to infer meaning from the structure of the piece; how to guess intelligently what is unknown from what is known (a key skill in foreign language work); how to get help from knowledge of other languages; and so on.

A similar process should be undertaken when teaching all skills – the process must be made overt for the students so that they learn techniques and strategies for working with language and thus can hope, by applying them in new contexts, to improve.

3.1.2 Developing Skills in Listening and Viewing

In listening and viewing, we cannot simply assume that listening a lot will develop listening skills automatically (Cauldwell, 2013). Developing skills in listening and viewing involves many processes: what to look out for in structure; how much language is redundant; what will come next; how a picture may support, or contrast, with meaning; what sounds to listen for; what pitfalls there are in the comparison between the sound system and the written system of the language; what intonation reveals; how, and where, to pick up meaning again if it has been lost.

3.1.3   Developing Skills in Speaking

Speaking can often produce anxiety for second language learners (Woodrow, 2006). Having to speak spontaneously with often scant knowledge of grammar and vocabulary can be daunting (Thornbury, 2012). Other factors need to be considered in any speaking interaction, whether this be a monologue or an extended response:

What are the rules of delivery?
How is a monologue to be made interesting and clear?
How can content be improved?
How can sentences be lengthened and developed (by the function or extension of, for instance, conjunctions)?

Or in conversation:

What are the 'turn-taking' rules?
How do you start, extend, review or finish a topic with your interlocutor?
How do you use repair strategies?
What are common repair strategies?
How do you recognise that you have been asked a question if you do not understand what has been said?

The analysis of video or audio recordings of performances in both presentations and conversations is a much-underused technique in the modern language classroom.

There may also be an issue of what to say, if the content of speaking is based on personal views and experiences rather than set up by the parameters of a transactional or interactional task. There must be a role there also for the teacher. It may start with exploring, if the students do not come with pre-formulated ideas.

In this way, the foreign language work contributes again to the development of the person as well as to their competence in foreign language use. For example, in response to the question often asked in the warm-up to a lesson 'What did you do last night?' a student operating at a simple level might say 'I watched TV' and that would be an adequate response (assuming it is correctly said in the foreign language). However, at a higher level it is inadequate unless followed up. 'What did you watch and what did you think about it?' is the next stage of development. Yet how many students could articulate why they watch a particular episode of a show on streaming platforms, such as Netflix? Perhaps that is the moment to explore views, and if none are forthcoming from the students, for the teacher to suggest them. You could ask whether they like it (or not!) because it is realistic, people seem friendly or help one another; or because it deals with everyday problems (but at a distance and thus 'safely'), the characterisation is strong, situations can be amusing and so on. Once this has been discussed, the necessary words and expressions can be given in the foreign language and thereafter practised every time a similar language situation arises during the warm-up or, indeed, as part of a task for a speaking or writing outcome. Such exploration of views, providing students with the means to create views and opinions then express them, is a key part of language – and personal development. Once again, making the process overt for the students is central to helping them progress in language work.

3.1.4 Developing Skills in Writing

Writing is not simply a matter of speech written down (Biber et al., 1999; McCarthy & Carter, 1994). It 'involves a complex mixture of linguistic and textual knowledge as well as strategic knowledge and sociocultural awareness' (Burns & Siegel, 2018: 8). Developing skills in writing can complement the other three skills. In seeking to develop learners' L2 writing skills, it is important to show learners how to plan their writing, to review and revise it, and to edit it.

Any teaching programme will inevitably also include grammar, teaching through the correction of work, advice on next steps and so on, but skills teaching is very important and it has perhaps become less well done or less frequently included in programmes for language learners of all ages. Once such processes are made overt to learners and they reach their own highest level of language competence, they will be able to transfer the processes to the same skills in any other foreign language they might learn in later life and thus be able to accelerate the learning process to their, and others', advantage.

Section 3.1 has looked at why skills development is important in the L2 classroom and given an overview of the features of different skill areas. Section 3.2 will look at strategies to develop different skill areas.

3.2 Strategies for Developing Different Skills in the L2 Classroom

This section will present strategies for developing the skill areas of listening, speaking and writing with examples for use in the L2 classroom. These are strategies that I have observed being used by students in classes of different age groups. The suggestions listed below for each skill area can and should be adapted for the level of the class and the different abilities of the learners in your class. (Differentiation is looked at in depth in Chapter 7.) You should also consider how these generic suggestions can be adapted for the particular topic of the class.

3.2.1 Developing Listening Skills

The following are suggestions for developing listening skills with learners. The suggestions are generic in nature and can be used in different topic areas and with different age groups. The accompanying instructions should be adapted or expanded accordingly.

Suggestions for developing listening skills

- Ask learners to draw what they hear.
- Get learners to participate in chain activities in which each person repeats what the preceding people said and then adds a detail.
- Have learners indicate the number of words heard in a sentence.
- Have learners follow oral directions.
- Learners should indicate incongruities in a passage.
- Supply possible titles for listening passages.
- Supply the missing portions of a telephone conversation.
- Supply the ending for a story.
- Engage learners in guessing games based on message content.
- Get learners to signal (by standing, raising hand, clapping, etc.) recognition of grammatical features (tense, gender, etc.).
- Ask learners to categorise words heard.
- Ask learners to respond to possible, impossible and unlikely statements.
- Learners should distinguish between homonyms.
- Ask learners to indicate the moment when they realise the topic of a conversation.
- Ask learners to paraphrase what is said.
- Learners should place items heard in proper chronological order.
- Get learners to distinguish sentences, questions and exclamations.
- Learners should repeat a description as accurately as possible.
- Learners should indicate which word doesn't belong in a given sequence.
- Learners should respond to nonsense questions (e.g., 'Did you eat socks for breakfast this morning?').
- Have learners respond to questions about message content in a variety of formats.
- Learners should participate in various types of dictation exercises.
- Get learners to act out what is said.
- Ask learners to listen for a particular word or piece of information.
- Learners should complete grids, pictures or sentences with missing information.
- Have learners indicate if they heard a particular statement in a passage.
- Learners should write what they remember.
- Ask learners to choose the picture that corresponds to a description.

The above list is not exhaustive and you may well have other suggestions.

Of course, although designed primarily to practise listening skills, the suggestions above involve other skills as well. The activities may produce a spoken or written response, or even a non-verbal response (such as carrying out an action), showing the interconnected nature of skills development.

3.2.1.1   Examples of Listening Activities

Below are more detailed examples of some of the suggestions listed above and how they may look in lessons.

Examples of Speaking Activities

Learners Respond to Questions about Message Content in a Variety of Formats

The teacher should choose a topic with which learners are familiar or are currently studying. Upon hearing the teacher's questions, the learners can either draw something as a response to the questions, write an answer in note form or in full sentences, or explain orally to their partner or group.

Example 3.1 (in French)

Qu'est-ce qui se passe au début de cette histoire? Où est-ce Pierre est allé après sa visite à Paris? Pourquoi est-ce que Marie veut parler avec sa mère?

What happens at the beginning of this story? Where did Pierre go after his visit to Paris? Why does Marie want to talk to her mother?

Have Learners Follow Oral Directions

After having taught the directions in the foreign language, the teacher (a) gives oral directions which learners follow on a map (paper format or on tablet) and the learners tell the teacher the destination they have arrived at or (b) the teacher blindfolds a pupil and guides the pupil around the class with oral directions. For both (a) and (b) the teacher can then ask a pupil to give the directions.

Example 3.2 (in German)

Gehen Sie gerade aus, nehmen Sie die dritte Straße links! Das Ziel ist auf der rechten Seite.

Go straight on, take the third street on the left. Your destination is on the right.

Learners Should Indicate Incongruities in a Passage

The teacher reads out a passage of text which contains things or events that do not seem to fit. This may be something non-sensical, such as 'I went to bed at 10 o'clock and then I brushed my teeth' or 'I got on a plane and started to play tennis' or 'I went to the sports shop and bought some salad and vegetables'. Pupils have to indicate what these incongruities are and why.

Example 3.3 (in Italian)

Sono andata a letto e poi mi sono lavato i denti. Sono salito su un aereo e ho cominciato a giocare a tennis. Sono andato al negozio sportivo e ho comprato dell'insalata e qualche verdura.

I went to bed and then brushed my teeth. I got on a plane and started to play tennis. I went to the sports shop and bought some salad and vegetables.

Learners Should Complete Grids, Pictures or Sentences with Missing Information

The teacher reads out lists or instructions or a passage of text and the learners should indicate what is missing. For example, the teacher could read out a recipe that has previously been taught and miss out some steps and the learners fill this in on a grid or a recipe card. The teacher could read out a well-known extract from a story or a news report and the learners write down the missing information.

Example 3.4 (in English)
Recipe for fruit scones
Take 350g of plain flour

_____

_____

Mix the flour and the butter together
Add 100g of raisins

_____

_____

Add the milk
Fold the entire mixture with a knife
Roll out mixture and cut into shapes
Baste the _____ with a beaten egg mix
Bake for _____ minutes at _____ degrees

3.2.2　Developing Speaking Skills

The following are suggestions for developing speaking skills with learners. The suggestions are generic in nature and can be used in different topic areas and with different age groups. The accompanying instructions should be adapted and expanded accordingly.

In terms of devising speaking activities, it is important to decide first of all what the purpose of the act of speaking is. Generally, most speaking acts will fall under one of the overarching categories below.

Speaking categories
- Introducing;
- Explaining;
- Negotiating;
- Seeking clarification;
- Checking;
- Helping the conversation along;
- Closing.

Here are some further examples of activities which combine information and which can be developed at various levels of difficulty:

Finding solutions or answering a need
- *Negotiating what to do for an evening or a day*

Each participant has searched for a 'What's on' list for the locality; the lists can contain different but not conflicting information; each participant has looked up what films are on and must decide on one to watch together by chatting with a partner.

- *Deciding where to go on holiday*

Similar to the task above, but this time each partner has looked up information about different holiday resorts and must decide together which resort to go to and give reasons why.

- *Deciding what to take on holiday*

This requires participants to discuss and reach agreement about what activities they may undertake. The language involved includes: 'Shall we …?; Let's … at about …?; The … needs/has got to be …'

- *Planning menus for a short holiday, a camp, weekend away, etc.*

This involves discussing what each participant likes to eat, whether they have any dietary requirements or food allergies, or are vegetarian or vegan.

- *Arranging to meet: where, when?*

Discussing where is convenient for all parties; do some of the group live further away? Does this affect where to meet (e.g., coming in by bus, so meeting at the bus station)? Does the weather affect the choice of meeting place?

- *Seeking hotel accommodation*

One participant has the hotel details while the other has requirements, which can be complex, for example one has a dog or one has a disability.

- *Seeking and providing information at an information office*

This could be excursions (times, costs, details of places to be visited, meals en route, amenities in the locality, etc.).

Splitting information as stimulus for speaking tasks using

- Timetables of any sort;
- Menus;
- Lists, the material for which will be selected according to the relevance of content and appropriateness of level. These lists can be presented as symbols or words, e.g., 'What's in the box?';
- Prices and items;
- Descriptions of anything or anybody;
- Life histories;
- Town maps. Each pupil has a simple, incomplete map. What is on one map is not on the other student's map, although blank spaces may be drawn in. Each has a list of places to ask for which are on the other student's map. All the directions start from the same spot on both maps.
- Changes in a town or village: each student has a map with the changes marked but the dates are divided between them. Students spot the difference. This is often used in History classes.
- 'What's on this week?' Students have information which they have to put together in the form of an information sheet, e.g., cinema, theatre sporting event, or concert.

- Giving information. As in the previous example, but this time students discuss and create together an information sheet about activities in a particular locality, e.g., riding, sailing, tennis or walking.

The above list is not exhaustive and you may well have other ideas. The suggestions above, although designed primarily to practise speaking skills, involve other skills as well. The speaking activities will often have arisen from reading a written stimuli or from listening to a partner(s), which is more evidence of the interconnected nature of skills development.

 The following are more detailed examples of some of the above suggestions and how they may look in lessons.

Examples of Speaking Activities

Explaining

The teacher should choose a topic with which learners are familiar or are currently studying. The teacher explains that the class will be exploring the town centre (either in person or virtually via maps and videos) and that pupils should find out certain information from staff in shops or collect objects in town.

Example 3.5 (in French)

Vous allez visiter le centre de la ville avec un partenaire. Il y a trois tâches à faire. Demandez les horaires des trains en direction de la prochaine ville. Découvrez cinq sites touristiques à visiter. Trouvez trois objets typiques de cette ville et rapportez-les en classe.

You are going to visit the town centre with a partner. Ask for the train timetables to the next town. Look for five tourist attractions to visit. Find three typical objects from this town and bring them to class.

Seeking Clarification

The teacher gives pupils a list of different leisure venues to phone. Pupils must find out if the venue is open today, what time it closes and how much the activity costs.

Example 3.6 (in German)

Entschuldigen Sie, bitte. Darf ich fragen, ob das Schwimmbad heute offen ist? Um wieviel Uhr sperrt das Schwimmbad zu? Wieviel kostet das/der Eintritt?

Excuse me, please. Can I ask if the swimming pool is open today? When does the swimming pool close? How much does it cost/How much is the entrance fee?

Checking

The teacher directs pupils to find out if it is okay to enter a certain building, use a facility or bring a pet.

Example 3.7 (in Italian)

Scusi, e permesso entrare in questo ufficio? Possiamo utilizzare i servizi igienici qui? Devo domandare, se posso entrare con il mio cane?

Excuse me, is it possible to go into this office? Can we use the toilets here? Can I ask if it is possible to come in with my dog?

Closing a Conversation

The teacher asks you to close a conversation with your partner, giving your reasons for doing so.

Example 3.8 (in English)

I'm very sorry, but I'm going to have to go now, as I am working at five o'clock. Please excuse me leaving now, I have to pick up my little brother from school. I need to leave you now, as I am so far behind with my homework. Sorry, I have to run, my bus leaves in two minutes!

3.2.3 Developing Writing Skills

When teachers try to develop writing skills in their learners, it is important that writing is not practised just for the sake of it. Like the other skills of listening, speaking and reading, developing writing skills should be set within a communicative framework. Writing activities should be authentic, where learners see that the writing task has a purpose. When learners see a purpose for writing, they are much more likely to complete it. Whatever the activity, it is useful to consider at the outset what the reasons are for writing. Is it initiation or response? Who is the audience? This second question will also have a bearing on the style of writing that teachers task their learners with completing. It is good to know that there is no shortage of opportunities to write, as writing occurs in many contexts for many people. Here is a list of different types of writing.

Types of Writing

Personal writing
- Diaries, journals, lists, reminders, addresses, recipes.

Social writing
- Letters, invitations, notes, emails, SMS texts, WhatsApp chats, social media posts.

Public writing

- Letters of enquiry, form filling, applications.

Study writing

- Notes from reading and listening, summaries, synopses, reports, reviews, essays.

Creative writing

- Poems, stories, rhymes, drama, autobiography.

Institutional writing

- Reports, reviews, adverts, posters, instructions, notes.

With advanced learners, there may be occasions when more extended writing is required and learners will need coaching in how to do this. This will involve helping learners with how to compose, communicate and craft their writing, namely:

- Getting their ideas together;
- Planning and outlining the main points they wish to get across;
- Making notes;
- Making a first draft;
- Revising and redrafting;
- Editing;
- Producing the final version.

Learners should be made aware that this level of extended writing is not something that just flows straight from the pen, but is rather a recursive, messy activity as they put down ideas, add to these, score others out and redraft. This type of mechanistic pre-activity is a necessary stage in producing a polished piece of writing.

The teaching steps may include the following:

1. Pre-writing: jotting down ideas and preparing initial plans.
2. Drafting and redrafting, involving reviewing and revising, i.e., working out what to say and how best to say it.
3. Editing the pre-final version, including assessing for clarity for the intended reader and checking accuracy.

Writing Frames These are specific approaches for different writing genres (Ferlazzo & Sypnieski, 2018; Wray & Lewis, 1997) and are recommended to help learners structure their writing. Examples of different types of writing frames (adapted from Wray & Lewis, 1997) are:

- **Recount** – inform or entertain audience by retelling events (Enumeration frames)
- **Report** – describe a range of natural, cultural or social phenomena (Compare and Contrast frames)
- **Explanation** – explain natural and social phenomena (practise the use of temporal and causal conjunctions)
- **Procedure** – describe how something is done in a series of sequenced steps (Goal → Equipment → Steps to achieve goal)

- **Persuasion** – promote a particular point of view (Thesis → Arguments → Reiteration)
- **Discussion** – present arguments from differing viewpoints (Statement of issue preview → Pro → Con → Recommendation)

This section has explored the development of the skills of listening, speaking and writing in the L2 classroom, accompanied by some examples in different foreign languages.

3.3   Developing Reading Skills

Developing the ability to read in the target language is a vital skill for the foreign language learner. Not only does it help expand the vocabulary of the language learner, it also helps cement the new target language structures and can present the language in a variety of contexts. Reading also helps to develop awareness in learners of discourse (or narrative) structure, it teaches cultural conventions (e.g., knowing it is bad manners to steal porridge) and also general knowledge (e.g., knowing that a straw house will be weaker than a wooden house).

This section takes an extended look at the skill of reading in L2. To do this, the process of developing reading skills in L1 is examined, which leads on to how L1 reading development can help the development of reading in L2. I have chosen to devote a whole section to reading. This is not because I want to promote it over any other skills or because I think reading is more important than other skills. My reason for this is that I have seen so many poor examples of developing reading skills in L2. What a lot of student teachers (and sometimes experienced teachers) do is to present learners with long texts in L2 as the learners' first encounter with the written version of L2. This invariably has the consequence of affecting the learner's speaking and listening skills. If there is no bridge made between the spoken and written versions of L2, then in most cases, learners will superimpose their L1 sound–symbol relationship onto the L2 text. In most cases, this results in false pronunciation of the L2 if asked to read the text aloud. What is extraordinary is that learners will pronounce the L2 in the written text wrongly, due to using their L1 sound system on the L2 text, even though they have previously been pronouncing the L2 properly in listening and speaking activities. If this is left unchecked, fossilisation of pronunciation occurs and affects not only how learners speak in L2, but also their listening and writing skills. In other words, if we do not introduce reading in L2 in a planned and structured way, we risk undoing learning and progress made in the other skill areas.

Note: The sections on listening, speaking and writing above contain examples and strategies that can be used in any language using the Latin alphabet, and I would argue that the strategies will also work for Chinese, Japanese and Hindi. The section on reading below, however, pertains to languages using Latin script. It is outside my expertise to explain how to teach the development of reading skills in languages with non-alphabetic scripts.

3.3.1 The Sound–Symbol Relationship

To help learners to develop reading skills in the target language successfully requires a systematic and planned approach. Even if the learner's mother tongue and the target language share a similar alphabet, learners cannot simply decode the written form of the target language, as they would with their mother tongue. Reading ability in the target language needs to include building up competence in decoding short familiar texts to progressively grappling with longer and denser texts. The initial shorter texts need to provide lots of exposure to familiar language before more complex and less familiar language is introduced. The move to presenting the written form of the target language to learners needs to be carefully managed and is normally most effective after learners have started to develop their listening and speaking skills. A planned approach where the teacher guides the learners to the written form of the target language should not be skipped and will pay dividends in skill proficiency almost straight away.

It is essential that the learners are aware of the sound–symbol relationship in the target language. This is true for all languages and teachers need a coherent plan to build up these recognition skills in their learners.

To assist learners to develop automatic recognition skills, learners should be given opportunities to develop letter recognition and sound–symbol correspondence skills. This is best achieved by using familiar language that the learners have practised orally or heard before. This is similar to the way in which learners have developed the ability to read in their mother tongue. Indeed, it is important to know how this process works in a learner's first language to support their reading ability in a second language effectively. It should be done in a structured way and requires the examination of L2 reading strategies for beginning learners.

3.3.2 Problems in Developing Reading Skills in L2

Why look at L2 reading strategies for beginning learners? Well, most people will first learn foreign languages at school, usually at secondary but sometimes at primary. As we have children in schools for a substantial number of years, it gives teachers time to develop skills gradually and progressively, as these skills are integrated – proficiency in one skill helps other skills. Lastly, if pupils cannot read in L2, it affects their speaking and other skills in L2.

So, what's the problem? Well, each year, I go into many schools to support and assess my student teachers of modern languages on placement in schools. What I have seen mainly in secondary or high schools with modern or foreign language departments is that a large majority of language teachers find teaching reading in L2 difficult.

This has several origins:

1. Teachers often say they have very little time in which to cover the syllabus expected of them.

2. They lack experience in classroom management.
3. There is pressure from colleagues to conform to the practices of other colleagues in the languages department.
4. When teachers are under pressure, they often go into survival mode and switch to how they were taught as learners of modern languages. If they were taught in a very traditional way, this is how they teach to get through the here and now of the situation. If they perceive that this 'works' to resolve the situation, then they will most likely do this again and again in similar stressful situations until it becomes their own pedagogy (Borg, 2003; Korthagen, 2010). It is hard to understate how powerful these prior learning experiences are on novice teachers.
5. This happens very quickly and teachers will switch to a very teacher-centred traditional Grammar–Translation Approach to teaching, which hinders the development of reading (and other skills), unless they are shown how to develop L2 reading skills in their learners successfully.

3.3.3   Development of Reading Strategies in L1

The following is a brief examination of why we need to look at L2 reading strategies and how learners develop the ability to read *in L1* and how this can help with developing reading ability *in L2*.

Why, then, do I suggest that we look at L1 reading? There are many techniques we can borrow from learning to read in L1 that can help develop reading skills in L2, for example top–down, bottom–up, analytical phonics and synthetic phonics. If we do not understand these approaches, we risk using ineffective strategies to teach reading in L2. Lack of success in learning the foreign language affects motivation and can turn pupils off the L2 very quickly. More importantly, if we get the teaching of reading in L2 wrong, it is something very difficult to undo or unteach.

3.3.3.1   Analytical and Synthetic Phonics

So, what are analytical and synthetic phonics?

The **analytical phonics** approach – often referred to as the *whole word* approach – largely relies upon children learning to recognise words straight away. By contrast **synthetic phonics** involves decoding and encoding with a systematic approach. This allows learners to read unfamiliar words and helps with comprehension.

Let's look at the skills for proficient readers in the learner's L1, namely:

- Automatic, rapid letter recognition;
- Automatic, rapid word recognition;
- The ability to use context unconsciously as an aid to comprehension;
- The ability to use context when necessary as a conscious aid to word recognition.

In terms of reading, if we take English as the learner's L1 as an example, then the beginning L1 learner needs to recognise the sound–symbol relationship. Let's use the word 'cat' as an example.

The learner recognises the letters in the following way. The first letter is the letter *C*. However, the teacher does not teach the learners the name of the letter, that is, the letter *C* (si:), but the learners are taught that this letter, this symbol, is pronounced as 'keh'. Similarly, the learners are taught that the second letter in the word is not the letter *A* (eɪ), but is pronounced 'ah', and the third letter of the word is not taught as the letter *T* (ti:), but is pronounced 'teh'. I have used 'keh', 'ah' and 'teh' as approximations of sound to show the contrast with the name of the letter, the precise standard pronunciation of which is represented by the International Phonetic Alphabet (IPA) notation in brackets after each of the letters (though this is not generally used in L1 teaching).

The next step is to *synthesise* these three letters. When you synthesise, you combine two or more things to create something more complex. The teacher does this by reading the letters aloud one after each other and blending the sounds 'keh', 'ah' and 'teh' into each other to give a new sound, using lots of repetition, for example with C̲ A̲ T̲: C̲ A̲ T̲, C̲ A̲ T̲, C̲ A̲ T̲, C̲ A̲ T̲ to give CAT!

The approach I have just illustrated is what we call 'synthetic phonics'.

The same approach is used with other common words, for example 'dog', again using the *sound* of the letter and not the *name* of the letter.

> d̲ o̲ g, d̲ o̲ g, d̲ o̲ g → dog
> s̲ e̲ t, s̲ e̲ t, s̲ e̲ t → set
> h̲ i̲ m, h̲ i̲ m, h̲ i̲ m → him

Essentially the learners are sounding out and blending the letters to form a word. Let us consider **digraphs**.

What about digraphs?

After the teacher is comfortable that the learners can sound out and blend individual letters, the teacher moves on to groups of letters. Two consonants together, for example *sh* and *ch*, are taught as one sound; for example, learners learn that *sh* is pronounced 'shih' and *ch* is pronounced 'chih' (again, these are approximations of sound). In this way, they learn that the word 'shop' is made up out of three distinct sounds, namely: *sh̲*, *o̲* and *p̲* blended together, as in the examples above, to make *shop̲*, or that the word *chip* is made up out of three sounds, namely: *ch̲*, *i̲* and *p̲* blended together to make *chip̲*. The learners still know, however, that *c* on its own is pronounced as 'keh' and that 'h' on its own is pronounced 'hih' (approximation).

What about vowel digraphs?

The same principle is used in **vowel digraphs**. Learners are taught how *o* sounds in 'hot', but they know that when it is combined with other vowels it makes a different sound, like *o̲o̲* in 'c̲o̲o̲l' and *o̲w̲* in 'h̲o̲w̲'. Similarly, they learn to distinguish between *e* as in 'set' and *ee* as in 'feel'.

Teachers also teach what they call 'tricky words'. Some words, such as 'the', are learnt as tricky words and are learnt as a whole, but these are very few.

So how do teachers manage this? Well, they do this progressively over about three months in the first class of primary or elementary schools. Letters and the sound–symbol relationships are learnt and used to make short words at first. Pupils have 'letter tins' with cut-up letters which are gradually added to. The pupils use these in a tactile way to form words. The teachers practise reading simple picture stories with the pupils with the words underneath. Big books (i.e., a giant version of pupils' books) are often used to demonstrate this for the whole class or in groups. Through this system, the pupils develop phonologic or phonological awareness (mental manipulation of sounds). They also develop phonemic awareness (recognition and manipulation of 'chunks').

3.3.3.2   Other Factors That Help Develop Reading Skills
As stated earlier, beginning readers need to know the following to develop their reading skill:

- The vocabulary and grammar of the language to be read;
- discourse structure (e.g., narrative structure);
- cultural conventions (e.g., knowing that it is bad manners to steal porridge);
- general knowledge (e.g., knowing that a straw house will be weaker than a wooden house).

They get this through pre-literacy activities in nursery school and from their parents or caregivers, largely through fairy tales.

Building up Reading Proficiency Teachers develop learners' reading proficiency in L1 by starting off with simple phrases and short sentences, reusing familiar language in easy-to-understand contexts, often with images As learners become more proficient and fluent in reading, text length can gradually be increased and more complex structures introduced. Learners can then be introduced to short, simple storybooks with illustrations.

Reading Schemes It is particularly useful to set the development of reading skills within a reading scheme. These schemes should include reading connected text: not simply workbooks, but a **pluralistic approach to reading**. This means not just fiction: factual books can also be added, and in fact a range of genres should be used. All this helps in developing reading practice in young learners. Teaching young readers to skim and scan to get the gist of a text is another essential skill, as is guessing words from the context and predicting what will happen next in a story. These are all skills that primary or elementary teachers use when developing reading skills in young learners.

3.3.4   Application of L1 Reading Strategies to Developing Reading Skills in L2
If a foreign language teacher does not manage the transition from the oral to the written form of the L2 in their teaching, then it can affect the development of not only L2 reading skills, but also other skills. Too often this transition is skipped over in class and long pieces of dense written text in L2 are presented to learners instead, without

the necessary attention having been paid to presenting the sound–symbol relationship in the foreign language. As a result, we then see interlingual interference occurring (Long & Hatcho, 2018). This is when one language (often L1) will affect the learner's production of L2. In the case of reading, if the learner has not been made aware of the sound–symbol relationship in the L2, then they will apply the only sound–symbol system they know, that of the L1. The language produced when read out loud often bears no resemblance to the L2. Indeed, the interference from the known L1 sound–symbol relationship is often so strong that words that the learners could previously pronounce perfectly well in L2 during listening and speaking activities are then mispronounced. It is important not to leave the introduction of reading in L2 too late, as this will lead to 'fossilisation' (Long & Hatcho, 2018), where the L1 sound–symbol relationship becomes dominant in the L2. This is particularly acute when the L1 and the L2 have a similar alphabet and where a large number of the letters are similarly pronounced. Apart from the problem of mispronunciation, the early introduction of long pieces of dense text in L2 can overwhelm the language learner.

3.3.4.1   How Can I Help My Learners to Read in L2?

To help language learners to develop proficient reading skills in L2, there are a number of steps in the process.

1. After your learners have acquired some competence and confidence in listening and speaking in L2, start to introduce the written form gradually.
2. Do this by introducing the written form of the L2 using language that the learners are familiar with.
3. Draw the learners' attention to how the written form is pronounced by reading the L2 out loud to the learners, if necessary pointing to the words.
4. Make sure to emphasise not only similarities with the sound–symbol relationship of the L1, but also the differences; for example, the completely different ways in which 'en' is pronounced in English and French. Indeed, 'en' in French can be pronounced in different ways, depending on how these letters are used or where they appear in a word. Give plenty of practice.
5. As with the advice for building up reading proficiency in L1 in Section 3.3.3.2 above, foreign language teachers should build up reading proficiency in L2 by moving from simple phrases and short sentences to progressively longer and more complex pieces of text. Encourage your learners to skim and scan in the L2, to guess from the context and to predict what will happen next. Do not rush this, however. This needs to be built up gradually.
6. Include in your lessons reading schemes where learners are allowed and encouraged to read a variety of text genres in L2. Encourage your learners to give regular feedback on what they read, perhaps through a simple evaluation form or booklet accompanying them on their reading journey. Start a class library corner and encourage a pluralistic approach to reading in L2. This could be through a commercial reading scheme, or an eclectic collection of books you have amassed, or both.

3.3.5   Some Suggestions for Simple Reading Activities in L2
These can be adapted to make them either easier or more difficult.

Examples of Reading Activities

Activity 3.1: Finding the word
Pupils work in pairs and have one copy of a text between them. The teacher calls out a list of words which the pupils look for in the text. One point goes to the pupil in the pair who finds and points to the word the quickest.

Activity 3.2: Finding the synonym
This is the same as the activity above, but the pupils must find a synonym in the text for the words the teacher reads out.

Activity 3.3: Running dictation
Stick a paragraph of text on the walls around the class and divide the class into small groups. Two members of the group run or walk up to the text on the walls, read or memorise a part of the text and come back to the group and whisper it to the group members sitting at their desks, whose job it is to write down what the runners say. This involves the runners having to run or walk back and forward to the text and to try to memorise short sentences or phrases of the text. The group that manages to write the complete text first wins. Points can also be awarded for accuracy.

Activity 3.4: Wrong words
Pupils are given a text which contains some wrong words. As the teacher reads out the correct text, pupils underline the wrong words. The teacher then reads the text out loud a second time and the pupils have to write in the correct words.

Activity 3.5: Word bingo
Prepare bingo grids with a selection of words from a text or topic with which the class is familiar. The grids should contain some similar words, but they should not all be the same. The teacher reads out a list of words and the first pupil to score out all the words in a line vertically, horizontally or diagonally wins. This game can be extended after the first line has been won by playing for a full house, that is, until all words on the grid have been scored out.

Activity 3.6: Jigsaw texts
Divide the class into groups of four pupils. Choose or prepare a text and cut it into different sentence strips. Pupils have to read their sentence and discuss which order the sentences should go in. When the order of sentences has been decided, the pupils should lay these on the desk and call the teacher to check if it is correct.

3.3.6   Some Useful Apps and Sites for Online Games to Develop Reading

Kahoot

https://kahoot.com

A free online platform where the teacher can recycle language in the form of a quiz or survey with multiple-choice answers that are displayed on the screen in class and simultaneously on pupils' smartphones or devices. This is a game played against the clock and answers and statistics are displayed after the timer for each question stops. This takes little time to prepare and pupils enjoy the competitive element. As well as practising reading, Kahoot is good for vocabulary building. There are paid versions of Kahoot which offer extra features.

Quizlet

https://quizlet.com

A useful online tool which includes digital flash cards, matching games, live quizzes and electronic assessments which teachers (and learners) can create to practise reading and vocabulary.

Blooket

www.blooket.com

Similar to Kahoot and Quizlet, Blooket is a web-based quiz game platform for group competition or solo study which teachers can use to help develop their pupils' reading skills.

Linguascope

www.linguascope.com

Linguascope is a very popular website offering interactive language content, such as multiple-choice questions, comic strips and games, amongst other things. It has ready-made content which teachers can add to or change and is offered at different levels of difficulty. As part of a wider suite of tools, Linguascope offers reproducible resources, such as story books, e-posters, songs and video resources which can be used to develop reading.

3.3.7   Using Literary Texts in the Classroom

An important point to note is that if literature is part of a course, it is there for a purpose, usually to help develop reading skills, as well as to introduce pupils to the literature, history and culture of the country or countries where the target language is spoken.

   If reading a book is part of the course, then use it to its full advantage. Do not treat it as something to be done, as part of questions in an oral exam. Do not skip over it or be tempted to give a summary of the book in the target language to your pupils to rote-learn in order to pass part of an oral for a mock exam, a commonplace occurrence over the years in many schools. Instead, exploit the book to its full potential! Here are some ways in which you can do this.

Spread the reading of the book over the whole teaching 'year'

- When introducing the book, capture the pupils' interest with a 'taste' or 'trailer' of the book!
- If it is situated in a certain part of the country, look at this with your class through readings, video clips (perhaps from tourist websites), news articles, web pages or personal accounts.
- If it is situated in a historical era, situate this in context with your learners, giving background and information about events.

Make the reading manageable

- Set chapters or sections to read by due dates – make these every few weeks.
- Give useful guides to aid their reading, i.e., points for them to look out for and note down, or things to report back on. This will help them to target their reading purposefully.
- Give useful or difficult vocabulary in advance.

In class

- Set tasks to allow pupils to report back on what they have read.
- Ask questions (whole class, group, individual) to find out pupils' opinions on events in the book.
- Allow them to ask questions and discuss in groups.
- If a section or chapter of the book introduces an interesting, unusual or complex topic, explore this in class.

After you have done all of this:

- Agree on a summary of the section or chapter that pupils can write into a specific section of an exercise book or on a dedicated space online, e.g., in OneNote.
- Identify any new language areas pupils encounter in their reading to help your pupils extend their linguistic ability.

 FOOD FOR THOUGHT

When you were learning languages in school, did you have regular exposure to the four skills of listening, speaking, reading and writing?

Did you have the opportunity to use these skills on a regular basis?

Did you feel more or less confident or able in any skill area(s) as a result?

This section has explored the development of reading in L2, looking initially at reading development in L1 and considering how strategies in L1 reading development can help the development of reading in L2. Guidance was given on how to make reading in L2 manageable and practical strategies explored as well as useful resources listed.

3.4   Multi-Skill and Multi-Task Activities

More often than not, if someone is speaking, then someone else is listening and if someone is writing something, it is for someone else to read. As you can see, learners are often engaged in multi-skill activities and the mix of skills used will vary depending on the task. Frequently, when using the foreign language in real life, we are carrying out a series of tasks. It is quite rare that these tasks are always uniform. Most times, we perform a variety of different tasks one after each other or simultaneously. This is referred to in language learning as multi-task activity. Although teachers may set discrete tasks which focus on one particular skill in class, in a communicative classroom what we often see is multi-skill and multi-task activities. If we look again at Communicative Language Teaching (Section 2.1.3) and Task-Based Language Teaching (Section 2.1.4), we see that much of the suggested teaching and learning involves multi-skill and multi-task activities, using real language in authentic activities.

Some examples of this include:

- Reading holiday brochures or websites, then phoning to book a holiday;
- Reading holiday brochures then discussing with others, agreeing on a destination and then writing an email or filling in an online form to book a holiday;
- Listening to a passer-by giving you directions then writing them down;
- Listening to voicemail then telling someone about it;
- Listening to voicemail and making notes;
- Discussing with others which restaurant to go into then studying the menu before ordering.

TRY THIS OUT

Try these multi-skill and multi-task activities!
Look at the four scenarios below:
Scenario 1
Listening leading to Speaking and Writing

Scenario 2
Reading leading to Speaking and Writing

Scenario 3
Writing leading to Reading and Speaking

Scenario 4
Speaking leading to Listening and Writing

Write a short description of what each scenario would look like in a L2 class.
- Choose the age group;
- Choose a topic for the scenario;
- Write a brief outline of this multi-skill multi-task scenario;
- Show your outline to a peer or to your tutor, supervising teacher or mentor and ask for feedback;
- Try this out in class.

....

SUMMARY

Chapter 3 has examined the importance of developing the skills of listening, speaking, reading and writing in L2 and explored a range of strategies for using these in class. This has included examples in different languages to show how these would work practically in class. The development of reading skills was explored in detail with an analysis of how strategies for developing reading in L1 can be adopted to develop reading skills in L2. This included an examination of analytical and synthetic phonics and a look at strategies to build up L2 reading proficiency in learners. Suggestions for simple reading activities were given, together with a list of useful apps and online sites to develop reading. A look at the use of literary texts in the classroom focused on more advanced learners. As skills seldom exist on their own, the chapter concluded with a look at multi-skill and multi-task activities with a task to try out creating multi-skill and multi-task activities for L2 classes. I recognise that many more examples could be given for each skill; indeed, whole books could be devoted to a particular skill. What I have attempted here is to raise awareness of how important it is to develop each skill and accompany this with some initial ideas to help student teachers develop the appropriate skills in their learners.

REFLECTIVE QUESTIONS

1. Do you consider there to be a hierarchy in the development of skills for the L2 classroom? Is it useful to develop one skill or skills before others? If so, why do you think this is the case?
2. How can we ensure that we develop the different skill areas in the L2 classroom effectively? Can we be sure that we do not overemphasise one skill to the neglect of others?

KEY TERMS

analytical phonics An approach to reading that largely relies on children learning to recognise words straight away.

digraphs Two letters that make one sound or phoneme when combined.

pluralistic approach to reading A pedagogical approach to reading that uses a variety of different genres of books including fiction and non-fiction.

synthetic phonics An approach to reading which involves decoding and encoding words within a systematic approach.

vowel digraphs Two vowels written together, sometimes to make a single sound, sometimes to form diphthongs.

FURTHER READING

If you are interested in themes and issues surrounding skills teaching, Burns and Siegel have edited a selection of articles with an international perspective in this publication:

Burns, A. and J. Siegel, 2018. Teaching the four language skills: Themes and issues, in A. Burns & J. Siegel (eds.), *International Perspectives on Teaching the Four Skills in ELT: International perspectives on English language teaching.* Cham: Palgrave Macmillan.

This excellent resource from Cambridge University Press and Assessment contains advice and practical ideas for teachers to develop listening skills in their learners and how to find out which approaches are most helpful to them:

Cambridge English, 2024a. *B1 Preliminary for Schools: Developing listening skills for Cambridge English Qualifications: A guide for teachers.* Cambridge: Cambridge University Press and Assessment. Online. https://bit.ly/42mFWyA

Cambridge University Press and Assessment has also produced a number of guides for developing reading skills. Although related to specific Cambridge exams, it contains useful advice for teachers:

Cambridge English, 2024b. *B2 First for Schools: Developing reading skills for Cambridge English Qualifications: A guide for teachers.* Cambridge: Cambridge University Press and Assessment. Online. https://bit.ly/4hmU0wr

Here are some activities devised by students to help develop speaking skills in L2. They are fluency-focused activities, language-focused activities, socio-culturally sensitive speaking activities and public speaking activities:

Willy's ELT Corner, 2021. Engaging speaking activities for L2 learners. Online. https://willyrenandya.com/engaging-speaking-activities-for-l2-learners

This TEFL site has a range of ideas for lessons which can be adapted for any language:

The Art of TEFL, 2021. Writing skills practice in the EFL classroom. Online. https://bit.ly/3CfIPGY

4 Modes of Teaching

Introduction

Chapter 3 examined the development of the different skills of listening, speaking, reading and writing, as well as how they interact in multi-skill and multi-task activities. The different ways in which they are used in class were explored and practical examples given.

Chapter 4 focuses on the different modes of teaching that teachers can employ in class and when and where to use them. Resource-Based Learning (RBL) and Task-Based Language Teaching (TBLT) will also be examined.

The learning objectives for this chapter are, therefore, as follows:

1. Examine the educational theories of behaviourism, constructivism, social constructivism and cognitive apprenticeship and how they are used.
2. Explore different modes of teaching and the features of each particular mode.
3. Look at the ways in which these modes of teaching may be used in the L2 classroom and to examine issues related to each mode.
4. Explore the uses of Resource-Based Learning and Task-Based Language Teaching in the L2 classroom.

Overview

This chapter looks at different modes of teaching that teachers can employ in class. Direct, Discussion, Activity, Enquiry, collaborative and group approaches are all examined in detail, considering the advantages and disadvantages of each mode and offering practical advice on when and where to employ the different approaches within a pupil-centred environment. The chapter examines why particular modes appear predominant in class and why it is important for teachers to use a wide range of learning and teaching modes, as well as what each mode is particularly suited to achieving. Resource-Based Learning and Task-Based Language Teaching are also explored in detail.

4.1   Exploration of Educational Theories

To understand what the different modes of teaching are and how they can be employed in class, it is necessary to look first at a number of educational theories and how they may influence the choices teachers make to use different modes of teaching. The educational theories that we will consider here are **behaviourism, constructivism, social constructivism** and **cognitive apprenticeship**.

4.1.1   Behaviourism

Probably the most well known of the theories popular in education is behaviourism. Associated largely with Burrhus Frederic Skinner (Skinner, 1957; Braddon-Mitchell & Miller, 2020), behaviourism is predicated on the view that people learn best when they are rewarded for correct responses: what has come to be termed 'positive reinforcement'. This is often displayed in class through the use of praise, merit marks or special privileges. In terms of teaching, behaviourism is very much a model where the teacher is seen as the transmitter of knowledge and the pupil receives and replicates this. The learner is seen as a 'blank slate', who accumulates fragments (facts and sub-skills) of knowledge and structures, absorbing what the teacher transmits. The learner is in a dependent, passive learning role, expected to listen, remember and answer. In second language learning, this type of stimulus–response language is believed to reinforce structures and vocabulary and has led to an approach to L2 learning and teaching that relies a lot on drilling and the memorisation of language patterns, rather than an authentic use of L2.

4.1.2   Constructivism

In contrast to behaviourism, constructivism deals more with patterns, as opposed to accumulating fragments of knowledge, where the learner actively constructs understanding, interacts with their environment and builds upon (or contradicts) prior knowledge and constructs. Generally associated with Jean Piaget, constructivism is a more pupil-centred approach to learning (Piaget, 1928; Hyslop-Margison & Strobel, 2007; Taber, 2019). The teacher will normally identify the level or stage of learning of each learner and set up appropriate learning opportunities to enable the learner to progress further in terms of their understanding of concepts. As opposed to behaviourism, the teacher is effectively an enabler, helping the learner with their own personal formation of knowledge. Instead of being mere accumulators of fragments, the learner will use pre-existing models and compare what they already know with new knowledge (see also 'noticing' in Section 2.5.2.2), often changing their beliefs or knowledge as they construct new knowledge, beliefs and concepts (von Glasersfeld, 1984). It is an active learning process, with supported autonomy where the learner does not just regurgitate knowledge, but learns to reason and interact.

4.1.3   Social Constructivism

Social constructivism shares many traits with constructivism, such as building upon prior learning, acknowledging the importance of comparing and contrasting new knowledge with what the learner already knows to construct new knowledge in an active and dynamic way (Bruner, 1996; Kukla, 2013). However, social constructivism takes this further. Lev Vygotsky, the pioneer of social constructivism (Vygotsky, 1978), maintained that learning is an essentially social activity and that learners make best progress when they interact with others, be this with their peers or with their teacher. Vygotsky put emphasis on recognising that we learn as members of a culture and that within that culture we use its tools, the prime tool being our shared language (Amineh & Asl, 2015). We do, we talk and then we internalise. As we talk and share ideas with others, we construct new ideas and knowledge or concepts, comparing what we know with what others present us with. This takes us into what Vygotsky termed the 'zone of proximal development', that is, the place between what a learner can do unassisted and what that learner can do with the assistance of someone more knowledgeable.

4.1.4 Cognitive Apprenticeship

Cognitive apprenticeship is a theory of learning inspired by traditional apprenticeship learning (Collins et al., 1987; Dennen, 2004; Ghefaili, 2003). Adapted to school conditions, it can be regarded as practical social constructivism. It is based on modelling, coaching and 'fading'. The teacher models the learning and coaches the learners as they carry out the new learning by prompting, encouraging and advising. As the learner becomes more proficient, the teacher can gradually start to withdraw (fade) this scaffolding.

FOOD FOR THOUGHT

How were you taught in your Modern Language (and other subjects) classes in school?
   Did your teachers' approaches resemble more behaviourism, constructivism, social constructivism or cognitive apprenticeship? Or was there a mixture of different approaches? Do you think your teachers' approaches helped you or created barriers to your learning?

4.2 Modes of Teaching

The four educational theories summarised in Section 4.1 above (behaviourism, constructivism, social constructivism and cognitive apprenticeship) are overarching approaches for guiding the practices of teachers in class. These often translate into different modes of teaching, which we will examine. The most common modes of teaching derived from the educational theories in Section 4.1 are Direct, Discussion, Activity and Enquiry. These modes differ from each other in terms of learning, organisation and resources, teacher and learner roles, teaching skills and typical assessment approaches. Assessment will be explored in more detail in Chapter 8.

4.2.1   Features of Different Modes of Teaching

To relate these teaching modes to learning, we can summarise this as follows:

Direct Teaching →having something explained directly
Discussion →through reason and argument
Activity Learning →through direct experience
Enquiry →through exploring and investigating

Each of the modes of teaching listed above has particular features, which also have an influence on why a teacher may choose them.

Tables 4.1 to 4.4 summarise the main features usually associated with Direct Teaching, Discussion, Activity Learning and Enquiry, followed by a list of possible issues.

Table 4.1 A summary of the features of Direct Teaching

Factors to consider	Specific features
Means of learning	Direct presentation of ideas, information, skills
Organisation and resources	Learners in rows facing the teacher
	Presentation via text (various types)
	Use of presentation aids
Teacher and learner roles	*Teacher* – giver/transmitter
	Learner – receiver
Teaching skills	Exposition, explanation, demonstration
	Structuring knowledge for learners
	Questioning to check understanding
	Motivating
	Holding attention, discipline
Typical assessment approaches	Worksheets, practice problems, exercises to apply and test understanding, oral questions to check understanding throughout lesson
Issues	Differentiation, holding attention, motivation, active participation

FOOD FOR THOUGHT

Think back to how you were taught modern languages in school.
Which mode of teaching did you experience most – Direct, Discussion, Activity or Enquiry?
Which mode of teaching did you enjoy most?
Through which mode of teaching do you feel you learnt best?

Section 4.2 has examined the modes of Direct Teaching, Discussion, Activity Learning and Enquiry, and the features of each mode.

Table 4.2 A summary of the features of Discussion

Factors to consider	Specific features
Means of learning	Learning through interaction, by reasoning and argument. Double aim of learning through Discussion and teaching to discuss
Organisation and resources	Stimulus or focus for discussion (scaffolding), interaction among all participants in small groups or whole class
Teacher and learner roles	*Teacher* – models discussion skills orchestrates, conducts and encourages participation, or may merely facilitate
	Learner – participates, listens, and argues constructively and reasonably
Teaching skills	Modelling effective participation in discussion
	Managing discussion without resorting to question and answer
Typical assessment approaches	Of *process* – quality of reasoning, discussion procedures (etiquette, turn-taking, confidence to express views)
	Of *outcomes* – usually through later activities (written work, practical projects, but also further discussion)
Issues	How to manage without dominating; how to encourage participation; what type of questioning to use

Table 4.3 A summary of the features of Activity Learning

Factors to consider	Specific features
Means of learning	Marked degree of autonomy
	Learning by doing – applying skills and/or knowledge and understanding
	Focus on direct experience – experiential learning with reflection and evaluation
	Learning *how* versus learning *what* (discovery)
	Thinking about action – not just doing, but also reflecting in action
Organisation and resources	Dependent on learning environment and activity
	Time required for planning and set up
	Management and maintenance of resources and equipment
Teacher and learner roles	*Teacher* – involves learners in planning, execution and reflection, helps learners to sustain the action, move things along
	Learner – follows the brief, sustains the action, remains engaged, employs skills effectively, applies and develops knowledge and understanding effectively, realises goals, reflects
Teaching skills	Support and challenge through commenting, questioning
	Offer feedback
	Judge when and when not to intervene
	Encourage and support without leading or dominating

Table 4.3 (cont.)

Factors to consider	Specific features
Typical assessment approaches	Observation of process Observation of product, presentation or performance Reflective self-assessment by learner Peer assessment in groups or whole class Structured feedback from teacher
Issues	Danger of pushing learners through the action and not involving them in the planning and reflecting phases How to interact without taking ownership from the learner Some activities may be tightly structured – implications for teacher about how much they instruct and/or facilitate

Table 4.4 A summary of the features of Enquiry

Factors to consider	Specific features
Means of learning	Learners find out for themselves – research, experiment, investigation. Double aim of teaching learners how to enquire and how to learn through Enquiry
Organisation and resources	Can be individual or group; resources are key – reference books, artefacts, realia, various types of instruments, equipment, components or tools such as library, internet or crib sheets as scaffolding
Teacher and learner roles	*Teacher* – adviser (scaffolding), resource consultant, modelling how to enquire (process) *Learner* – tries relevant strategies, being confident to experiment and reflect on evidence, learning how to address enquiry questions, learning how to be systematic
Teaching skills	Clarity of exposition Modelling effective enquiry Encouraging disciplined pupil enquiry Sound management and organisation
Typical assessment approaches	Commonly through observation of the process and of the learners Reporting back on results of investigations Presentation of the results of the enquiry
Issues	How to support and challenge learners' thinking and their enquiry process, how to encourage pupil questions, role of subject understanding, e.g., can you enquire in modern languages without some basic language knowledge?

4.3 Using the Different Modes of Teaching in Class

This section will examine the use of different modes of teaching in class and how to achieve a balance of the modes used. It will also examine which modes of teaching are suited best to promoting communication in class.

An examination of the features of the four modes of teaching outlined in Section 4.2 reveals the different ways in which they might be used in class. For teachers wishing to keep the entire class at the same point and to control the amount of knowledge delivered, then Direct Teaching, with its highly controlled mode of teaching often rooted in behaviourism, sees the class being taught in a whole-class lock-step manner at a rate determined by the teacher. By contrast, if teachers wish to encourage learners to work collaboratively in groups, then Discussion is a more obvious choice, allowing to learners to share and learn from each other in a socially constructivist way, at the same time as developing social and negotiating skills. Where the objective is more learning by doing, then Activity Learning with its focus on learning through direct experience will be more appropriate. If the aim is to develop more research-oriented skills in the learners, then Enquiry will be the most suitable path to choose.

In most classes, teachers will find themselves employing a number of these modes, often within a single lesson. This may start with some expository Direct Teaching to teach a particular point or to explain something, which may then be followed by discussion, where pupils negotiate meaning and their shared level of conceptual understanding. This may in turn lead to pupil-centred activity or enquiry supported through scaffolding (structured parameters, worksheets or working to a specified brief), and conclude with a plenary session including discussion-based feedback and reflection or evaluation.

4.3.1 Issues to Consider in the Choice of Mode(s) of Teaching

The choice of which modes of teaching to use will depend largely on what the aims of the particular lesson or lessons are, and it may be that one or more modes are dominant. Part of the craft of the teacher lies in determining what the most appropriate modes of teaching to choose to develop knowledge, understanding and skills in the learners for a particular lesson are.

4.3.1.1 Overuse of a Mode of Teaching

As an essentially practical subject where it is important to give regular practice in a range of skills, choosing the appropriate mode to develop competence and confidence in learners' abilities is crucial. Overuse or underuse of a particular mode of teaching may lead to an imbalance in learners' skills, as well as limit their knowledge and understanding. A particular mode of teaching which I have found is perhaps the most often overused in Modern Language classrooms is Direct Teaching. In classrooms where this approach is dominant and used for most (sometimes all) of the lesson, new knowledge, language structures and vocabulary are presented in a teacher-centred, whole-class fashion, where the pace is set by the speed at which the teacher presents or explains topics and language. All pupils progress through work at the same rate and the teacher asks frequent questions to check comprehension. While this approach may have some value in a lesson introduction, I would caution against using this as the only approach in a lesson. The problems with overuse of a Direct Teaching approach are manyfold, namely:

1. All learners in the class are expected to progress at the same rate and level, regardless of their ability – for some learners this may be too complex, for others too easy.
2. Learners are mainly in receptive mode, either listening or reading, with few opportunities for output.
3. It is difficult for teachers to monitor the progress of individuals in a whole-class environment.
4. It is difficult for learners to concentrate for long periods of time, which may lead to inattention and/or disruption.

In terms of point 1, this means that it is harder to differentiate input, so differentiation often only comes in the form of graded tasks or exercises (easy, middle, more difficult, etc.) after a core presentation or explanation. For more on differentiation, see Chapter 7.

Point 2 highlights the obvious situation that if the teacher is in expository mode, giving or transmitting information, the pupils are in receptive mode and are denied the opportunity to use or to practise and improve their productive language skills of speaking and writing. Advice on skills development was provided in Chapter 3.

This whole-class approach makes it very difficult to monitor the learning of individual pupils, affecting the ability to gauge comprehension reliably (point 3), and at best the teacher gains a rough idea of whether the class 'as a whole' is following the lesson or not. With very little opportunity for output, it is impossible to judge whether input has been successfully transformed into intake and there is minimal opportunity to assess spoken or written performance (see Chapter 8 for advice on formative assessment). Consider this: in a fifty-minute lesson using a Direct Teaching approach with a class of thirty pupils, even if the teacher does not speak, each pupil – assuming all are given the opportunity to speak – would only be able to do so for just over a minute and a half. This would leave no time for feedback and also raises the question of what the other learners may be doing while waiting for their turn to speak.

Connected to this, point 4 highlights a particular problem for teachers when using this mode of teaching as their primary approach, namely, how to hold the attention of the learners and prevent or minimise disruption. Paradoxically, teachers who often use whole-class Direct Teaching as their main approach believe they have more control in terms of behaviour management. Many teachers also feel it is easier for them to give explanations, teach grammar and have social chat with their classes in this more controlled whole-class setting. More information and advice on classroom and behaviour management will follow in Chapter 12.

4.3.2   Influences on Teacher Choice of Approach or Teacher Cognition

There are a number of reasons why teachers, especially beginning teachers, choose to make Direct Teaching their dominant approach. Most importantly, the influence of how they learned foreign languages themselves as young learners is very power-ful. Despite studying educational theories and modes of teaching during teacher education, it frequently transpires that when under pressure, teachers will often switch to how they were taught themselves (Borg, 2003; Korthagen, 2010). This can be observed particularly with teachers at the beginning of their career, where not only are they coping with a fuller timetable than they had during their teacher education programme, but they are also faced with new practices in their first school, pupils (and colleagues) who may use a different approach, a burgeoning amount of administration – all of which can cause stress and affect decisions they take in class. Often these novice teachers may be experimenting with different modes of teaching, perhaps more discursive, activity or enquiry-centred approaches. However, they may face obstacles in terms of pupil resistance to their modes of teaching and lack of pupil motivation or discipline problems, especially if the pupils are already accustomed to a different mode. It is then that teachers often switch to a more traditional, expository type of teaching mode in an almost 'knee-jerk' reaction to get them through the 'here and now' of the classroom situation (Borg, 2003; Richards & Pennington, 1998). If this becomes a default reaction to dealing with perceived problems, it can soon become the teacher's main, or only pedagogy (Korthagen & Lagerwerf, 2001; Lynch, 2020). This situation is well known and has been explored by educationalists and researchers of the field of **language teacher cognition** (see Section 2.3 and Chapter 2 Further Reading).

4.3.3   Modes of Teaching That Encourage Communication

In order to help learners make progress in their knowledge and understanding of the foreign language and also in the different skills of listening, speaking, reading and writing, the modes of teaching used in class must provide opportunities to use the foreign language in authentic situations or wherever there is a purpose in using the language. This is more difficult in a whole-class, Direct Teaching mode where the focus is largely on the teacher, who may often be explaining the workings of the language, as opposed to giving practice in using the language. The other modes of teaching outlined above (Discussion, Activity and Enquiry) are more suited to a communicative approach to language teaching, offering more opportunities for use of the language in realistic contexts.

It is important that teachers have a coherent plan to ensure that *what* is to be taught is done so in a logical order and makes sense to the learners. It is also the teacher's duty to plan linguistic progression for learners, so that new learning is based on previous learning in a constructivist way. Chapter 5 looks at ways in which teachers can develop a coherent plan, taking account of what is to be taught (topics and themes, etc.) as well as linguistic progression. Alongside the subject matter teaching, there must be ample opportunities for learners to develop and improve both their receptive (listening and reading) skills and their productive skills (speak-ing and writing). This may be a good point at which to review Chapter 3.

4.3.3.1   Using Discussion to Encourage Communication

If we look firstly at Discussion, there are a number of features of this mode of teaching that make it suitable for a communicative approach to language teaching. In orchestrating and encouraging learners to engage in discussion, teachers are not only providing opportunities for learners to develop and practise their listening and speaking skills, but they are also teaching valuable skills of negotiating in a safe environment, where learners listen to each other and learn to form reasoned and constructive arguments. The learners learn how to participate in a conversation, acquire the rules of conversations, and develop confidence to express themselves. Effective discussion often takes place in smaller groups, which is less stressful than speaking in front of the whole class and leads to learners being more willing to speak, thereby developing their listening and speaking skills. All of these factors contribute to the overall development of social skills within learners. Developing effective skills to take part in discussion means, of course, that the classroom teacher has an important part to play. This may involve modelling the process, providing support materials, such as useful prompts, and monitoring the process. Teachers can encourage more reticent speakers by providing specific areas for individual group members to speak about, or to ask questions about. This can be supported with cue cards or other resources. This task can be delegated eventually to a group leader.

Example 4.1 (in French)

Topic: *Planning what to do on Saturday afternoon*

Vous travaillez en groupe de trois personnes.
Chacun choisit une carte avec un loisir (cinéma ou concert ou piscine).
Parlez avec les deux autres dans votre groupe.
Essayez de les persuader de faire l'activité sur votre carte.
Vous devez arriver à un choix qui est convenable pour tout le monde.
You are going to work in groups of three.
Each person chooses a card with a leisure activity on it (cinema or concert or swimming pool).
Speak to the other two members of your group.
Try to persuade them to do the activity on your card.
You need to choose an activity that suits all three of you.

Points to Note for Effective Discussion Activities

1. Make sure the task is well defined, with realistic steps and a clear goal to be achieved.
2. Supply appropriate and authentic source material (i.e., for above task, information on the leisure activities, locations, opening times and prices).
3. Provide phrases on cue cards to aid the discussion, for example: 'Why would you like to go to …? Isn't that on too late? How would we get there? I like going to X, but I prefer Y. Ok, agreed, let's go to …'
4. Set a timescale for completion of the task.

4.3.3.2 Using Activity Learning to Encourage Communication

It is important for learners to have regular opportunities to use their knowledge, understanding and skills, as opposed to being passive receivers of knowledge, which is often the case where Direct Teaching is overused. Apart from making pupils more autonomous in their learning, a more active mode of learning allows pupils to use their language learning in authentic situations. This gives the pupils opportunities to see the language in action, to try out their newly acquired knowledge of topics, vocabulary and structures and gain a feeling of achievement as they realise that they really can communicate. Language learning is not just about vocabulary and grammar, which admittedly are necessary to language learning, but is also a skills-based subject, so the vocabulary and grammar are mere items of knowledge if not used in a practical way. This is why it is essential to include as much and as regular practice as possible in all four skill areas of language learning. Skills need to be practised and built up to develop fluency, which means teachers must plan to include these opportunities to use the language.

Example 4.2 (in German)

Topic: *Surveying the class to find their favourite food and drink*

In dieser Aktivität redest du mit allen in der Klasse!

Du nimmst deinen Fragebogen und du fragst jede Schülerin/jeden Schüler, was sie gern essen und trinken.

Du notierst die Antworten in der Tabelle auf dem Fragebogen.

Schließlich machst du ein Diagramm aus den Ergebnissen.

In this activity you will talk to everyone in the class.

Take a questionnaire and ask each pupil what they like to eat and drink.

Note down their answers in the table on the questionnaire.

Finally, make a diagram of your results.

Points to Note for Effective Activity Learning

1. Make sure the task is well defined, with realistic steps and a clear goal to be achieved.
2. Make sure any language to be used is clear and unambiguous. You may wish to provide some revision in advance of the activity.
3. Provide phrases on cue cards to aid the discussion, for example: 'What do you like to eat/drink? What is your favourite food/drink? My favourite food/drink is ...' etc.
4. Ensure that the classroom allows safe movement. If not, consider using another accessible part of the school or location.
5. Take steps to ensure there are no barriers, physical or otherwise, that would disadvantage any member of the class.

4.3.3.3   Using Enquiry Learning to Encourage Communication

A method which is useful in its own right, but which can be used in combination with Discussion and Activity Learning, is Enquiry Learning. Some obvious benefits of Enquiry Learning are developing investigative and research skills amongst learners, as they use a variety of resources to learn more or search for answers to particular questions. The enquiry that learners are asked to do can be pitched at different levels, that is, from a simple search for information of what there is to do in a holiday location through looking at brochures and websites, to a more detailed project, perhaps focusing on an aspect of life or culture in a country where the target language is spoken, for example using realia, the library, online sources or through interviews with locals. Depending on the type of task set, this may involve the learners using a specific set of skills (e.g., reading and writing) or all skills in an interactive and communicative manner. Results of such enquiry can then be used more actively in a discussion forum with other members of the class to negotiate a particular desired outcome.

Example 4.3 (in Italian)

Topic: *Finding out what there is to do or visit in town*

Fa' un po' di ricerca sulla città che hai scelto di studiare.

Trova delle informazioni utili ed interessanti sull'internet e negli opuscoli.

Scrivi un rapporto sulla città per presentare al tuo gruppo.

Rispondi alle domande degli alunni nel tuo gruppo.

Research the town that you have chosen to study.

Look for useful and interesting information on the internet and in brochures.

Write a report about the town to present to your group.

Answer questions from your group.

Example 4.4 (in English)

Topic: *Researching cultural aspects of a location*

Work with a partner and each of you choose a site, monument or location of cultural significance in your nearest town or city (e.g., Edinburgh).

Find out all you can about this site through a web search. Look to see if the site has a website and contact addresses for staff.

Write an email requesting an interview with this person online (i.e., on Zoom, Teams, etc.) explaining that you are researching this site/monument/location.

Carry out the interview and make notes of what you find out.

Finally, use the information you have found on the internet and through your interview and make a presentation to give to the class or your group on the cultural aspects you have researched.

Points to Note for Effective Enquiry Learning

1. Make sure the task is well defined, with realistic steps and a clear goal to be achieved.

2. Provide a list of sources/materials to be used in the enquiry, e.g., websites, apps, brochures.
3. Remind learners where to get help if they come across language that they do not understand, for example, word banks, glossaries, dictionaries.
4. Define the format of the presentation.
5. Set a timescale for completion of the task.

In Section 4.3 we have looked at the use of different modes of teaching in the L2 classroom, the issues affecting the choice of mode(s) that teachers make, and explored which modes are most effective for promoting communication in class.

4.4 Other Approaches to the Learning and Teaching of L2 That Promote Communication

This section will examine two further approaches to the learning and teaching of L2 that are used in many schools, namely Resource-Based Learning and Task-Based Language Teaching, and how they are used.

4.4.1 Resource-Based Learning

Resource-Based learning (RBL) is a form of learning which generally encompasses any learning or teaching resource for a particular subject discipline that can be used in the classroom (Butler, 2012). This can be worksheets, booklets, commercial materials, such as textbooks, as well as audio files, videos and online sources. It has been interpreted over the years in a variety of ways. To some it is a method of teaching which is tightly controlled and sequenced by the teacher. To others it is a way to organise very open-ended work in an activity- or enquiry-type approach. The common element in most RBL classrooms is that the teacher is responsible for gathering appropriate resources for the programme of learning appropriate to the needs of the particular class. This needs to take into account the ability needs of the learners, the range of interests, any additional support needs and the levels of maturity. It was initially very popular in Modern Language classrooms in the 1970s and 1980s in the UK and USA and indeed, as a young teacher starting out in language teaching, I myself found it a refreshing and liberating change from the traditional grammar-based textbooks on offer in most schools. Now a lot of the elements of RBL have been subsumed into general learning and teaching advice in Modern Language Teacher Education courses.

4.4.2 Task-Based Language Teaching

Task-Based Language Teaching (TBLT) has become increasingly popular over the past few decades in the field of second language learning. A well-established pedagogical approach in modern language teaching, it focuses on both communication and functional use of L2 and owes a lot to the work of Jane and Dave Willis

(Willis & Willis, 2007). So, why use Task-Based Language Teaching? The answer to this question is that TBLT provides optimum conditions for language learning and provides the following necessary ingredients for an effective L2 learning classroom environment:

- *Exposure* to a rich but comprehensible input of real spoken and written language in use;
- *Use* of the language to carry out actions, i.e., to exchange meanings;
- *Motivation* to listen and read the language and to speak and write, i.e., to process and use the exposure;
- *Instruction* in language, i.e., opportunities to focus on form.

If we define a task as an activity where learners use the foreign language purposefully and communicatively to achieve a goal, then this opens up a multitude of learning opportunities that the teacher can set up or facilitate across any number of topic areas. See Section 2.1.4 for a definition of a task goal.

Types of Task

Listing: thought showers; fact-finding, for example finding what there is to do in a holiday location and sharing these with a partner or group/class.

Ordering and sorting: sequencing, ranking, categorising, classifying, e.g., categorising food groups to decide where to eat in the TL country (for vegetarians/vegans, meat-eaters, fish lovers).

Comparing: matching, finding similarities, finding differences, e.g., conducting a survey of peoples' likes and dislikes to use in decision-making, or matching personal traits to specifications in job adverts.

Problem solving: analysing real situations, analysing hypothetical situations, reasoning or decision making, e.g., looking at how we can reduce waste.

Sharing personal experiences: describing, narrating, exploring and explaining attitudes, opinions, reactions, e.g., saying what you did at the weekend or on holiday or how personal experience of the lesson topic affected you personally.

Creative tasks: designing, writing, composing, e.g., imagining your ideal place to live, composing a song, writing a poem or a short story based on a theme.

The TBLT Framework Within the TBLT framework, there are a number of steps:

A pre-task: This would be an introduction to the topic and task, where the teacher might provide useful and necessary information or resources; ideas on subject content or possible activities; activate relevant prior learning.

The task cycle: This is typically setting the task for the learners, allowing time for planning and task completion and reporting back on the task.

Language focus: This should be as is appropriate and as it arises inductively in the task, analysis and practice of language items or structures.

This is not an exhaustive list, but hopefully it provides you with ideas that you can adapt and add to. As is evident from the description of the tasks above, many of these TBLT tasks can be used in Activity, Enquiry and Discussion mode.

An **Example TBLT Lesson** This would be suitable for an intermediate level ESL (English as a Second Language) class.

The task
To choose where they would like to go on school trip.

Pre-task
Divide the class into four groups and provide each group with brochures and websites of the different places – a local castle, a museum, an outdoor activity centre, and a hill walk. Pupils should read the information for comprehension. Provide help sheets for any tricky vocabulary.

The task cycle
From their reading of the brochures and websites, pupils should:

1. Discuss their place in their allocated group and come up with arguments for why their place should be chosen for the class trip.
2. Once each group has agreed on a set of convincing arguments, they should prepare a short presentation for the other groups.
3. Each group should present their arguments to the class.
4. The whole class votes for one of the places.

Note: groups cannot vote for their own place, which should motivate them to make their place sound the most attractive.

Language focus
Help pupils with any language problems as they arise. This may require you to earmark certain language structures or grammar for a future lesson.

▐▐▷ TRY THIS OUT

Plan a TBLT activity for a class of your choice.

Start by choosing a task type (listing, ordering, comparing, etc.).

Use the TBLT Framework to guide your planning.

Make sure you include exposure to comprehensible input and use of language.

SUMMARY

This chapter has presented educational theories (behaviourism, constructivism, social constructivism and cognitive apprenticeship) that have to a greater or lesser extent had an influence on teachers' practices over the past few decades, as well as different modes of teaching (Direct Teaching, Discussion, Activity Learning and Enquiry) used in schools to teach modern foreign languages. Although an exact matching is not always possible, we can generally associate the modes of teaching with an educational theory. With its emphasis on direct presentation of ideas and the teacher as the transmitter of knowledge, Direct Teaching has been shown to share features with behaviourism where the learner is a passive receiver of fragments, facts and sub-skills.

By contrast, Activity Learning would seem to share some aspects with constructivism using experiential, active learning to help build knowledge and understanding in learners who reflect on what they are learning as they construct new knowledge, ideas and theories. Activity Learning also shares aspects of cognitive apprenticeship, as the pupil, through working on tasks and supported by a more expert other, progresses in learning and learns to climb quite naturally into the zone of proximal development.

Discussion and Enquiry Learning sit very comfortably with social constructivism, where the gathering of new knowledge through working and discussing with others in a social and collaborative setting is recognised as important and transformative in terms of knowledge and understanding, but also in the development of skills.

Ultimately, it is my hope that, in presenting these educational theories and modes of teaching with an indication of how they can be used in modern languages classes, teachers will use this chapter to reflect on and choose the most appropriate ways in which to plan for the learning and teaching in their classes, which will often be a mix of one or more educational theories and modes of teaching as judged appropriate to the aims they have for their different classes.

REFLECTIVE QUESTIONS

1. Considering the educational theories and modes of teaching presented in this chapter, which educational theories and modes of teaching do you see yourself using in your future teaching and why?
2. Do you see any difficulty in using specific modes of teaching? If so, which ones and why?

KEY TERMS

Activity Learning Learning by doing and direct experience.

behaviourism The theory that people learn best when they are rewarded for correct responses.

cognitive apprenticeship Regarded as practical social constructivism, based on modelling, coaching and fading.

constructivism Where learners use pre-existing models and compare what they already know with new knowledge to construct new learning.

Direct Teaching Direct presentation of ideas, information, skills.

Discussion Learning through interaction, reasoning and argument.

Enquiry Learning by carrying out an investigation or research.

social constructivism Like constructivism, but maintains that learning is essentially a social activity and that learners make best progress when they interact with others.

FURTHER READING

If you are interested in looking in more depth at models of teaching and learning, particularly behaviourism, constructivism and social constructivism, then Moore (pp. 1–32) provides quite an accessible read:

Moore, A., 2001. *Teaching and Learning: Pedagogy, curriculum, and culture*. Abingdon: Routledge.

The following publication provides a good overview of cognitive apprenticeship:

Collins, A., J.S. Brown & S E. Newman, 2018. Cognitive apprenticeship: Teaching the crafts of reading, writing, and mathematics, in L.B. Resnick (ed.), 1989, *Knowing, Learning, and Instruction: Essays in honor of Robert Glaser*. New York: Routledge, 453–94. Online. https://doi.org/10.4324/9781315044408.

This article looks at using TBLT online to create collaborative writing tasks:

Lynch, M. & N. Wang, 2022. Creating effective goals in TBLT for online collaborative English (as a foreign language) writing tasks. *Pädagogische Horizonte*, 6(2): 85–105.

Unit Planning

Introduction

Chapter 4 focused on the different modes of teaching that teachers can employ in class and when and where to use them. It also looked at the educational theories related to the different modes of teaching.

Chapter 5 will look at why successful learning and teaching depend on careful planning. It will consider the place of long-term planning and how this feeds into mid-term planning and unit construction. Unit planning will be explored in detail, leading into the development of more detailed short-term plans.

The learning objectives for this chapter are, therefore, as follows:

1. Consider the place of long-term planning and its stage in the process of unit planning.
2. Examine the rationale for creating unit plans within the mid-term plan.
3. Explore the steps in creating a unit plan.
4. Explore the use of textbooks in unit planning.
5. Explore practical steps and approaches to planning units.
6. Consider how to move from mid-term planning to short-term planning.
7. Consider progression and coherence in planning.

Overview

The construction of a long-term and a mid-term plan is vital to successful learning and teaching and a necessary preliminary stage to lesson planning. In order to ensure successful progression in pupils' language learning, careful thought is necessary in terms of deciding what pupils need to learn and in what order (Irfani, 2017). This involves planning not just what topics should be included in the learning programme, but also careful thought given to the sequence of language (vocabulary, function and notions, grammar and skills development) that is to be taught. Deciding what to teach across the year for a particular class needs to be given consideration in terms of what the logical progression of language within the hierarchy of needs of the learners is (Maslow, 1943), while also taking into account the stage they are currently at in their learning (Sinor & Kaplan, 2012). This needs to be set within a communicative framework and promote an authentic use of language, which is best achieved when language structures, grammar and vocabulary are introduced and practised in meaningful settings (Krashen, 1989). This chapter looks at the fundamentals of syllabus and unit planning with the aim of providing meaningful progression through the foreign language that is directly related to appropriate pedagogy. It walks student teachers through the stages needed to create successful unit plans and mid-term and long-term schemes of works for learners. It also contains tasks for student teachers aimed at giving them practice in producing those plans and schemes of work for teaching modern languages.

5.1 Long-Term Planning

Before we reach the stage of planning the individual lessons that we are going to teach our pupils, there are essential pre-requisites to consider. Effective learning, where learners build up their knowledge and skills, will only take place if this is planned for appropriately. In an established modern foreign languages department in a school, it is normal to expect that there will be a coherent **long-term plan** that allows for progression through the years of learning and teaching. Each year will have a set range of topics or themes considered appropriate to learners' needs and as learners move through the school, each new year of learning will be built upon the previous year.

In successful programmes of study, this is managed through effective teamwork between teachers in the modern foreign languages department, who plan what is to be taught, how this is to be taught and at what point in the school year for each class it will be taught. Depending on the curriculum in the school and the predicted length of study (which could be two, four or six years in a secondary school or across seven years in an elementary school), teachers will plan what the overall objectives will be for each year of study in terms of the topics studied and linguistic progression. This needs to consider the age, interests and terms of reference of the learners.

A typical long-term plan for a language class in their first year of secondary school may look like Table 5.1.

With these decisions taken in terms of objectives for each academic year, the next step is to plan the learning and teaching that is to go into each segment or part of the annual course. Many schools opt for a topic-based approach and plan the learning and teaching around what they perceive to be necessary to carry out the communicative aims for particular topics. The label given to these topics may vary from school to school. Some schools call these 'topics', others 'themes' or 'modules'. Whatever the nomenclature, these topics, themes and modules are essentially distinct units of work. For the purposes of this chapter, we shall use the term 'unit of work'.

Table 5.1 An example long-term plan for a first year language class at a secondary school

Week	Topic
Weeks 1–3 (4 Sept–22 Sept)	Self and family Name; age; where you live; brothers and sisters; extended family; pets
Weeks 4–6 (25 Sept–13 Oct)	School School subjects; timetable; what subjects you like or dislike and reasons; daily routine
Weeks 7–10 (16 Oct–3 Nov)	Hobbies and interests Sports; music; films; hobbies; likes, dislikes and reasons; frequency and location of hobby
Weeks 11–14 (6 Nov–1 Dec)	Holidays Where you want to go; why; attractions (mountains, sea, rivers, lakes); sightseeing (castles, monuments, museums, galleries)
Weeks 15–18 (4 Dec–22 Dec)	Christmas and other winter festivals Customs and traditions; holiday events; presents; music and dance
Weeks 19–22 (8 Jan–2 Feb)	'Finding your way about town' Places in town; asking and giving directions; opening and closing times
Weeks 23–26 (5 Feb–1 March)	Travel Means of travel; buying tickets; bus and train times; sustainable development and caring for the environment
Weeks 27–30 (4–31 March)	Accommodation Finding a place to stay; booking a youth hostel, AirBnB, hotel, campsite; facilities (plot, showers, toilets, cafes, restaurants, pool); at reception.
Weeks 31–34 (17 April–12 May)	Food and drink Looking at food and drink in target language country; buying food in shops or at stalls; understanding menus; ordering food in cafes, restaurants; paying the bill; problems with the food and drink
Weeks 35–38 (15 May–2 June)	Getting help Illnesses; accidents; at the chemist's; going to the doctor's or hospital
Weeks 39–41 (5 June–23 June)	Project work related to target language country Culture and traditions; food; music; geography; history

5.2   Rationale for Creating a Unit of Work

Section 5.2 will look at the rationale for creating units of work within a mid-term planning framework.

   If an annual plan can be thought of as a school's long-term plan, then the individual units of work are what we could safely call mid-term planning. These units may be of varying lengths and this will be decided by the teachers, depending on their views about what is necessary and appropriate to teach at each specified point in the pupils' learning. Typically, a unit of work may be of two, three or four weeks' duration. From the **mid-term plan**, you will be able to create **short-term plans**, each being component parts of the mid-term plan.

So, why make a unit plan? Well, there are a number of reasons why this is important, namely:

1. Most importantly, to make sure you cover all the learning outcomes for the particular unit.
2. To organise and sequence the learning and teaching.
3. To specify the aims, content and skills for the unit.
4. To avoid vagueness.
5. To have specific activities or tasks that can be used for regular assessment of pupil performance, whether this be formative or summative assessment (see Chapter 8 for detailed guidance on assessment).

If we look at point 1, it is essential to set out what it is that you want the pupils to learn in the unit. Bearing in mind that since most topics could continue for weeks or months, the action of agreeing the outcomes and setting limits on what is to be learned will make the planning and resourcing of lessons more manageable. Just as important as deciding what you want your learners to learn is deciding how this will be organised and sequenced (point 2) and this requires thought, not only in terms of what the most logical order of the subject matter is, but also in terms of pedagogy. This requires careful planning, as the language points, structures and items of grammar required to carry out the communicative purposes within the unit need to be considered in terms of supporting pupils' linguistic progression, that is, some structures or language items may require another language point to be learned first (Rahimpour, 2010). This entails careful consideration of how to plan for this within the framework of the unit without it appearing out of place or contrived, but instead integral and authentic. This affects the aims, content and skills to be practised that will be included in the unit (point 3). It is important that these aims and the general structure of the unit are shared with pupils at the beginning of the unit to assure them that you have a route plan through the learning that avoids vagueness (point 4). Pupils want and need to know what is expected of them throughout their learning and sharing your unit plan helps them with this and gives them confidence. It also helps pupils to identify when they have achieved the learning outcomes for the unit or for particular parts of the unit (point 5).

5.3 Developing a Unit of Work

As a starting point for any unit of work, it is important to consider who the course is for and what they require in terms of language learning. This means carrying out an analysis of needs.

5.3.1   Needs Analysis

The steps to creating the unit of work should be appropriate to the age and stage of the learners. It is important to determine what the learner wants to and needs to know for the programme of study (Yana, 2016).

There are, therefore, a number of factors that need to be considered before going through the steps above, namely:

What are the overall aims of the class? Is it to develop conversational fluency? Is it transactional to obtain services? Is it to go on holiday? Is it for further academic study of the language (at college or university)?

What are the pupils' learning needs? Why do they want to learn the language? Is this a language class in a school (elementary or secondary)? Are the learners adults? Do the learners need the language for work, leisure or specific purposes? Even if the learners are adults learning the language for leisure, or indeed for any purpose, the language, activities and resources must be appropriate to their interests and level of maturity. You cannot merely use the same language course which has been designed for young children.

Length of course: How many weeks or months are planned for? Is this a short course, or part of a sequence of courses taken over a prolonged period of time?

Prior learning: What do learners already know? Has this class already completed courses in the language? How many years, months or weeks? At what level?

Level of competence: Are the learners in your class all roughly at the same level of competence, or do you have a mix of ability levels in your class? Are there learners in your class with additional support needs or specific learning disabilities? (See the discussion of differentiation in Chapter 7 for more advice on responding to these needs.)

5.3.2   The Title

Although this is rather obvious and will perhaps be almost automatic as you decide on what to include in your long-term or annual plan, it is important to choose a title that is indicative of the purposes and content of the unit. For example, a unit simply called 'Town' might not say much to your learners, but 'Finding your way about town' gives a much clearer idea to pupils of what they can expect to learn in the unit.

5.3.3   Aims of the Unit

Having chosen a title for the unit, the next step is to decide on the main aims of the unit: what it is your pupils should expect to learn. If we take 'Finding your way about town' in an English as a Foreign Language class as an example, then your main aims may be as follows:

1. *To be able to ask for places in town.*
2. *To be able to ask for directions to a place.*
3. *To be able to give directions to a place.*

It is important to keep these overarching aims manageable. Don't be tempted to create an unending list of aims; rather keep the list manageable and decide what you think is realistic, given the time you have allocated to this topic.

5.3.4   Functions

From the aims that you have specified, you will be able to work out which functions are most suited to achieve these aims. Functions or notions can be thought of as language structures to enable a particular aim to be met (Finocchiaro & Brumfit, 1983). Each aim may have one or more possible functions that are appropriate to carrying out the aim. Within the unit of work above, 'Finding your way about town', the first aim *To be able to ask for places in town* could be met through the functions:

'Excuse me, is there a ... . . nearby?' or by 'Where is the (nearest) ... ... ?'

The second aim *To be able to ask directions* could be met through the functions:

'Can you direct me to ... ?' or 'How do I get to ... ?'

And the third aim *To be able to give directions* could be met through the functions:

'Go straight ahead ...'
  'Turn left/right ...'
  'Take the first/second street on your left/right ...'
  'Cross over at the junction/traffic lights/corner ...'

Note that some functions may also be found in other contexts or topics, so you may be able to activate prior learning.

5.3.5   Language Area

Once the functions have been decided upon, a number of general language areas will be obvious. These language areas are broad categories of vocabulary needed to complete the functions. Identifying these and making a conscious note of these in your planning will help keep you focused. Staying with our topic of 'Finding your way about town', an obvious language area for the first function above would be *Names of town buildings*. For the second function the language area would be *Directions* and for the third function it would be *Directions, parts of streets, roads, etc.*

5.3.6   Lexicon

Connected directly to language areas is lexicon. This is where you specify the actual vocabulary for each language area. This is not just a list of words, but may include short phrases, too (although not be confused with functions above). This may seem superfluous when you have just identified the language area (in Section 5.3.5), but both steps are necessary. Identifying the language areas and not choosing too many of them will help to keep work manageable while still carrying out the aims and functions of the unit. It is very easy to go off on a tangent if you do not set these parameters. Equally, the lexicon coming from the identified language areas needs to be chosen. This involves working out which words and phrases are most likely to be needed for communication and task completion. Given that you will have set an allocation of time or number of lessons for the unit, then choosing which lexicon to use will keep tasks manageable and avoid the temptation to teach every single related piece of lexicon that exists for a particular function. This will be of value in planning to keep your lessons varied and interesting and prevent them becoming never-ending lists of vocabulary to be learnt. As the learners master the language for each unit, they will have a sound basis upon which to add new words and phrases as they progress through their language learning. When choosing the lexicon for a particular class, you will be guided by what is appropriate language for their age and stage and your knowledge of prior learning (if any) your pupils may have in this area. A useful starting point is to consult the long-term plans and unit plans for classes your pupils have previously taken. In many schools this may mean looking at the long-term and unit plans from the previous year.

For the lexicon for the function above *Excuse me, is there a ... nearby?*, you may decide to limit this to *hotel, restaurant, bank, post office, train/bus station, sports centre, cinema, chemist.* Learners will easily be able to add other places they need once they have had thorough practice of these initial words in communicative settings in class (or you may come back to this area in a future unit or in the following year).

5.3.7   Grammar

If you go through the process of setting your aims for the unit and conse-quently the **functions**, language areas and lexicon, the grammatical knowledge required will be self-evident. It is important that you identify the grammar that will come up in the unit and that you specify what grammatical items are needed. You will also need to decide just how much of a particular grammatical point needs to be taught – you may not need to cover all aspects of a grammatical point at this moment in time, rather just enough to help your learners to use the language appropriately. This grammatical knowledge can be expanded later as required.

How you approach the grammar is very important. It is not necessary to embed a 'grammar lesson' to teach a particular point. It is far more effective if this is done in an inductive way, where learners can work out or acquire the grammar without being required to demonstrate a declarative (and often out-of-context) knowledge of a grammatical rule. For more on how to do this in a communicative way, have a look at Chapter 2 again.

Thus, the grammar necessary to fulfil the functions of the unit above may look like this:

- Question forms/interrogatives;
- Adverbs;
- Adjectives;
- Singular/plural nouns;
- Command forms/imperatives;
- Ordinal numbers.

You need to decide just how much of the identified grammatical points are useful for your learners to know *at this point*, knowing that this can be built on and expanded later in their language learning. Resist the temptation to explain everything about the point of grammar in question, as this will detract from the communicative focus of your lesson and may eat into the time allocated to cover your chosen aims and functions.

5.3.8   Activities and Games

Although this is still the point at which you are doing mid-term planning, it is advisable to give some thought to possible activities and games that could be included in the lessons as you teach the unit. You may, of course, change or add to these, but this is an opportunity to pool and share your ideas with other colleagues in the department. This means you are not starting from cold and having to come up with all the ideas yourself. It also helps you in terms of thinking about resources, allowing you to examine what you already have and what you must create. It is far less stressful to be working on this in advance than worrying about not having the appropriate resources the day before you teach the lesson.

Possible activities and games for the unit 'Finding your way about town' may include:

- Matching activities (directions with places on a map);
- Role-play (asking your way);
- Map or street plan activities (asking/giving directions);
- Flashcard activities or games (to introduce/consolidate vocabulary and structures);
- Blind man's buff (a fun way for pupils to practise understanding and giving directions).

5.3.9   Keeping the Learner at the Centre

Although you may have gone through all the steps above and identified aims, functions and language areas, it is important to remember at each stage of the planning process that the pupil is at the centre of this learning. Are you responding to the needs of individual learners? Not all learners may be of the same ability level. Indeed, the majority of classes in schools tend to contain quite a wide mix of ability. In addition, you may have pupils in your class who have specific additional support needs, which you will have to find out. Have you made sure that learning and teaching activities are pupil-centred? Have you specified ability levels for different functions? Do all pupils need to learn all the language, or will some language functions, grammatical points, resources be targeted at certain pupils according to ability? Have you considered how to support any additional learning needs that individual pupils may have? Is this clear from your unit of work? (See Chapter 7 for advice on differentiation and responding to pupils' needs.)

5.3.10   Review and Revise

As is the case for individual lessons, a teacher must always reflect on how well the unit of work meets the needs of their learners. What worked well? What did not go so well? Were the aims appropriate? Did I include too much or too little in the unit? Should I remove anything? We always hope that our planning will bear fruit, but to make sure that the learning and teaching are appropriate for the age and stage of the learners, that they are fit for practice, teachers need to regularly review the units of work to see what is working and what is not. This will largely be through reflection after having taught a lesson or a sequence of lessons. It may be something that occurs to you in the middle of teaching a lesson – reflection in practice – and you adjust your teaching on the spot. Or, you may revise your unit on the basis of assessment of pupils' performance, whether formatively or summatively, or both.

Where this works well is when Modern Language departments engage in a process of continual review. This does not mean changing everything all the time or being in a continual state of flux, rather planning as a team regular review points in the year to amend and improve each unit of work based on the evidence you collect through evaluations and assessments.

5.4   Use of Commercial Textbooks in Unit Planning

In conversations with student teachers and serving teachers in schools, I am often asked why teachers should write their own units of work when there are commercially produced coursebooks which they can use. There is certainly a myriad of coursebooks on the educational market, many of which claim to be the only resource you need to help your pupils learn the language for your class's particular level or to pass a particular national exam. The reality is, no matter how attractive and comprehensive these coursebooks aspire to be, it is not possible for a coursebook to respond to the wide and differing needs of all the learners in a particular class, let alone for the needs of all language learners of a particular year group in a school, or in all schools nationally. The very nature of a coursebook is that it is literally bound by its covers, and the author must decide what to include and what to leave out. Indeed, some coursebooks do a good job of providing an appropriate range of topics with learning and teaching resources at a range of ability levels. However, due to their finite nature, no coursebook is able to meet all needs of all learners in all schools.

This does not mean that I am dismissing coursebooks out of hand. Where you find that a particular coursebook offers appropriate and attractive material to meet the needs of your learners, you should include this with your other materials to provide the best learning experience for your pupils. Part of the craft of a teacher is knowing what your learners need and being able to respond to those needs. This often means a combination of *selection and creation* of appropriate resources. What is essential is to plan the learning around the learners: to fit the learning around the learners and not to fit the learners into the constraints of a particular coursebook or textbook.

5.5   Ways of Approaching the Planning Process

This section will look at the practical steps involved in designing and creating units of work for the L2 classroom. It is often difficult to know where to start when writing a unit of work and you may find yourself staring at a blank piece of paper, unsure how to begin the planning process. Happily, I can report, this does not need to be the case, as there are a number of easy steps that you can follow.

Step 1
Carry out your needs analysis. This will often be very simple to do, particularly if you are required to respond to a national curriculum or prescribed guidelines. If the class is for a particular group, then the participants will often have a list of their needs. Where this information is not available, you can find out their needs through discussion or via a survey or questionnaire, or indeed through prior assessments of their learning. This is also an opportunity to find out any prior knowledge the learners may have in the language.

Step 2
Having carried out the needs analysis, you will have a very good idea of what the learners wish or need to know and this will guide your planning. This is the step in which you can allow yourself to throw ideas onto the table. A number of ideas or requirements will have come from assessments, from your discussion with participants or surveys, or, often for school classes, from an examination of prescribed national curriculum guidelines.

Using the headings and sections outlined above (aims, functions, language areas, etc.), share your ideas. This could be as simple as taking a large sheet of paper or a flipchart and making a spider diagram where you have different headings emanating from the centre, as schematised in Figure 5.1. Figures 5.1, 5.2 and 5.3 and Tables 5.2 and 5.3 are examples of different layouts used for planning units of work.

Section 5.5 has examined practical steps in the unit planning process and proposed a variety of different layouts and approaches to help you plan your units of work for a junior class in a secondary school.

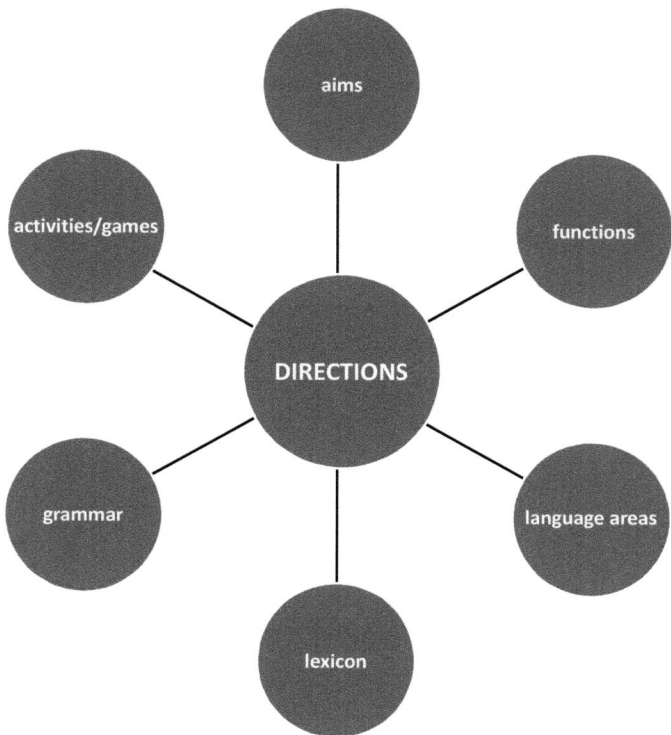

Figure 5.1 An example of a spider diagram approach to unit planning

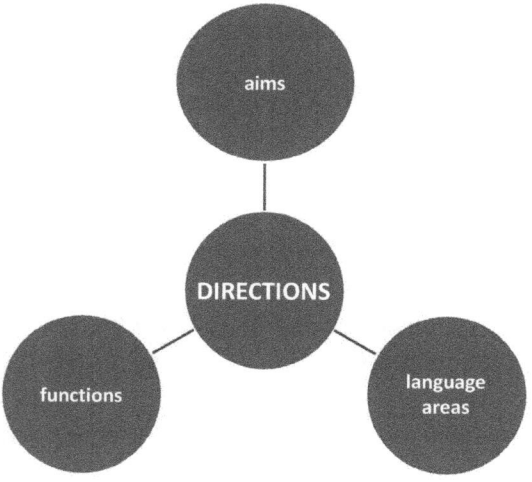

Figure 5.2 An alternative layout for planning a unit of work

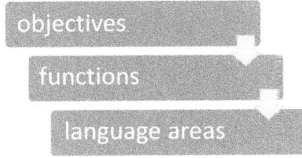

Figure 5.3 An approach to unit planning using step boxes as a unit planning template

Table 5.2 An example of using a grid planning template to design a unit of work

Title of unit	Aims	Functions
Extra	Class profile	Language area
Activities/Games	Grammar	Lexicon

You can view and download this table at www.cambridge.org/lynch.

5.6   Short-Term Planning

Whatever approach you take to create your unit plan, the principles are the same and you need to include the same or similar features in your planning as in the examples in Sections 5.3–5.5. The next step, which will act as a detailed reference upon which to base your individual lesson plans, is to create short-term plans from your unit plans. Short-term plans are what you hope to achieve in blocks of time that you allocate to the different sections of your unit plan. These can vary in length depending on the topic and where you can identify a natural set of sub-topics. Or, where this is not obvious, you may decide to create several short-term plans in order to assist you with managing your planning and where there may be obvious overlap, or continuation, of a sub-topic or topics, which lead from one short-term plan into the next short-term plan.

Short-term planning is the stage at which you will look at the calendar and decide how best to meet the learning and teaching challenges that you set in your unit plan. This is a necessary step and should not be neglected, as here you will be setting the parameters of what you hope to get through in terms of delimiting the aims, functions, language, skills and the amount of time to devote to each part of your unit plan. Good teaching is the result of careful planning and preparation. The best learning and teaching that I have witnessed has always been by teachers who have sequentially gone through these steps in long-, mid- and short-term planning, producing lessons which look natural and seamless.

Table 5.3 A tabular approach to planning a unit of work

Topic: Finding your way about town

Aims	Functions	Language areas	Lexicon	Grammar	Activities	Resources
To be able to ask for places in town	Excuse me, is there a ... nearby? Where is the ... (nearest) ...?	Names of town buildings	(1) hotel, restaurant, shops, chemist's, train station, sports centre, theatre, cinema	Question forms Adverbs	Matching activities	List of resources to meet these objectives
To be able to ask directions	Can you direct me to ...? How do I get to ...?	Directions	(2) & (3) Go straight ahead; turn left/right/ take the first/ second/third/ fourth/fifth street; on the/your left/ right; traffic lights, junction, pedestrian crossing	Adjectives Singular/plural nouns	Role-play Map/street plan activities	List of resources to meet these objectives
To be able to give directions	Go straight ahead, ... Turn left/right ... Take the first/second street on your left/ right ... Cross over at the junc-tion/traffic lights/ corner ...	Directions, parts of streets, roads, etc		Command forms/ imperative Ordinal numbers	Flashcard activ-ities/games Blind man's buff	List of resources to meet these objectives

Table 5.4 An example of a first short-term plan for a unit of work in a sequence of short-term plans

Week	Aims	Functions	Language areas	Lexicon	Grammar	Activities	Resources
1	To be able to ask for places in town	Excuse me, is there a ... nearby? Where is the ... (nearest) ...?	Names of town buildings	(1) hotel, restaurant, shops, chemist's, train station, sports centre, theatre, cinema	Question forms Singular/plural nouns	Matching activities Map/street plan activities Flashcard activities/games	Flashcards of places in town Printed town maps Online town maps interactive whiteboard (IWB)/ video/audio files

Table 5.5 An example of a second short-term plan for a unit of work in a sequence of short-term plans

Week	Aims	Functions	Language areas	Lexicon	Grammar	Activities	Resources
2	To be able to ask directions	Can you direct me to ...? How do I get to ...?	Directions	(2) & (3) Go straight ahead; turn left/right/ take the first/ second/third/ fourth/fifth	Command forms/ imperative Ordinal numbers	Role-play	Printed town maps Online town maps IWB/video/audio files
3–4	To be able to give directions	Go straight ahead, ... Turn left/right ... Take the first/second street on your left/ right ... Cross over at the junction/traffic lights/corner ...	Directions, parts of streets, roads, etc.	street; on the/ your left/right; traffic lights, junction, pedestrian crossing	Command forms/ imperative Ordinal numbers	Blind man's buff	Printed town maps Online town maps IWB/video/audio files

Examples of short-term plans based on the unit of work above ('Finding your way about town') may look like Tables 5.4 and 5.5. The layout is tabular, but other layouts which contain the necessary features are also possible.

All these are necessary steps to respond to the needs of your learners. Remember, no two classes are exactly the same, so it is unlikely that a commercial textbook will answer all those needs. At best, it will be part of a wide range of resources that you have selected or created to teach a particular class or year group. Your long-term and mid-term plans will serve as starting points from which you will be able to develop the short-term plans, tailored to the needs of the learners in your classes. Indeed, even if you have two classes from the same year group, the composition and needs of each class and the individual learners therein may be slightly (or vastly) different, which means that care must be taken in producing your detailed short-term plans. Preparing all of this in advance will be invaluable when you move to write your individual lesson plans, as you will not be starting with a blank sheet of paper; rather you will have detailed plans of what you need to teach at each stage of your pupils' learning and suggestions of how to go about this.

Section 5.6 has explored how to create a sequence of short-term plans derived from a detailed unit of work. Section 5.7 will consider how the same topic may look when planning for an older, more advanced group of learners, further along in their language learning.

5.7   Progression and Coherence in Planning

As learners progress in the language and their language ability develops and improves, their cognitive ability also improves, as well as their level of maturity. This must be reflected in the growing cognitive demands made of the learners as they progress in their language learning from one year to the next. It is safe, then, to say that if an older pupil in a more senior class studies the topic of 'Town', they will be able, and indeed will want, to study the topic at a deeper, more mature level. In terms of the topic of 'Town', a more advanced learner will be able to consider this at a higher level than the transactional level illustrated in the example above. This may involve, among other themes:

- A comparison of town and country life;
- Environmental issues in town and country.

In terms of comparing town and country life, learners may be asked to consider:

- Facilities that the town offers young people or society generally that villages and remote locations cannot offer, and vice versa, e.g., access to shops, entertainment, institutions, hospitals or work;
- Transport links;
- Sports and leisure.

In terms of environmental issues, learners may be looking at:

- Pollution, air quality, climate change;
- Access to nature;
- Quality or pace of life.

This will inevitably also involve making long-, mid- and short-term plans. However, these must be at a higher cognitive level and reflect the maturity and depth of understanding that older learners bring. This has obvious implications for planning, that is, finding or creating resources that will stimulate the interests of older learners; offering activities and tasks that deepen learners' understanding; using more complex and mature language; studying grammar in greater depth and with more accuracy.

 TRY THIS OUT

Let's practise creating mid- and short-term plans.

Part 1

- Think of a class you are currently teaching or will be teaching (this can also be a class you recently taught or helped teach on placement).
- Next choose a topic.
- Plan a four-week mid-term plan, i.e., a unit of work on the topic for this class. You can choose whatever layout you wish (see above for ideas). Remember to specify the class and the class profile.
- Add details of the target language aims, functions, language areas, lexicon, grammar, possible activities and resources (if you have access to resources and materials).

Part 2

Develop appropriate short-term plans arising from the mid-term plan or unit of work.

Part 3

Show your mid- and short-term plans to one or more of your peers (or your mentor if on placement) and ask them for feedback.

Part 4

Make any necessary changes to your mid- and short-term plans in light of feedback.

SUMMARY

In this chapter we have considered a rationale for why it is essential that you engage in detailed planning. In doing so, we have examined the key stages in planning and explored the reason for incorporating each stage. The key stages of identifying functions, language areas, lexicon, grammar and activities have been defined and we have explored what each stage entails. This chapter has taken you through the important steps in this planning process, from long-term and mid-term planning, through to how this feeds directly into the detailed short-term plans upon which you will base your individual lesson plans for the learners in your classes. Examples were given for planning for a junior class and consideration was also given to progression and coherence by considering the implications of planning the same topic for an older, more mature class. There are examples and templates in this chapter, but, whichever model you adopt, it is crucial for successful learning and teaching that you adhere to the principles and features of effective planning as laid out in this chapter. This will help you to devise individual lesson plans, which are the subject of the next chapter.

REFLECTIVE QUESTIONS

1. Assuming you arrived in a school where no unit plans existed, how would you ensure that you created effective and coherent learning opportunities for the pupils in your classes?
2. How would you find out the previous learning of your pupils or class if no long-term or unit plans for the previous year exist?

Possible answers to question 2: Look at pupils' exercise books from last year's class, talk to previous teachers, give a diagnostic test, or use a combination of these.

KEY TERMS

functions or **notions** An approach to L2 teaching focusing on the communicative meanings of words and structures as opposed to grammatical structures.

long-term plan An outline plan detailing the main areas of learning and teaching for an academic year for a specified class or year group.

mid-term plan A unit of work of usually 2–4 weeks derived from a long-term plan, which contains details of aims, functions, language and activities.

short-term plan A more detailed plan of work where a unit of work is broken down into a sequence of shorter segments of shorter duration, i.e., of 1 week/3 lessons.

FURTHER READING

For information on the functional-notional approach, please see the seminal work:

Finocchiaro, M. & C. Brumfit, 1983. *The Functional–Notional Approach: From theory to practice.* Oxford: Oxford University Press.

For information on the use functions and notions introduced in Section 5.3.4, please see the seminal work:

Mickan, P., 2012. *Language Curriculum Design and Socialisation.* Bristol: Blue Ridge Summit: Multilingual Matters.

6 Lesson Planning

Introduction

Chapter 5 considered the importance of long-term and mid-term planning and presented ways in which this can be done to feed into the development of detailed lesson planning. Chapter 6 builds on this and analyses the fundamentals of modern foreign language lesson planning and the features of a successful lesson. It emphasises the importance of planning learning across a series of lessons and walking through your planning in advance.

The learning objectives for this chapter are, therefore, as follows:

1. Consider the principles of successful lesson planning.
2. Examine the steps you must take to plan lessons.
3. Analyse ways in which evaluative feedback can be obtained to support teachers both before and after lessons.

Overview

Chapter 2 looked at how we acquire language and how effective target language use is vital to successful language learning. Code-switching and communication strategies were examined and advice given for use of the target language in class and how to promote its use by learners. Chapter 4 then looked at a range of teaching modes and examined which different approaches can be employed in the most effective way within a pupil-centred environment. Chapter 5 looked at the fundamentals of syllabus and unit planning and the relationship between long-term and mid-term plans. These three chapters are important for a number of reasons. They give us an understanding of pedagogy, they explore modes of teaching, examine what is most appropriate to use at a given moment, and they highlight the sequence of stages necessary to help you develop effective lesson planning skills. These are the building blocks upon which to base your planning of individual lessons and series of lessons. Successful lesson planning must be based on a sound knowledge of pedagogy (Beckmann & Ehmke, 2023). This implies that teachers need to know the most effective ways to learn and teach languages. This in turn needs to be coupled with skilled use of the appropriate modes of teaching used at the appropriate time. This all needs to happen within a planned framework, which allows and supports pupils' development and progress across a sequence of learning goals.

6.1   Principles of Successful Lesson Planning

In terms of creating effective lessons for your pupils, it is important to consider the principles upon which successful lesson planning is based. It is important to know that learners make the best progress when:

- The learning tasks you ask them to do are related to what they already know;
- Lessons are based on a sound understanding of the curriculum content and the nature of the learning process, in this case on a sound understanding of effective pedagogy for language learning.
- Tasks cater for the different needs, styles and preferences of all the learners in your class;
- Assessment is formative and summative;
- Learners are clear about the purposes and goals of the lesson;
- Learners are appropriately supported in their learning;
- Feedback is given and received continuously, based on achievement and attainment;
- Learners can see that their experiences promote self-esteem and that you as a teacher value their progress and achievement.

6.1.1   Promoting Self-Esteem

Success breeds success, therefore it is important that learners have the opportunity to experience this on a regular basis. By creating short, achievable tasks (Willis, 1996) that learners can understand and complete, as opposed to long complicated exercises, your learners will get a feeling of satisfaction, which will spur them on to learn more (Dörnyei, 2020). When you show your learners that you value their efforts and what they have achieved, which may be different from one learner to the next, this gives learners that extra 'kick', helps their own individual feeling of self-worth and encourages them to do more, so make sure that you regularly praise your pupils for their work. This should not be confined to only praising your pupils when they produce a right answer – they should be praised for effort, even if the answer is not always correct.

FOOD FOR THOUGHT

Think back to when you were taught modern languages in school.
   Which teachers motivated you most to learn?
   Did your teachers do anything specific that made you feel good about your learning?

6.1.2   Building on Prior Knowledge

No learner comes into the class as a blank sheet. Even if the class is a beginners' class in a particular foreign language, your learners may already have some knowledge or experience of the foreign language, as well as eleven years of L1. It may be that some learners have been taught some of the language in primary school or at a language club. They may have parents who take them regularly abroad on holiday to a country or countries where the foreign language is spoken and they have picked up some words or phrases. Through music and film, they may have developed an interest in the target language country, or they may have older brothers and sisters who are learning the language and who have shared their enthusiasm with them. You can tap into this at the beginning of lessons by asking what learners already know and giving them an opportunity to share this with their classmates. Establishing your learners' existing level of knowledge rather than assuming they know nothing will help you to tailor your teaching to their needs and help learners to co-construct new learning from what they already know (Vygotsky, 1978).

6.1.3   Making the Purpose of the Lesson Clear

To help the learners in your class to succeed in their learning, they need to know what the purposes and goals of the lesson are. This means that you need to share the aims, that is, the **learning intentions** of your lesson with them (Wiliam, 2018), so that they know what it is that they are to achieve. At the beginning of the lesson, it is important to set out what these learning intentions are to give an overview of the lesson. You can display this on the board or screen and you should take the time to go over this with your learners at the beginning of each lesson, so that they know what is expected of them. Do not skip this step or rush it by diving straight into 'work'. What they are learning needs to be relevant and contextualised. By sharing the learning intentions of the lesson(s) with your learners, you are showing them the purpose of the lesson(s), which will guide them in their learning. It also shows that you have a *coherent plan* for their learning and will gain support from your learners as they see not just *what* they are to learn, but also *why* they should learn it – in short, it will show *the relevance of the tasks to their learning.*

6.1.4   Supporting Learning

Each learner is different and comes with different learning needs (Convery & Coyle, 1993; Florian et al., 2017), learning styles and learning preferences (Kolb, 1984). There is no average pupil, and each learner will learn at different rates commensurate with their investment in the lesson (Norton & McKinney, 2011), their ability, their needs and how much they enjoy, or see a purpose to, their learning. Acknowledging that there is no average pupil means that you cannot simply 'pitch' your lesson at what you consider the level of the class to be, to some imagined 'middle' level. Whether you have been told that the class is 'set' or 'streamed' (in other words that the learners have been placed in the class due to being judged to be at the same ability level), this does not mean that you can simply teach to the one level. Any class is an administrative grouping based on pre-determined eligibility criteria. Quite frequently, past performance in a previous class will be used to decide to which class a learner will be allocated. If we take the first four years of a typical secondary school language class in Scotland, it is common for classes to have thirty pupils. This class, however, is not a homogenous class of similarly skilled and similarly knowledgeable learners. There will be a number of pupils who scored very highly on eligibility tests for the class, or whose past perform-ance puts them among the more able in the class. There will also, however, be pupils who, based on past performance or test scores, just made it into the class and no more, indeed who possibly may be more suited to being in a lower-ability class. And there are all the levels in between in this grouping of thirty pupils.

6.1.5   Planning for Mixed Ability and Mixed Needs

Ability level is just one consideration in a class. If we acknowledge that, even within a class with a so-called set ability level, not all the pupils are as able as each other, then this has implications for our lesson planning. In most schools, rather than teaching a language class set by ability level, you will often be teaching full mixed-ability classes. If we consider that there will also be a range of learning styles and learning preferences in your class, this has implications for the tasks and activities that you design or choose, for the materials and resources you choose and for the expectations on the learners. In addition, you may have learners with a particular additional support need, for example a hearing or visual impairment, mobility issues or a medical condition (see Chapter 7, which looks at differentiation in the classroom and how best to support all learners). Part of the job of an effective teacher is responding to the varying needs (physical, cognitive and emotional), abilities, learning styles and preferences of the learners in our classes. We need to recognise these factors as we plan for our classes. Part of this is being able to identify what constitutes progression in pupils' learning. This could be observing how pupils move from more familiar language to less familiar language, how they move from short simple texts and tasks to increasingly longer and more complex ones. This could also be seen in how pupils show an increased aptitude in understand-ing and producing spontaneous talk.

6.1.6   Assessment and Feedback

To help pupils know if they are understanding and are on track with their language learning, they need regular feedback on their progress (Black & Wiliam, 1998). As mentioned above in Section 6.1.3, knowing *what* is to be achieved should be made clear through the learning intentions that you explain to the class at the beginning of the lesson. It is just as important to know if or how far pupils have achieved these. To make this clear you should clarify for your pupils at the beginning of the lesson what the **success criteria** are. For example, if the learning intention is:

We are learning to say the parts of the body and height in French (etc.).

Then the success criteria may be:

I can correctly label the parts of the body and say how tall someone is.

Table 6.1 An example of learning intentions and corresponding success criteria

Learning intention	Success criteria
We are learning the members of the family in French, German, etc.	I can correctly identify members of the family through pictures and listening.
We are learning animals in French, German, etc.	I can match the picture to the correct name and pronounce it correctly.
I can talk about my school day.	I can say at what time my different lessons are.

Consider the learning intentions and corresponding success criteria in Table 6.1. Not all lessons lend themselves naturally to assessment, especially summative assessment. Nevertheless, you will find yourself continually monitoring how your pupils are doing throughout the lesson, whether this be how they answer questions, listening in to pair or group work, taking in pupils' worksheets or workbooks and so on. As part of this ongoing informal assessment of pupils' work, you will often give feedback, advice and support. This is what is known as **formative assessment** and takes place almost automatically in every lesson. It differs from **summative assessment** in that with formative assessment you will give comments – qualitative feedback – on how pupils are doing and how they can improve. Summative assessment, on the other hand, is normally used to generate a mark or report on progress, often for a report card, or as part of examination requirements. Formative assessment is very useful and provides valuable information on pupil progress, which in turn informs future planning. Advice on how to plan for and manage assessment of learners' progress is examined in detail in Chapter 8. Advice on how to use assessment for learning within a framework of dynamic formative assessment is detailed in that chapter, including self-assessment and peer-assessment techniques.

 TRY THIS OUT

Choose a lesson to teach to a first-year beginners language class. (It may help to situate this within a topic, so choose a topic first.)

Write two or three learning intentions (not a full lesson plan) for this class.

Write the corresponding success criteria for these learning intentions.

6.1.7 Knowledge of Pedagogy

All the principles above are vital to successful lesson planning, but just as important as this is to make sure that you base your lessons on a sound understanding of curriculum content and the nature of the learning process in general, in this case with a firm grasp of effective pedagogy for language learning. Although *what* you choose to teach should correspond to what is advised in what is often a prescribed curriculum, *how* you teach this is vitally important and *lies at heart of effective language learning and teaching.* It would be useful now to revisit communicative approaches to language learning in Chapter 2 and modes of teaching in Chapter 4. What you choose will depend on what is appropriate to the aims of your lesson, but it is important that the methods you choose sit within the framework of a communicative approach to language learning and teaching.

Section 6.1 has considered principles of successful lesson planning and the required elements for this, analysing each of these in turn and presenting arguments for their inclusion.

6.2   How to Plan Your Lesson

This section will take you through the necessary steps to plan successful language lessons, discussing the importance of each step.

Taking account of the principles of successful lesson planning outlined in Section 6.1, you are now ready to start thinking about writing your lesson plan. However, before you start you need to consider a number of factors that will influence firstly *what it is* that you are going to teach in your lesson and secondly *how you are going to teach it.* Effective lesson planning is best seen as part of a learning cycle, as can be seen in Figure 6.1.

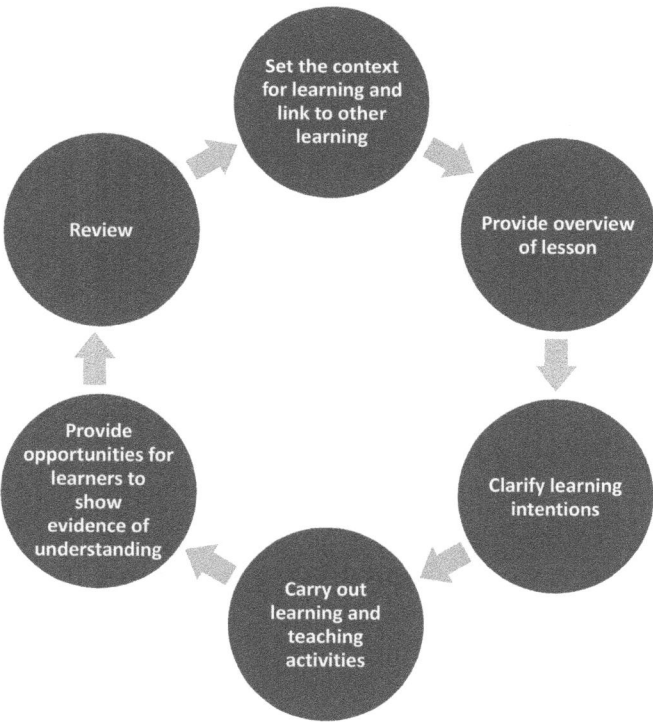

Figure 6.1 A suggested lesson planning cycle

6.2.1   Setting Objectives for Language Learning

As a first step, the framework for learning must be explicit, setting a context for the learning and linking to other or previous learning. After providing an overview of the lesson, as a teacher you must make absolutely sure that the expected learning intentions of the work to be undertaken are clearly set out for the learners and, where practicable, negotiated with them (Leung & Scarino, 2016). You should make clear how you expect these will be achieved. Normally, you will be working on topics, themes and areas over a longer period of time and will find yourself outlining what the learning is for a *series of lessons* and *not* single lessons. That having been said, you still need to follow these steps at the start of each individual lesson: set context; provide lesson overview; clarify learning intentions.

6.2.2   Writing Your Lesson Plan

Many people may tell you that they do not need a lesson plan, as they have been teaching for many years, or that they have taught the class so often before they do not need a written lesson plan. However, preparation will lead to confidence and inspire confidence in your learners. Experience will help you in terms of reflecting on what has worked well in similar lessons in the past for similar classes and for avoiding things that have not worked well, which will help you as you prepare new lessons.

So, what should your written lesson plan look like? Well, your lesson plan needs to contain enough information so that you, or any colleagues co-teaching the lesson with you, know straight away what is going to happen in the lesson. It should be a working document and to that end it needs to be concise yet comprehensive. By concise, this means that learning intentions, tasks and activities should be readily identifiable. By comprehensive, this means that there should be enough information for the smooth running of the lesson. This is part of the craft of a teacher and you will get better at achieving this balance (being *concise*, yet *comprehensive*) with experience, as long as you make sure you include the key points and do not skip steps. If you are working with colleagues (e.g., teacher colleagues, learning support assistants or foreign language assistants) you should share your lesson plan with them in advance of the lesson and, where practicable, include them in the planning process, or at the very least, ask them for their advice. Other colleagues may have useful ideas that you can incorporate into the lesson, which inevitably benefits the learners. Remember, it is unprofessional *not* to share your plans with other practitioners in the class, quite apart from the obvious problem that, if your colleagues have not seen the lesson plan, they will have no idea what to do and will be less effective than they otherwise could have been in the lesson.

The Pre-Planning Stages

Before you start the detailed planning and writing of individual lessons, you must ask yourself a number of questions.

Questions

Previous learning

1. What have the pupils been learning previously?

Next steps

2. What are the (next) stages and objectives in the course?

Amendments and follow up

3. Are there any amendments or follow up needed as a result of the previous lesson?

The answers to these questions should be easy if you have planned and created your course in advance (see Chapter 5), or for student teachers on placement, if you have consulted the department unit plans.

Answers

Previous learning

As a first step, consult your record of work to find out at what point the learners are in their learning and at what point in the course they have arrived. This should be straightforward and easily accessible if you have been reviewing and evaluating your lessons on a regular basis.

Next steps

You should then consult your course plan, looking at topic areas and themes, functions or notions, objectives and language areas to help you to decide what the next stages in the learning process should be.

Amendments and follow up

Here, it is a question of reviewing the evaluation(s) you or any teaching assistants, colleagues or assessors have compiled on your previous lesson or lessons.

Once you have gone through the preliminary stages mentioned above, you are ready to start planning your detailed lesson.

Key Points to Include in Your Lesson Plan There are certain key points to any lesson that you will want to focus on, and each of these require detailed consideration of the basic principles of the learning and teaching of foreign languages. It may be a good point to revisit some of these sections now before reading the general advice on how to write your lesson below (see Chapter 2).

Topic of the Lesson Define your area of study by giving your lesson plan a title indicative of the content, for example *Talking about hobbies*.

Learning Intentions In this section you should clearly and concisely state your overall aims for this lesson and specific objectives. These should be shared with the learners in your class. This section should be fairly brief and to the point. Do not set out a long list of learning intentions which your learners will not be able to accomplish. It is important to distinguish here between general aims and not to confuse these with tasks and activities, which is a common occurrence amongst novice teachers. Be aware of the constraints of *time, pupils' concentration spans* and *interest levels*, and their *level(s) of ability*.

Figure 6.2 shows an extract from the start of a typical lesson plan.

Lesson Plan

Language	Teacher
French	Mike Lynch

Class	Date
S3	24/03/2025

Class Profile:

This is a mixed-ability class of 28 pupils, 12 boys, 16 girls.

There is a wide spread of ability with some very chatty pupils.

One boy has been absent for the last week.

> Important to give profile of class, as has bearing on activities and materials used

Context:

The class have been working on topic of sport for 2 weeks. They are familiar with the present tense and days of week.

Detailed Lesson plan

> Details prior Knowledge

Rapid Revision:

Practise days of week with diary.

Practise sports with flashcard games.

> Do not have too many learning intentions per lesson

Learning Intentions:

1. To introduce talking about what you have done last week.

2. To ask friends in class what they have done last week.

3. To talk about what other people have done last week.

Figure 6.2 An extract from the start of a lesson plan

Methods and Teaching Sequence

It is important that you decide *what* it is you wish to accomplish. It is also very important to realise *how* you are going to do this. This is the very heart and soul of learning and teaching and the methods you choose should be in accordance with best practice and accepted principles and theories of learning and teaching foreign languages. This may mean:

- teaching in groups;
- use of pair work;
- individual learning;
- whole-class teaching;
- use of technology;
- skills practice;
- multi-skill activities;

- multi-task activities;
- differentiation;
- working with colleagues.

It will certainly require a mixture of the above and the teaching will all be taking place in the target language. As a teacher, you should draw on your knowledge of theories of learning and teaching foreign languages to decide on the appropriate learning and teaching approaches to use in individual lessons.

A typical learning and teaching sequence may look like Figure 6.3.

Steps in teaching sequence			
Teaching and Learning	**Mode**	**Skill**	**Time**
Use this week's diary page to practise known structures: **This week I play at …+ 5 sports,** pointing to icons of sports and miming sports, e.g. "Lundi, je joue au football; mardi je joue au golf…"	Direct	L, S, R	5 mins
Ask questions/elicit answers from pupils, e.g. "Qu'est-ce que tu joues mercredi? Tu joues au golf jeudi?"	Activity	L, S, R	5 mins
Then use **last week's diary page** to introduce idea of past and introduce **Last week I played at …,** pointing to icons of sports and miming sports, e.g. "Lundi dernier, j'ai joué au rugby; mardi dernier j'ai joué au volley…"	Direct	L, S, R	5 mins
Introduce **question form/introduce 2nd person (perfect tense)** with lots of question and answer and repetition to consolidate new structures	Activity	L, S, R	10 mins
Extend to **introduce 3rd person masculine and feminine** using answers from class Lots of oral practice, i.e. *Qu'est-ce qu'il a joué, Chris?/Il a joué au rugby?/Qu'est-ce qu'elle a joué, Marie ?* *Oui/Non, il a joué au…/elle a joué au…*	Direct/ Activity	L, S, R	10 mins
	Details of mode, skills covered and duration in minutes of each step in lesson plan		

Figure 6.3 An extract from the middle of a lesson plan

Differentiation On your lesson plan you should note any differentiation strategies you intend to use, for example those in Box 6.1.

Materials You should make clear on your lesson plan which materials you will be using. This will largely be determined by the topic, functions or notions, objectives and language areas appropriate to the particular lesson. Remember to tailor your

---

Box 6.1 Example of differentiation strategies on lesson plan

- Vocabulary sheets for those struggling;
- Picture prompts for paired conversations if needed;
- Encourage more able pupils to use 3rd person of past tense, as well as 1st and 2nd person.

---

materials to the needs of your learners. Do not try to 'make the learner fit the materials'. Where there is a deficit in your main resources, you will need to *search for*, or *create*, new materials to plug this gap. Course book authors and publishers often claim that a particular textbook will satisfy 'all the needs of all learners' in your classes. It is important to realise that, good though some course books may be, due to their size, this is an exaggerated claim and these textbooks will rarely fulfil all the needs of all the different learners in your class. It is impossible to cater for all learners in all classes in all schools within the confines of a single textbook. It may well have a range of activities and materials suitable for a range of abilities, but they are limited by the amount of pages allocated to each topic, theme or section. It is up to you to find or create suitable materials and to use appropriate methods to respond to the various ability levels, learning styles and interest groups in your class. The craft of a teacher lies in being able both to *select* appropriate existing material and to *create* suitable material where there is a deficit.

Assessment You need to include a note of your assessment strategies in your lesson plan, whether this is informal or formal assessment, ongoing or end-of-unit assessment, formative or summative assessment. Any assessment you do needs to be carefully planned and managed. Another consideration when incorporating assessment into your lesson is to decide on the purpose and scope of such assessment(s). If not prioritised, assessment often becomes an afterthought in lesson planning. It is all too common to read on lesson plans phrases such as:

Formative assessment through listening in to pupils working/parish visiting
Formative assessment of answers round class
Checking exercise books as I walk round class

But what does this *mean*? Will you informally, through listening to multiple exchanges in class, be able to keep an accurate and reliable record of pupils' progress (of groups, individuals or the whole class) in your head as you walk around the class? These phrases are often found pro forma-like on lesson plans, but do not mean anything unless you have decided in advance what you will specifically look for:

- Will you target specific pupils or groups?
- How will you record this information?
- What will you do with this information?

Box 6.2 Example of formative assessment strategies on lesson plan

- Monitor Group A and give feedback on speaking task;
- Self-access marking sheets for reading task;
- Traffic light cards to get feedback from pupils on how easy/difficult they found listening task.

An example of assessment strategies within a lesson plan is given in Box 6.2, but see Chapter 8 for a more detailed look at how to plan for and manage assessment in your lessons.

Follow up In planning your individual lessons, you must always be conscious of where each lesson fits into the overall unit or course plan and objectives. When you plan an individual lesson, indicate briefly what the next stages will be. This is important in terms of your own organisation, but it is useful for the learners in your class to know as well. This reassures the learner that the learning will be a coherent progression and helps the learner to identify a route map for the areas to be studied and the learning outcomes.

Figure 6.4 provides a graphical overview of the steps required for effective lesson planning.

Section 6.2 has illustrated the vital steps necessary to produce effective and successful lesson plans, providing examples of their use.

6.3 Ways to Obtain Evaluative Feedback and Support Both before and after Your Lesson(s)

It is important to remember that as a beginning teacher you are not alone. When you are at university, your tutors are there as a source of support and advice. Similarly, on placement you will normally have a mentor who will be an invaluable guide on your journey to becoming a teacher. Indeed, each teacher you work with in your placement schools (and there will often be several teachers with whom you will work) will give you advice and ideas on how to develop your knowledge, skills and craft as a teacher. As such, there are a number of ways in which you can obtain evaluative feedback to support you both before and after your lessons.

Support *before* Your Lesson: Feedforward Make sure that you plan far enough in advance and send your draft lesson plan(s) to the classroom teacher or your mentor (or both) to allow them enough time to look at your plans and to give you advice, for example on what they think will work well in class and on any potential problems they may see. This type of advice is called feedforward and it is important that you do this. Firstly, because doing so allows you to take

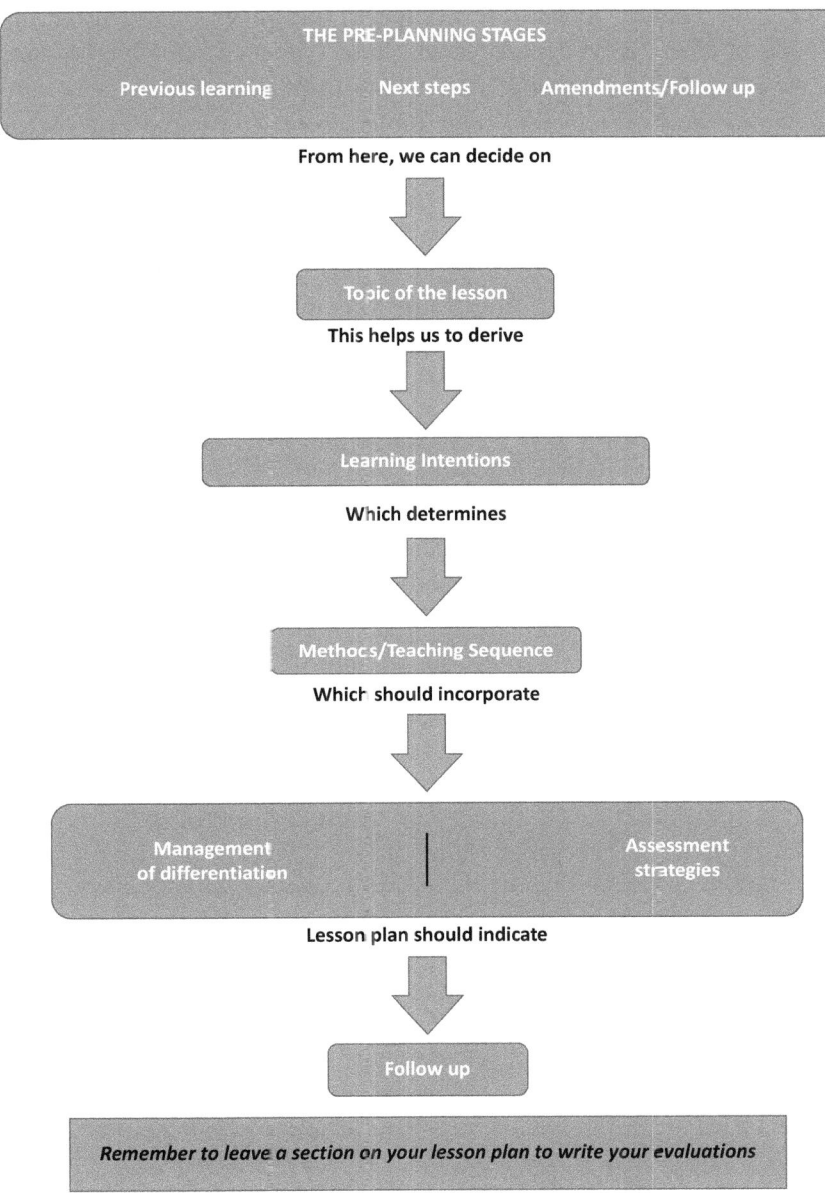

Figure 6.4 An at-a-glance summary of the main steps in lesson planning

advantage of the knowledge and skills of experienced teachers who can spot anything that may be problematic in your draft lesson plans, giving you time to make amendments before you have invested lots of time and energy in detailed final planning and material production. Secondly, because you are learning a lot in terms of the planning process through these collegiate discussions with colleagues.

Support after Your Lesson: Evaluative Feedback This means evaluating the extent to which, and the ways in which, teaching has been effective (or not, as the case may be). It is an integral part of the professional activity of any teacher to examine ways of teaching their subject continually and to look for ways of introducing improvements. This type of advice is called feedback. This necessitates a degree of experimentation and experiments are, by their very nature, not always successful. To have any chance of knowing whether your teaching can be improved (and if so, how), you need to know what its current strengths and areas that can be improved are. This general attitude of critical self-questioning is often referred to as being a *reflective practitioner* (Schön, 2017).

Sources of Evaluation There are many different people who can give you evaluation. There is your mentor, your pupils, your peers and, of course, you yourself. These sources of evaluation can be seen at a glance on Figure 6.5.

As you plan your lesson, use the at-a-glance checklist in Table 6.2 to help you make sure you have included necessary elements in your lesson plan.

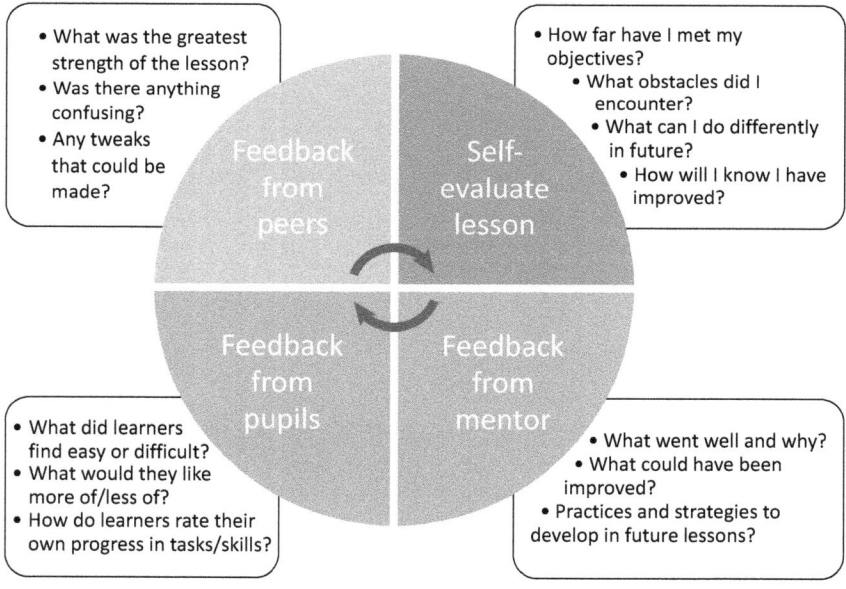

Figure 6.5 Sources of evaluative feedback

Table 6.2 An at-a-glance checklist of things to consider when planning your lessons

Core language	Grammar	Activities
• Have you decided what the core language will be for the lesson? • Have you decided what extra language may be needed for more able learners? • Have you decided on what the bare minimum is for those having difficulty?	• Does the lesson help develop pupils' knowledge of the language system? • Has this been done in a communicative way? • Have you provided opportunities for practice/for using it in other contexts?	• Do they foster communication? • Are they authentic? Do the pupils see the point/relevance? • Are the tasks suited to the variety of learners? • Have you differentiated the activities to respond to the needs of all learners?
Pedagogy • Have you thought about learning and teaching approaches? • Are the pupils learning what they need, or is it just rules? • What is the best way to help learners acquire/learn any new language for this lesson? • Have you capitalised on the language they already know? • Have you provided opportunities for output?		**Monitoring performance** • Have you thought about how to monitor what the pupils are doing/where they are doing well/where they have difficulty? • How will you record this? • What will you do with this information? • How will you share this with the pupils so that they know what they are doing well and where they need to improve?
Classroom management language • Have you thought the lesson through? • Have you planned how to manage the lesson in L2, taking account of their levels? • Have you provided support for classroom management language? • Have you varied your techniques for making language comprehensible (gesture, mime, cognates, vocabulary sheets, posters, sandwich technique)? • If you use L1, have you thought about when to use it and how/why, without it becoming the lingua franca?		**Assessment** • Have you incorporated formative assessment? • What is the purpose? • Is this varied? • Have you incorporated summative assessment? • What is the purpose? Is this varied?

🢂 **TRY THIS OUT**

1. Choose a class you are currently teaching.
2. Consult your record of work or the MFL department's record of work to find out at what point in their learning and at what point in the course the learners have arrived.
3. Next, consult the course plan for that class, looking at topic areas and themes, functions or notions, objectives and language areas to help you to decide what the next stages in the learning process should be.
4. Plan a series of three linked lessons for the class. Make sure to use appropriate learning and teaching strategies within a communicative framework, as well as ensuring continuity across the three lessons.
5. Be sure to include a profile of the class and give contextual information.
6. Include details of

   • how you will manage differentiation
   • your formative assessment strategies

Format of lessons

You may choose to use or adapt the lesson plan template in Table 6.4 for these three lesson plans, or use any lesson planning template from your modern foreign languages department. To help you in this planning process, you may find the checklist in Table 6.3 helpful in writing your draft lesson plans.

Table 6.3 A checklist for writing draft lesson plans

Questions to ask yourself on your draft lesson plan	✓	✗
Learning intentions		
Are learning intentions and success criteria clear and unambiguous?		
Is it clear where this lesson fits into a series or sequence of lessons?		
Have links to previous learning been included or taken into account?		
Is the learning realistic and contextualised?		
Pedagogy		
Is my lesson based on a sound understanding of communicative language learning and teaching?		
Is there opportunity for ample practice of new language?		
Have I included a variety of skills?		
Communication		
Are instructions to pupils clear? Will they be displayed on the board, on worksheets, be given verbally, or in multiple ways?		

Table 6.3 (cont.)

Management and organisation		
Does the normal room layout need changed?		
Have I specified the mode of teaching (group, individual, pair, team, etc.) for the different parts of the lesson?		
Will pupils have to move around the class? Have I thought how to manage this safely and in a way that avoids disrupting learning?		
What technology is involved (IWB, computers, tablets, listening posts)? Am I and are the pupils familiar with it?		
Have I checked the technology works? Do I have a backup plan if the technology breaks down?		
Have I checked my documents and recordings are compatible with the technology?		
Are my documents clear and easy to read by all pupils? Are my materials produced to a high standard?		
Will there be other colleagues involved in the lesson (Learning Assistants, Foreign Language Assistants)? Have I thought how to make best use of their expertise? Have I shared my lesson plan or ideas with them in advance?		
Differentiation		
Have I planned how to support learners?		
Is there a variety of tasks and activities?		
Does the lesson cater for the variety of ability levels and learning styles in the class?		
Assessment		
Does my lesson contain summative or formative assessment?		
What is the purpose of the assessment?		
How will I monitor performance?		
How will I record performance and achievements?		
What will I do with this information?		

You can view and download this table at www.cambridge.org/lynch.

Table 6.4 A suggested lesson plan template

Language	Teacher	

Class	Date	Time

Class profile	Context

Other relevant info

Learning intentions 1. 2. 3.	Success criteria 1. 2. 3.

Teaching and learning Differentiation Classroom organisation and management Assessment	Mode	Skill	Time

Homework

Follow up

Evaluation of lesson

Self-evaluation

Feedback from supervising teacher/tutor/peer

Next steps for me Next steps for class

You can view and download this table at www.cambridge.org/lynch.

Table 6.5 A feedforward sheet for mentors

Feedforward template for mentors			
Use this form to give advice to student teacher on draft lesson plan in advance of lesson			
Student teacher name Class			
Date of lesson			
Comments on learning intentions (i.e., clarity of learning intentions and success criteria, previous learning, context)	Problem	Needs work	Good
Pedagogy (Is this appropriate and communicative; is there a variety of skills?)	Problem	Needs work	Good
Communication (Clarity of communication; are intentions and instructions clear?)	Problem	Needs work	Good
Management and Organisation (Layout, mode, practicalities, technology, quality of resources, collaboration with colleagues)	Problem	Needs work	Good
Differentiation (Provision of support, task variety)	Problem	Needs work	Good
Assessment (Purpose, relevance, monitoring of performance)	Problem	Needs work	Good

You can view and download this table at www.cambridge.org/lynch.

When you have written a draft of your lesson plan, show it to your mentor, colleague or peer student teacher and ask them for constructive advice or criticism. Give them the mentor's feedforward sheet (Table 6.5) to allow them to make their notes.

You can view and download this table at www.cambridge.org/lynch. Make any necessary adjustments to your lesson plan as a result of advice from your

Table 6.6 A lesson feedback sheet

Student teacher name	Class	Date
Comments on lesson		Recommendations for development
Learning intentions and success criteria (i.e., clarity of learning intentions and success criteria, previous learning, context)		
Use of appropriate/effective pedagogy (Is this appropriate, communicative, is there a variety of skills?)		
Communication (clarity of communication, are intentions and instructions clear?)		
Management and organisation of class (layout, mode, practicalities, technology, quality of resources, collaboration with colleagues)		
Differentiation (provision of support, task variety)		
Assessment (purpose, relevance, monitoring of performance)		
Overall		

You can view and download this table at www.cambridge.org/lynch.

mentor, colleague or peer student teacher and finalise your lesson plan, materials and equipment. Ask your mentor, department colleague or student teacher peer to observe you and to give you feedback using the lesson feedback sheet in Table 6.6.

Finally, you should use the self-evaluation sheet (Table 6.7) to reflect on your lesson(s) critically.

Table 6.7 A self-evaluation sheet*

Self-evaluation
Use this form to reflect on what went well in your lesson and what can be improved.

Student teacher name	Class	Date of lesson

Learning intentions (i.e., How clear were my learning intentions? Were they relevant and appropriate? How far were aims achieved?)

Communication (Did effective communication take place? Was there a range of skills? Could pupils understand and express themselves in L2?)

Management and organisation (Pace of lesson, resources. Were pupils on task? Was it a safe learning environment?)

Differentiation (Did I respond to the needs of all learners? Was there a range of differentiation strategies? How well were learners supported?)

Main action points for future

*This is an alternative to the summary section of the Table 6.4 lesson plan template.
You can view and download this table at www.cambridge.org/lynch.

SUMMARY

This chapter has built on Chapters 2–5 and taken a step-by-step approach to help you begin to develop your skills of lesson planning. An examination of the principles of successful lesson planning in Section 6.1 was followed by advice in Section 6.2 on the practical steps which you must take in order to write effective and successful lesson plans. The advice and guidelines in these first two parts have hopefully led you to try out writing your own lesson plans and encouraged you to share these with mentors, colleagues or other student teachers, thereby helping you to refine your skills of lesson planning and encouraging you to adopt a reflective approach to the whole process (Section 6.3).

REFLECTIVE QUESTIONS

1. In Section 6.3, one of the sources of evaluative feedback that you can obtain on your lesson(s) is from pupils. Reflect on any factors that may influence the pupils in their evaluation of your lesson and how this could be interpreted.
2. Can you come up with any other sources of evaluative feedback that may be useful to you in addition to the sources mentioned in Section 6.3?

KEY TERMS

formative assessment Evaluation of learning to provide feedback to students on how to improve their learning and for teachers on how to improve their teaching.

learning intentions A statement of what it is hoped learners will achieve in a lesson.

success criteria A statement that describes what learners will say, do, make or write to demonstrate that they have met the learning intentions.

summative assessment Evaluation of student learning to provide a mark or a grade against a defined benchmark.

FURTHER READING

If you are interested in reading more about lesson planning in the L2 secondary school classroom, refer to:

Mackay, C., 2019. *Learning to Plan Modern Languages Lessons: Understanding the basic ingredients*. London: Routledge.

If you are interested in learning more about teaching languages in primary or elementary schools, then have a look at this website, which brings together work by researchers, teacher educators and policy makers:

Research in Primary Languages. 2020. Online. https://ripl.uk

7 Differentiation and Responding to Pupils' Needs

Introduction

Chapter 6 examined the principles of effective lesson planning for modern foreign languages classes and analysed the necessary steps to do so. The importance of evaluative feedback was also discussed, highlighting ways in which to obtain this both before and after lessons. Chapter 7 will analyse why it is important to differentiate work for classes, which will be followed by an exploration of a range of differentiation strategies. The chapter will also examine a range of additional support needs, and determine ways in which you can support your learners.

The learning objectives for this chapter are, therefore, as follows:

1. Analyse why it is important to differentiate work for classes.
2. Explore a range of differentiation strategies to use in class.
3. Illustrate a number of specific additional support needs and examine ways in which to support pupils who have those needs.
4. Consider how information and communications technology and digital tools can be used to support learners with additional support needs.
5. Illustrate the overarching skills teachers need to be able to make effective use of the differentiation strategies outlined in this chapter.

Overview

This chapter looks at why it is necessary to differentiate learning, as well as how to plan for and manage **differentiation** in the language class. A range of strategies is given with practical examples of how both content and skills can be differentiated in terms of reception and production of the foreign language. Areas studied include differentiation by length, presentation and density of text; design of task, graded tasks, parallel tasks, branching tasks; differentiation by outcome, differentiated expectations; and the organisation of classes and appropriate use of teaching modes. The chapter examines how to respond to the needs of all learners, from helping pupils with specific learning difficulties (SLDs) to using appropriate strategies with more able learners, and provides examples. It will discuss a wide variety of **additional support needs (ASN)** and gives advice on how to respond to multiple needs within a mixed-ability class setting. Advice is also given on collaborative working with expert colleagues in the field of additional support needs. Fallacies and misconceptions concerning differentiation are also considered to help students avoid common pitfalls. The chapter includes tasks designed to help student teachers develop skills in differentiating the learning and teaching of modern foreign languages.

7.1   Why Differentiate?

This section will analyse the importance of differentiation and why it is necessary to differentiate your teaching.

Differentiation is a framework for learning which seeks to provide each individual with what they need to achieve their full potential (van Vijfeijken et al., 2023). It means supporting and challenging pupils to do their best. It is the entitlement of every learner to have their needs catered for in the programme of learning. The teacher has a responsibility to try to find appropriate and effective ways to address each individual pupil's needs in the planning and delivery of their lessons (Florian et al., 2017). This is not just about supporting learners who may be struggling, but is also about extending learners to the best of their ability, the less able learner, the more able learner and everyone in between. In order to be able to do so, teachers need to understand the principles of differentiation and develop strategies to integrate it with their teaching.

What differentiation is *not* is the provision of separate schooling for pupils with particular abilities or disabilities, *nor* is it the provision of alternative curricula for those with special educational needs. Rather, it is the process by which curriculum objectives, teaching methods, assessment methods, resources and learning activities are planned to cater for the needs of individual pupils. It is the matching of work to the abilities of individual learners so that they are stretched but still achieve success. Differentiation as a term is sometimes criticised as some see it as a practice of setting work and tasks at different ability levels, which may limit some learners and place barriers in front of others. *Adaptive teaching* is sometimes a preferred term as it advocates adapting teaching and learning to the needs of individual learners (Glazzard & Green, 2022). However, many teachers use the term differentiation to describe this adaptive process, which is why I have chosen it as an umbrella term for responding to the varying needs of learners. The Center for Applied Special Technology, now simply known as CAST, has created the widely used Universal Design for Learning (UDL) framework, which advocates for the design of curricula, methods, resources and assessments to be as flexible and inclusive as possible to respond to the needs of individuals (see also Section 9.3.2). These principles are used worldwide, promote inclusive practices and are also endorsed by UNESCO (UNESCO, 2018a).

It must be emphasised that differentiation is *not someone else's responsibility*, but the responsibility of teachers and other education professionals in the classroom. Programmes of initial teacher education incorporate differentiation into their courses, offering strategies, techniques and resources to help novice teachers develop the skills necessary to respond to the often wide-ranging abilities, needs and interests of pupils in class. Likewise, schools, local education authorities and national curriculum bodies and agencies all offer guidance in differentiation and support to teachers of all subject areas and sectors, for both elementary and secondary schools.

There are many reasons why differentiation is necessary. Most classes are not homogenous in nature, but come with a wide range of abilities. Even in so called 'set' or 'streamed' classes, where schools have grouped pupils with the same ability, there is still very often a considerable range of ability in each class. This is because the decisions on placement within specific ability groups are often the result of a summative assessment with a cut-off score. It may be useful to think of classes as 'convenient administrative groupings': there will be some pupils in the class who scored very well in the summative assessment and some who did not do so well and who may have been better placed in a lower-ability set, but the lower-ability set already has its maximum number of pupils. Differentiation by setting classes will not necessarily respond to the needs of all pupils, as setting can only ever give a crude approximation of ability. A very real problem with setting or streaming pupils into classes by ability level is the danger of reinforcing a deficit model (Swann et al., 2012).

Ability level is not the only reason why differentiation is necessary. In many classes you may have a learner or learners with additional support needs. This can be for a variety of reasons, such as:

- Dyslexia;
- Dyscalculia;
- Visual impairment;
- Hearing impairment;
- Emotional issues, e.g., distress in home environment;
- Illness or injury.

This is not an exhaustive list and you will have pupils with other needs as well.

Often a learner may have a combination of additional support needs. It is also worth noting that additional support needs are not always permanent. A learner may need additional support for a short period of time due to illness or an injury. There may be issues at home that affect learning, for instance family breakdown or bereavement.

7.2 Differentiation Strategies

There are many generic strategies which can be used across a wider range of subjects, for example differentiation by support, differentiation by task and differentiation by text. However, for the purposes of this chapter, we are going to look at a number of effective strategies that are used in language classrooms.

7.2.1   Differentiation by Length, Presentation and Density of Text

Here it is a question of choosing or creating texts in L2 that relate to the topic in question, but where accessibility for differing pupil needs is ensured through producing a longer text for more able learners, with more complex language or ideas where the meaning is not as easy to unearth. For less able learners, a shorter text on the same topic could be used with less complex language structures, fewer distractors and where the meaning is easier to deduce. The density of the text is also a factor. Less dense text with shorter sentences is easier to understand than lengthy dense texts consisting of long sentences with multiple clauses. Presentation can also be used to differentiate a text, for example by adding graphics or photographs as visual clues. Text can also be spoken text and again length, density and presentation play a part in how accessible a text is. An authentic audio recording of a food advert may be suitable for most able learners, whereas it may be useful to produce something similar with the aid of a native speaker for less able learners, where the language used is authentic, but shorter with simpler sentence structures. This would address the different ability levels in the class while keeping the learning intentions the same, supporting some learners and extending others. In terms of spoken text, the speed of delivery can also play a part, so choosing or creating audio files with variable speeds according to ability level will help respond to differing pupil needs. If the recording is actually audiovisual, this can greatly increase the chances of comprehension for the pupils through contextual and visual clues.

7.2.2   Differentiation by Support

Another way of differentiating learning in class is by the amount of support a teacher can offer. This support can come in the form of time, materials, tasks or human support, where a colleague, additional support needs (ASN) teacher or foreign language assistant (FLA) can assist the learning and teaching in class, helping specific pupils or groups of pupils. In some schools, senior pupils often help teachers with junior classes, which has the dual function of consolidating the learning of the senior pupils while supporting the younger learners. Where this works well is when you include those helping you in your planning. This means that the planning has to be carried out sufficiently in advance to allow colleagues to contribute, acquaint themselves with the roles expected of them and to prepare for the lesson. As a matter of course, anyone involved in helping should have a copy of your lesson plan where their expected contribution is clearly indicated. If you do not include your colleagues at the planning stage by consulting them, not only is it a professional discourtesy, but you also miss out on valuable ideas they may have for the lesson. I have observed in some schools situations where other staff assigned to help in class (ASN teachers and FLAs) have not been included in any discussions prior to arriving in class and indeed have not even been given a lesson plan. The result has often been a poorer learning experience for pupils through this wasted opportunity.

The mode of teaching that is employed can also aid differentiation. If the class is working semi-autonomously in a group setting, this can free the teacher to work with small groups of learners, either to assist with a task or to present new language at different levels according to the ability of the group(s). It is not always the case that you will have others supporting you in class. Indeed, you may be on your own for the majority of the classes on your timetable. However, you can still provide support in other ways. This can be done by providing help sheets with vocabulary and phrases that learners can choose to use if they need to, instructions for tasks and self-access answer sheets to check progress. Other ways to support leaners can come in the way of functional posters of wall displays where common classroom language and useful vocabulary and phrases are on view for pupils, who can choose to refer them if needed without recourse to the teacher.

7.2.3   Differentiation by Outcome

For this type of differentiation, learners work on the same task, but what they produce can vary quite considerably. A simple example of this would be where all learners respond to a task, but some by completing a matching exercise, multiple-choice questions or a gap-filling exercise, while more able learners might produce a more extended piece of writing or an audio or video recording. Other forms of output may be an oral response, to draw a picture, or learners acting out a role play or other performance.

A popular misconception of differentiation by outcome is that this relates to how far pupils will get with a particular piece of work or task. For example, a teacher will set a task which may involve reading or listening and will set comprehension questions on the text. The lesson plan will often state 'Differentiation is by outcome – the more able learners will manage to answer all questions and the least able just a few.' This is not differentiation by outcome. All it means is that the questions or the tasks have not been differentiated and that some learners will fail to reach the end of the task. This often leads to feelings of low self-worth among learners and can be demotivating. When this approach is applied to homework, these same learners will take much longer to complete a task that may have taken their more able peers very little time to do. Indeed, this may result in learners spending all evening on tasks. Added to this is the possibility of getting lots of answers wrong if the task is not suited to their level, so those learners then have a failed experience that can often discourage them from learning languages. Homework, like classwork, *must* be differentiated.

7.2.4   Differentiation by Task

This is the area of differentiation that offers the most variation, as tasks can be graded tasks, parallel tasks, branching tasks or differentiated by entrance level. Table 7.1 summarises the features of these different types of task and provides examples.

Table 7.1 Different task types and examples

Task type	Features of task	Example of task
Graded tasks	Task is graded by level of difficulty, and is dependent on whether this involves the learner in *remembering, understanding, applying, analysing, evaluating or creating*. Pupils have the chance to progress to cognitively more challenging levels.	Within the topic of holidays, a simple task could involve understanding the language in an online holiday advert (*understanding*). A more difficult task for this topic might be asking your pupils to design an advert for their home town (*creating*).
Parallel tasks	A similar task can be adapted so that different learners or groups of learners can work on the same topic with the same learning intentions, but may use different resources to do this.	While working on the topic of Hobbies and Leisure, you may wish to teach/practise structures around likes/dislikes, where they carry this out, with whom, when. Different stimulus material/content can be given to different learners or groups of learners in the class that respond to their particular interests, but which use the same core language structures/grammar. This may vary from providing resources related to sports, music and concerts, films, indoor pursuits, computer gaming and board games.
Branching tasks	All pupils do core work then move on to extension or simpler tasks after diagnostic assessment.	In the topic of School, after learning the basic vocabulary for school subjects, an extension task may be to say which school subjects you like or dislike and why. A simpler task to consolidate the school subjects may be a matching game, Pelmanism or a multiple-choice activity.
By entrance level	For the language area being looked at there are a number of tasks at different levels of complexity. Learners choose (or are guided to choose) a particular task suited to their ability level. There is the opportunity to move on to more difficult tasks if they find the entry level task too easy. Similarly, learners can choose easier tasks if they find the entry level task too difficult.	Learners may be learning about Food and Drink. There could be a range of tasks, such as: • Discuss in pairs/in a group healthy eating options • Write a menu for your school canteen • Say what you like eating/drinking and why • Identify the food and drink in a photograph

7.2.5 Differentiation by Questioning

Just as there are several types of task that can be used in differentiation, the use of questioning can be used to differentiate learning. Some types of questioning can be thought of as being part of a continuum, as Table 7.2 shows.

Table 7.2 Different question types and examples

Question type	Features	Example
Concrete questions to abstract questions	Concrete questions requiring simple recall of facts are generally easier to answer, whereas more abstract questions on the same topic may require analysis or evaluation by the learner.	Asking if a learner plays sport or likes playing sport is usually easy for learners to answer. A more abstract question asking learners to discuss the health benefits of doing sport will lead them to analyse and evaluate.
Leading questions to non-leading questions	Leading questions may carry clues and point the learner to certain easier answers, whereas non-leading questions may be devoid of contextual clues and require learners to exercise choice or their imagination.	A question asking where learners want to go on holiday accompanied by a choice of destinations displayed on screen will support learners and lead them to give an answer. To get learners to use their imaginations, you could ask them to speculate where they think their teachers go on holiday.
Personal to impersonal questions	Personal questions are often easy to answer as they relate to self, whereas impersonal questions may require speculation.	Asking what learners like to do at the weekend will be easy to answer. A more difficult task may be to guess what a certain celebrity likes to do at the weekend.
General to specific questions	A more general question about what a learner likes doing is relatively easy to answer, whereas giving details requires more thought.	Learners could be asked what they like to do at the weekend, which requires a relatively simple answer. More demanding is asking why they like to do this, where and with whom.

7.2.6 Learning Styles

An area worth mentioning when considering differentiation is learning styles. Kolb (1984) maintains there are four distinct learning styles:

1. concrete experience
2. reflective observation
3. abstract conceptualisation
4. active experimentation

Kolb claimed that effective learning takes place when a learner can complete all four stages in order. Peter Honey and Alan Mumford adapted this to what they called the learning cycle, where learners have an experience, review the experience, conclude from the experience and plan the next steps. Honey and Mumford (1989) align these stages to the following learning styles:

1. activist
2. reflector
3. theorist
4. pragmatist

They maintain that if you identify a learner's preferred learning style, it is important to focus on developing the underutilised style to enable effective learning.

There are different views on this theory, with no real conclusive evidence (Kamińska, 2014). Indeed, it may be very difficult to establish pupils' learning styles in any case. What perhaps it does show is that people learn in different ways.

Another theory of learning style typology popular in the 1980s is the visual, auditory and kinaesthetic model (VAK). This model proposed that some learners respond better to visual stimulus, others to learning presented via audio means, whilst a third group prefer more hands-on, tactile learning. Although very popular, most psychologists dismiss it due to lack of empirical evidence (Fallace, 2023). Howard Gardner's theory of multiple intelligences argues that everyone has a wide variety of intelligences, of which Gardner cites nine, which includes linguistic intelligence (Gardner, 2006). These intelligences, Gardner argues, impact the way we learn and interact with others.

It may be impossible to respond to all learning styles, but perhaps it is a reminder that we should use as many different approaches as seems appropriate, so that at some point(s) a learner's preferred style is used, while still exposing them to others.

7.2.7   Some Useful Online Sites and Digital Tools

The following is a list of online sites and digital tools which can be used for whole-class work and also adapted to support learning at different levels of ability and need.

Kahoot: https://kahoot.com
Kahoot is a very popular online site which can be used on a laptop, tablet or smartphone and allows teachers to provide a variety of games and learning activities that are interesting, fun and easy to use. In very little time, teachers can create topic-based quizzes, true or false games, polls, puzzles and slides, amongst other activities. Most features are free and the activities can be used as practice and consolidation of language and structures.

Quizlet: https://quizlet.com
Similar to Kahoot, Quizlet can be used to make quizzes and games and provides the opportunity to create flashcards to help pupils learn material, whether to study for a test, or simply to consolidate language learned in class.

Linguascope: www.linguascope.com
Linguascope is a subscription-based platform used by many schools. It offers thousands of activities in different languages to assist with language learning. Resources and tools are fun and interactive and can also be printed as worksheets for extension or consolidation.

Blooket: www.blooket.com

Blooket is a gamified learning platform where teachers can devise web-based games for their pupils, which pupils access and play on their own devices. There are various game modes to choose from and through the competitive game element, pupils review language learnt in class. Blooket provides score reports and question analysis to enable the teacher to identify areas where pupils are doing well and learning that may need to be reviewed again.

Genially: https://genial.y.com

Similar to Kahoot and Quizlet, Genially can be used to make quizzes and games, although it is mostly used to design and share media creations. There is a wide range of templates, games and quizzes on different topics to download that teachers can customise to suit their pupils' needs.

The list of technologies, websites and tools above is not exhaustive and such resources are constantly being improved and added to. The best way to find what is useful to you in your learning and teaching is to try out as many as you can. You should also chat to colleagues and share new technologies, websites, platforms and apps that you come across. (For more on technology, see Chapters 9 and 10.)

⟫ TRY THIS OUT

Create a series of differentiated tasks and resources for a mixed-ability class for a year group of your choosing.

Choose three different tasks appropriate for the topic chosen.

- For each topic, create three activities where the learning intentions are the same, but the input (activity and materials) is differentiated for a wide variety of learners.
- Focus on differentiation by text and by task and use as many different techniques as you can, i.e., by task (graded tasks, differentiated entry level, parallel tasks, branching tasks, etc); by text (changing degree of difficulty, i.e., denser texts, supported texts, varied types of text).
- If possible, discuss this with your mentor or peer.
- Make any adjustments based upon your discussions.

This section has explored a wide range of strategies for differentiating the learning and teaching in modern language classes and provided examples of how this can be done.

7.3 Additional Support Needs and How to Respond to Them

This section illustrates the wide range of specific additional support needs that teachers will experience in their classes and offers guidance on how to support pupils with these additional support needs.

In most classes, there will be a number of pupils with additional support needs and some pupils may have multiple additional support needs. Listening to pupils' feedback on your lessons will help you to gauge how well you are responding to their needs. It is important to listen to your learners and discuss with them what works well for them and what does not, within a learner-centred framework. This will help you to work with the learners to find the optimum ways of learning for individuals.

Although not an exhaustive list, here are a number of specific support needs often present in class and ways in which you can support your pupils.

7.3.1   Dyslexia

According to the British Dyslexia Association, dyslexia 'is a learning difficulty that primarily affects the skills involved in accurate and fluent word reading and spelling. Characteristic features of dyslexia are difficulties in phonological awareness, verbal memory and verbal processing speed. Dyslexia occurs across the range of intellectual abilities' (British Dyslexia Association, 2023: What is Dyslexia? para. 3).

Dyslexia is very common in learners. Common signs in reading are hesitant or laboured reading, omitting words or not recognising familiar words. In writing, a pupil with dyslexia may have a poor standard of written work compared to their oral ability, may have problems with spelling, punctuation or grammar, or may have difficulty taking notes in class. Please see the British Dyslexia Association website for a full list of signs.

There are a number of ways in which you can help your learners, for instance:

- Provide audio recordings of sounds to give listening practice. Encourage learners to listen to and say pairs of words where only one sound is different. Forvo.com is a free audio database of language to play or download recordings in different languages.
- Use flashcards with pictures, colours, shapes around words to associate a word with an image or colour.
- Colour-code grammar, e.g., different colours for masculine, feminine and neuter.
- Use word cards, mix them up and have pupils sort them into the right order to make sense.
- Use online platforms such as Quizlet to help pupils remember words and phrases.
- Research has shown that a Multisensory Structured Learning (MSL) approach to foreign language learning, bringing together auditory, tactile, visual and kin-aesthetic pathways, can help foreign language learning in learners with dyslexia (Kormos & Smith, 2012; Nijakowska, 2008, 2010).

7.3.2   Dyscalculia

Although dyscalculia is a learning difficulty in understanding numbers, this is not just a difficulty for a maths lesson but may present problems for pupils in your languages class. In language classes, we frequently talk about quantities, prices, distances and time, and this can be difficult for some learners. Some strategies that can be useful are breaking down the steps in a lesson involving numeracy into simpler steps, providing concrete materials to help pupils visualise number work and connecting learning to real life, for example following a recipe and weighing out the ingredients.

Both dyslexia and dyscalculia are conditions belonging to a paradigm known as **neurodiversity**, a framework for understanding how the brain functions. The neurodiversity framework argues that people's brains work in different ways and that this is normal. The framework, which started to appear in the late 1980s and early 1990s, provides a means of understanding how differences in brain processes can affect social interaction, learning and communication. Other common examples of neurodivergent conditions include:

- Attention Deficit Hyperactivity Disorder (ADHD);
- Autism Spectrum Disorder (ASD);
- Dyspraxia;
- Dysgraphia;
- Tourette's Syndrome (TS).

Understanding the particular features of neurodivergent conditions helps teachers to prepare appropriate lessons which respond to the needs of individual learners (Clouder et al., 2020).

7.3.3 Visual Impairment

In terms of visual impairment, this may range from partial visual impairment to major loss of vision to blindness. For most mainstream schools, the majority of pupils with visual impairment will have some vision. Pupils with no vision still tend to be taught by specialist teachers in schools for the blind, although this is not always the case. The British Childhood Visual Impairment and Blindness Study 2 (BCVIS2) found 'that childhood visual disability is a marker of vulnerability and should be considered a sentinel child health event' (Teoh et al., 2021).

In most modern foreign languages classes, the meaning of a word or sentence is often carried out with the help of visual stimuli, for example pointing to an object and naming it in L2 (comprehensible input). However, for pupils with visual impairment, this does not work due to not being able to see (or see clearly) the visual stimulus. As a result, teachers of pupils with a visual impairment must look for other ways to facilitate meaning.

There are general strategies that teachers of all subjects can use to assist learning for the visually impaired, for example:

- Addressing the class when entering and leaving the classroom;
- Calling students by their name to attract their attention;
- Being precise with descriptive words, such as left, right, straight on, and not using vague terms;
- Describing visual events in sufficient detail orally;

- Using a classroom assistant to help visually impaired learners with classwork;
- Not giving lots of information to copy down. Notes from the board can be printed in large text or emailed to pupils for enlarging on their devices.

Reading a foreign language can be facilitated for the visually impaired learner by using a laptop, tablet or other device with text to speech function. The use of large print or braille texts can also help pupils with a visual impairment. For some learners, it may be necessary to change the background colour for any documents they may be using. There is no 'one size fits all' technique. Classroom teachers should seek help from specialist teachers in their school to work on strategies collaboratively and prepare resources to provide appropriate, targeted support to visually impaired learners in their class.

7.3.4   Hearing Impairment

Hearing impairment is another very common issue in schools. Like visual impairment, the degree of hearing impairment can range from slight to severe. There are, however, a number of learning and teaching strategies that can be incorporated into a teacher's practice. Consider these strategies from Hilary McColl on the Scottish Sensory Centre website at the University of Edinburgh:

- Be prepared to use whatever amplification best suits the student's hearing loss.
- Always face the hearing-impaired student when pronouncing key phrases, and make sure your face is not in shadow.
- Write on the board any proper names that occur, as these are difficult to work out from context.
- Provide lots of repetition and opportunities for consolidation.
- Indicate clearly when you are switching between L1 and L2.
- Use flash cards and other visuals which can be shown or pointed to as an aid to comprehension.
- Use mime, gesture and facial expression to illuminate meaning.
- Arrange for extra 1-to-1 tutorials so that the student has a better environment and more time in which to practise listening with lipreading in L2.
- Consider learning which speech sounds are not lip readable so as to become more aware of which words may need to be written on the board or screen.

(Scottish Sensory Centre, 2023, What the tutor can do section of table)

As with visual impairment, classroom teachers should seek help from specialist teachers in their school to work on strategies collaboratively and prepare resources to provide appropriate, targeted support for hearing-impaired learners in their class.

7.3.5   Mobility Issues

Another thing to take into consideration when planning your class is mobility issues. You may have in your class pupils who have restricted mobility. This could be as a result of a number of things, for example an accident, cerebral palsy, or another condition that makes walking difficult or impossible. Not only must you take this into account in the physical layout of the classroom (e.g., consider whether pupils with mobility issues can obtain their own resources, equipment and materials, and if furniture is suitable), but you need to ensure that activities you have planned are such that all learners can accomplish these and that there are no barriers to learning placed in the way of pupils with disabilities. It may also mean that you need to plan for the use of specific equipment, or involve the use of a classroom support assistant or specialist teacher.

7.3.6   Emotional Issues

At times, pupils may come under particular stress that affects their concentration, attendance and their learning, for example when there is upset at home. This could be due to a member of the pupil's family being seriously ill, family breakdown, or a bereavement. This may also be due to particular mental health struggles that a pupil may be experiencing. Such events cause great distress in pupils' lives and may affect their learning, resulting in extra measures having to be put in place to support their learning. This could be extra support for classwork (resources or help from a classroom assistant), amongst other strategies. These needs may often only be on a temporary basis, but still require planning. Working with colleagues who are involved in pastoral care for pupils will help you plan accordingly to support these pupils in your classes.

7.3.7   Mode of Teaching

There are many ways in which you can achieve effective differentiation in your classes. The strategies outlined above have focused on particular techniques (differentiation by text, task, support, etc.) but alongside devising these learning and teaching activities, you need to consider how to manage the differentiation in your classes. A teaching style which consists largely of the teacher standing at the front of the class and explaining everything to the whole class in a lock-step fashion will make differentiation difficult. If we take explaining as an example: we cannot speak at multiple different levels at the same time, so teachers using this approach have to pitch the level of language in their explanation at a certain standard. This often results in the language being pitched to an imagined 'middle' ability level of the class. The problem here is that the less able learners in class will not be able to understand, while the more able learners may find the language too simple, or even boring. Far more effective is working in groups where, if working in ability groupings, you can explain and use the L2 at different levels of complexity with different groups as they come to you in turn. This is relatively easy to organise and has the advantage that each group will be able to work directly with the teacher. While not working directly with the teacher, groups could be working on tasks or resources pitched at their level, which is often more difficult to manage in a whole-class, lock-step arrangement. On other occasions, you may wish to place the pupils in groups of mixed ability to help more able pupils stretch less able pupils. (For more details and advice on working with groups in your classes, please see Chapter 12.)

7.3.8   An Inclusive Approach

The list of additional support needs in this section is not exhaustive, but it is similar to those commonly found in schools. There are other additional support needs and to address each one requires careful research and planning. The important thing is to make sure that your pedagogy is inclusive. The Salamanca Statement of 1994 (UNESCO, 1994) acknowledges that children are different and that learning should be adapted to respond to learners' needs, rather than making the child fit into a standard classroom model of teaching and learning (Armstrong et al., 2010). Furthermore, in 2006, the UN Convention on the Rights of Persons with Disabilities (United Nations, 2006) enshrined the rights of children by stating that no child should be discriminated against on the grounds of disability and that countries should work together to raise the aspirations and achievements of children with additional support needs (Hodkinson & Vickerman, 2012). This places a legal responsibility on schools and teachers to provide appropriate education for all children. As well as the legal responsibility, this is surely what we want for our pupils and these principles should be engrained in our teaching practices.

FOOD FOR THOUGHT

When you were learning modern languages in school, did you or any of your classmates have specific learning needs?
   How did your teachers respond to your needs?

7.4   Information and Communications Technology and Digital Tools to Support Learners with Additional Support Needs

While we should not look to technology and the internet as a universal panacea, it is useful to explore the growing number of websites and online tools to help respond to the needs of learners. We will consider how **Information and Communications Technology** and digital tools can be employed to support specific additional support needs.

   Most operating systems for computers, laptops, tablets and other devices have accessibility features or assistive technology built into them as standard and are easy to access. Some operating systems have a wider range of accessibility features than others, but most offer similar support. Here are some of the ways in which technology can help respond to the needs of learners. For convenience, links to full details of the support offered by each operating system and web browsers are listed at the end of this chapter.

7.4.1   Vision

With relative ease pupils can use their device's sight-related accessibility tools to get support. This includes using colour filters, changing contrast, magnifying what is on the screen or choosing how text is displayed (e.g., text spacing and line focus). This is particularly useful for people with low vision, or people with a vision disability, such as colour blindness. In addition, pupils can choose to hear text read aloud with built in text-to-speech (tts) functions. Alt text (alternative text) is a function of screen readers which describes the appearance or function of an image on a page, a valuable tool for learners with visual impairment.

7.4.2   Hearing

Support here ranges from hearing all sounds on a device in one mono audio channel to generating captions or subtitles for text on screen or within communication apps. Users can also use the language of the subtitles which will be translated in real time. A handy function is being able to increase the length of time notifications are displayed on-screen, giving pupils more time for comprehension.

7.4.3   Neurodiversity

To make learning more accessible for pupils with dyslexia, seizures, autism, Attention Deficit Hyperactivity Disorder (ADHD) or other cognitive differences, a number of operating systems offer the possibility of simplifying screen menus, or decluttering the screen to reduce distractions to learning. This can include reducing or customising notifications. Enabling suggested text and also spelling and grammar checkers all add support for learners.

7.4.4   Mobility

A number of operating systems offer support to suit mobility needs. These include the use of sticky keys to enable commands that normally use multiple keys, filter keys to set keyboard sensitivity, on-screen keyboards, dictation (converting voice to text) and eye- and head-tracking technology to control one's screen.

7.4.5   Mental Health

To help learners with certain mental health conditions, such as anxiety, depression or bipolar disorder, it is possible to minimise distractions. This can be through disabling notifications and animations, but also by clearing up the desktop to make it less cluttered. Immersive readers also help by focusing on lines of text and with layout to reduce or remove elements that may distract.

A number of the support features listed above are built into or usable with popular web browsers, such as screen readers, closed captioning, screen magnification software and alternative input devices.

FOOD FOR THOUGHT

Think back to how you were taught in your modern languages classes at school.
Were you taught in set or streamed ability classes?
Were you aware of your teacher using any differentiation strategies or were you taught in a whole-class lock-step manner?
Did you experience any barriers to your learning? How did this make you feel?

7.5 Overarching Teacher Skills for Effective Differentiation

Using the proposed strategies above will help you to respond to the needs of the learners in your classes; however, these must be coupled with a number of skills and detailed knowledge of the learners in those classes and of their individual needs. Importantly, you need to:

- have a clear understanding of the ways in which children learn a foreign language to make sure that you use effective and communicative strategies (see Chapter 2);
- analyse the knowledge and skills which comprise a particular learning task, to be able to devise appropriate learning and teaching;
- have a heightened awareness of possible obstacles to successful learning to make sure that you include help and support that address potential problems that some learners may face;
- develop procedures for observing pupils on task in order to see how well, or otherwise, pupils are coping with tasks to help you make any adjustments to teaching;
- have an understanding of ways in which this data can be used to provide for additional support needs, so that you plan effectively to meet these needs;
- work closely with colleagues with specialist knowledge, who will be able to advise and support you in meeting your learners' needs;
- develop expertise in designing and implementing structured programmes which consider the needs of all learners.

SUMMARY

Section 7.1 of this chapter analysed the importance of differentiation and why it is necessary. This led on to Section 7.2, which explored a range of differentiation strategies to use in modern language classes, providing examples of many of these. The necessity of addressing additional support needs was considered in Section 7.3 together with ways by which to support pupils with specific or multiple additional support needs. Section 7.4 considered how teachers can use information and communication technology and digital tools to respond to particular support needs of pupils, while Section 7.5 explored the overarching skills teachers need to be able to differentiate effectively. Differentiation is not an afterthought. It is not something that should be ignored or dismissed. It must be built into your daily planning of units of work and lessons. All learners are entitled to access to the same curriculum, and it is up to teachers and educators to integrate this as a pedagogical strategy to address the needs of classes and individuals. This is best achieved when teachers work collaboratively with colleagues and with as wide a range of educational specialists to which we have access. In this way, teachers will build up the knowledge, skills and experience that will help them make the curriculum accessible to all learners in an inclusive and supportive environment where diversity is welcomed and celebrated.

REFLECTIVE QUESTIONS

1. It is sometimes assumed that pupils with learning difficulties or additional support needs should not be offered modern language teaching but more teaching in L1 instead. How would you respond to colleagues who may put this view to you?
2. There exists the view among some teachers that specific additional support needs are best supported by placing learners in special units or special schools. What is your perspective on this view?

KEY TERMS

Additional Support Needs (ASN) These are specific needs where learners may need more or different forms of support to assist in their learning.

differentiation Techniques, strategies and approaches which ensure that learning and teaching meet the needs of individual learners.

information and communications technology A broad term to describe communication devices and technology to transmit, store, create, share or exchange information.

neurodiversity Provides a framework for understanding how differences in brain processes can affect social interaction, learning and communication.

FURTHER READING

For general advice on differentiation, refer to this online title:

Tomlinson, C.A., 2014. *The Differentiated Classroom: Responding to the needs of all learners.* Alexandria, VA: Association for Supervision & Curriculum Development.

Center for Applied Special Technology (CAST), 2024. Universal design principles. Online. https://udlguidelines.cast.org

UNESCO, 1994. The Salamanca Statement and Framework for Action on Special Needs Education. Adopted by the world conference on Special Needs Education: Access and Quality. Salamanca, Spain, 7–10 June. Online. https://unesdoc.unesco.org/ark:/48223/pf0000098427

United Nations, 2006. Convention on the Rights of Persons with Disabilities. Adopted by the United Nations General Assembly, 13 December. Online. https://bit.ly/4gz24dn

For detailed advice on assistive technology and accessibility in Microsoft Windows, macOS, Android OS, Linux OS and the Chrome browser go to the respective vendors' websites and search for 'assistive technology' and 'accessibility'.

8 Assessment *of, for* and *as* Learning in Modern Foreign Languages

Introduction

Chapter 7 analysed the importance of differentiation and explored strategies for differentiating learning and teaching in the modern foreign languages class and responding to additional support needs. Chapter 8 will consider the important area of assessment *of, for* and *as* learning in modern foreign languages and explore practical strategies for the use of different forms of assessment in the MFL class.

The learning objectives for this chapter are, therefore, as follows:

1. Analyse the connection between learning and assessment.
2. Evaluate the features of summative and formative assessment and their use in class.
3. Explore the relationship between assessment *of, for* and *as* learning in modern foreign languages.
4. Explore ways in which to develop metacognitive strategies in assessment.
5. Examine the importance of providing learners with feedback and recording their progress.

Overview

It is very important that teaching and learning activities and assessment are designed to cater for the needs of schools and pupils. This chapter looks at the connection between learning and assessment and includes approaches and strategies for both formative and summative assessment. How to plan for and manage assessment *of* learners' progress is examined in detail with practical advice on how to do this in a structured way. Advice on how to use assessment *for* learning within a framework of formative assessment is detailed, including self-assessment and peer-assessment techniques with practical examples for use in class. Developing metacognitive strategies in learners is explored and advice is given on how to promote and develop this in learners in a staged approach.

8.1   Connection between Learning and Assessment

We have looked at effective ways of learning and teaching modern languages (Chapter 2), how to develop different language skills (Chapter 3), the importance of choosing appropriate modes of teaching (Chapter 4), planning coherent lessons and programmes of study (Chapters 5 and 6) and responding to pupils' needs (Chapter 7). This chapter will examine an integral part of teachers' work, that of assessment, exploring how intertwined it is with learning and teaching.

There are many different types of assessment that teachers use in class and normally teachers will have a specific purpose for the particular type of assessment they choose to use in a particular class. The two most widely used types of assessment are **summative assessment**, which is usually administered at the end of a topic or unit with the goal of measuring performance (Andrade & Cizek, 2010), and **formative assessment**, in which evidence of pupil performance is gathered and analysed to help decide the next steps in their learning (Black & Wiliam, 2009).

Just as important as how we teach modern languages is how we assess learners' progress and what we do with the information. Learners need to know how they are doing in their language learning, areas in which they are performing well and areas in which they are not doing so well. Most importantly, they need to know *how to improve*. The process by which teachers convey this information to the pupils in their class is also known as formative assessment (see above). I like this term, as it implies helping the learners to *form* or *shape* their learning to make improvements. This should be a continuous process whereby learners are given feedback on their learning and performance and should be built in as an integral part of lessons and their planning. This is regularly done well in many schools, and not only helps learners understand how they are learning and how to improve, but also provides valuable information on pupil progress to the teacher, which in turn informs future lesson planning.

8.2   Choosing between Summative and Formative Assessment

This section will evaluate the features and use of summative and formative assessment in the modern foreign languages classroom.

We often see summative assessments being used predominantly in class and there are a number of reasons for this:

- summative assessments are the easiest to understand;
- teachers are inexperienced in the management of assessment;
- teachers lack confidence in identifying attainment levels;
- teachers are under pressure over exam results;
- they summarise pupil attainment at a simplistic level.

These aforementioned reasons are the drivers behind some teachers frequently using summative assessment where they often feel pressurised to provide information to

Table 8.1 An example of typical mark ranges for summative assessments

Mark range	Grade	Grade description
70–100	A	well above average
60–69	B	above average
50–59	C	average
40–49	D	below average
39 and below	E	well below average

school managers, national bodies and parents about the level at which individual pupils are working, and due to their simplistic nature, summative assessments are most easily understood by the general public (Andrade & Cizek, 2010).

However, although summative assessments may seem to provide data on pupil performance, much valuable information is lost. Summative assessments are what the name implies: the sum total of what a pupil has achieved in a test. It is a snapshot in time and really only states what a learner is able to demonstrate on a particular day. As such, summative assessments relate often more to performance and are not a guarantee that deeper, more lasting learning has been achieved. In addition, the majority of summative tests are designed to show the total mark, percentage or grade a learner has achieved. If we say that a learner has scored 54 per cent in a test, what information are we really obtaining? Admittedly, we may be able to say that a learner with 54 per cent is performing at an average level, as most summative tests generating a score tend to use a description of mark ranges similar to the one in Table 8.1.

In norm-referenced tests, the grade description is sometimes related to the position of the learner in a cohort. This leads us to the question: if the cohort one year performs a lot worse than a previous year, what value do these marks and grades have? Does a score of 54 per cent one year really indicate *average*, if the relation of the learner to other learners in the class in a different year taking the same test indicates that the learner has performed *above average* for the class? And can we really discriminate between 54 and 55, or 42 and 43 per cent?

The numerical value gives little information to the learner about what they have achieved. It does not give a description of what the learner can and cannot do in relation to the curriculum. There is no attestation of what content has been learned to earn this mark or grade, nor is there a description of the level of proficiency in a particular skill area. Often, summative assessments are regarded as a deficit model of assessment, that is, showing what deficiencies there are in a pupil's learning. It also does not give any advice to the learner as to what they need to do to improve. Formative assessment, however, can be diagnostic. It can give a lot more information. It can describe what the learner has actually learned, give an indication of level of skill and give advice on next steps and how to improve (Wiliam & Thompson, 2008). Below is an extract from a descriptor of performance in listening and talking in Scotland's

Table 8.2 Extract from the modern foreign languages experiences and outcomes in the Scottish Curriculum for Excellence

Listening and talking	First	Second	Third	Fourth
Listening for information	I explore the patterns and sounds of language through songs and rhymes and show understanding verbally or non-verbally. **MLAN 1–01a** I am learning to take an active part in daily routines, responding to simple instructions which are accompanied by gesture and expression. **MLAN 1–01b** I can listen to and show understanding of language from familiar voices and sources. **MLAN 1–01c**	I explore the patterns and sounds of language through songs and rhymes and show understanding and enjoyment by listening, joining in and responding. **MLAN 2–01a** I take an active part in daily routines, responding to instructions which are accompanied by gesture and expression. **MLAN 2–01b** I can listen to and show understanding of familiar instructions and language from familiar voices and sources. **MLAN 2–01c**	I can listen to and show understanding of mainly familiar language and instructions from a variety of sources, where the sentences are longer and where there may be more than one speaker. **MLAN 3–01a**	I can listen to and show understanding of language from a variety of sources, including unfamiliar speakers, where the sentences are more complex, less predictable, and contain some unfamiliar language or known language used in unfamiliar contexts. **MLAN 4–01a**
Listening and talking with others	I am beginning to identify key information from a short predictable conversation and react with words and/or gesture. **MLAN 1–02a** I am beginning to share information about myself using familiar vocabulary and basic language structures. **MLAN 1–02b**	I explore how gesture, expression and emphasis are used to help understanding. I can listen and respond to familiar voices in short, predictable conversations using straightforward language and non-verbal techniques as appropriate such as gesture and eye contact. **MLAN 2–02a**	I can listen and respond to others in mainly predictable, more extended conversations using familiar language and non-verbal techniques as appropriate. **MLAN 3–02a**	I can listen and respond to others, including sympathetic fluent speakers of the language, in extended conversations that are less predictable. **MLAN 4–02a**

Source: Education Scotland, 2017. Contains public sector information licensed under the Open Government Licence v3.0.

Curriculum for Excellence (Education Scotland, 2017). It helps teachers to identify where learners are in terms of what they have learned and their skill proficiency.

Of course, you may not necessarily be teaching a class within a national learning framework, but you will still want to know how your learners are doing and equally you will want to be able to give your learners feedback on their progress and how to improve. This is not difficult. What is required is that you develop a framework with descriptors related to identifiable stages in the pupils' learning. It does not have to be overly wordy, but it must give enough detail to indicate where pupils are in their learning. This is best achieved when teachers work together in a school, or across schools, to discuss, establish and agree on a framework that charts learners' development. Through using a framework for learning, whether a national one, or one that has been created in-house, it is relatively straight forward to identify in which areas learners are doing well and in which they are not, and from this be able to offer advice and guidance as to what learners need to do to improve.

8.2.1 Features and Use of Summative Assessment Strategies

There will be many times when you will be required to use summative assessment, notably if you are asked by your head of department or head teacher to provide a grade for a school report or to provide evidence for national grading systems. If this is the case, there are a number of types of summative assessment that you can use, depending on what you wish to assess. These are often taken at the end of a unit or chapter, or at the end of a course. Such summative assessments may take the form of, for example:

- a written test, i.e., creative writing such as a poem or a story, or an essay;
- a reading comprehension;
- a listening comprehension;
- a speaking test;
- a closed book exam;
- a presentation – oral or written;
- a conversation with an interlocutor;
- a group task;
- a project;
- a portfolio of work.

Some examples of the above could be similar to the following:

Written test
Write an essay of no more than 250 words describing your recent holiday in Venice. Say what you did there, what you liked about it and present reasons to persuade others to visit the city.

Speaking test
Deliver a short oral presentation in L2 of no more than three minutes where you outline what can be done in your local area to protect the environment.

Conversation with interlocutor
Using the brochures of what is on in your town or village, discuss with your partner what you would like to do this weekend. Discuss reasons why you would like to do a certain activity and listen to what your partner would like to do. Agree with your partner what you are going to do, how to get there and when and where you are going to meet.

Project
Create a project showing an aspect of successful sustainable development in your local area. The project must contain written text, oral text and video together with other artefacts that you consider essential to present your information.

As with any assessment, teachers should ensure that these assessments are marked and results returned to the pupils as soon as possible to allow pupils to see where they need to improve.

8.2.2   Features and Use of Formative Assessment Strategies

If we look at formative assessment, there are a number of reasons why it is regarded as useful for helping pupils in their learning.

- It is qualitative in nature.
- It is a useful tool for diagnosing pupils' strengths and development areas.
- It is valuable in evaluating the effectiveness of teaching.
- It can help diagnose pupils' progress in skill areas.
- It can show teachers how much of a topic has been mastered or remains to be covered.
- It can show if, or how far, language structures have been successfully acquired.
- It can show which areas are accessible or proving difficult for pupils.

All of the above provide very useful information about pupil learning, both for individuals and for the class as a whole. This can help to inform future lesson planning, either by allowing the teacher to adjust planned learning to revise an area pupils find difficult, or to look at a different way of approaching the learning or teaching of an area. Similarly, this allows teachers to move on more quickly if pupils have acquired something more easily than expected.

8.2.2.1   Using Formative Assessment during Unit of Work

As we can see from the list of features of formative assessment strategies above, formative assessment can be used at set points in pupils' topic learning and also on a daily basis. During the course of a unit of work, regular formative assessments can help both pupils and teachers to review learning and to keep track of progress. It is of far more use to do this at several points *during* a unit of work than to wait until the *end* of a unit of work. Assessing progress during the learning and teaching of a unit enables pupils and teachers to spot any problems in learning early on and allows opportunities to develop strategies to address these in a timely manner. Waiting until the end of a unit of work to assess or review learning can lead to what can sometimes appear to the learner to be too many points to focus on at the same time. It is easier to address problems in learning as they occur, rather than gather them all together in a list at the end of a unit. There may also be areas of language learning early in a unit upon which subsequent language learning is based. In such a case, if learners have difficulty with a language point early in a unit and it is not addressed, then this may have a knock-on effect on other learning. Early intervention in a small area early on will pay dividends in subsequent learning.

The ways in which this can be done can easily be planned into a series of lessons. Firstly, you need to decide what you would like to assess. Is it acquisition of language structures, knowledge of a particular topic, development of a skill area or areas, or the ability to carry out certain communicative tasks? Next, you need to identify the points within the unit of work at which you wish to carry out the assessments. These will usually be points at which a number of language structures or items and skills have been introduced and practised, and where a point of review will appear obvious, for example it may be at the end of a sub-section, or a sub-topic of a larger topic, or where you would like to know how much or how well your pupils have understood a language area, as the next area builds on this. Finally, you need to decide on the method by which you will assess the learning. This method does not need to involve a break in learning and a formal test to be administered. It can easily be part of their classroom learning. For instance, from work carried out through the normal course of a lesson:

- You may decide that you will take in work on a reading or a listening task (completed on a worksheet or in pupils' exercise books) to assess.
- You could decide to assess a short piece of writing which is part of the normal planned work of the class.
- You could ask pupils to record a short audio piece on recently learned language to upload or send to you (either individually or as part of a conversation).

The assessments should all be based on authentic and communicative tasks which are part of the planned learning and teaching for the class. The parts of classwork that you choose to assess then serve the dual function of simultaneously providing an assessment opportunity, while not interrupting or taking time away from the learning in class. An important consideration is that there should be enough time between the teaching and practice of the new language and the assessment thereof to allow pupils consolidation time, otherwise you will not get a true indication of what pupils can do. Another point in terms of ensuring that you get a true picture of pupil performance is that you do not need to tell learners in advance that they are going to be assessed. Not knowing they are being assessed will allow you to get a true reflection of their normal performance, as opposed to a test that they have crammed for, the language for which they may forget immediately after the test. I would advise, however, to let the learners know soon afterwards that you have used part of their classwork for assessment. This approach works best and gains support from the pupils when you have agreed this with the class as a way of working at the beginning of the year or course.

A very useful strategy to help you manage regular formative assessment is through group work. You may, for example, have your class working in groups, perhaps in different skill areas (or where one skill is predominant), for example in a listening group, a speaking group, a reading group and a writing group. Pupils may be working on tasks in each area for a set amount of time and then move on to another group. For assessment purposes, you may decide to take in the work completed by say, one or two of the reading groups to assess, although not from all four groups. Similarly, you may decide to work with the speaking group and monitor pupils from one or two of the rotations while they carry out communicative speaking tasks and assess them according to set criteria, or perhaps merely write qualitative comments. Although you will not have assessed every pupil, you can choose other pupils the next time you are teaching the class. It does not matter that you will not be using exactly the same material or tasks for assessing others or the rest of the class the next time. The important thing is that the material or classwork you choose for assessment purposes is of comparable standard and that you use the same assessment criteria. In this way you will have assessed the whole class in different areas without taking time out of teaching. Detailed guidance on how to manage this as part of carousel group work is given in Chapter 12. If you do this at several points through the unit of work, you will build up a valuable amount of information on the progress of each individual pupil, which will help you to work with them to plan the best next steps in their learning.

8.2.2.2   Using Formative Assessment during Individual Lessons

Using formative assessment in your daily teaching will provide a lot of valuable information to both you and your pupils as to their progress, allowing time to address any difficulties as they arise, as well as inform your future planning. You may decide to use similar strategies to Section 8.2.2.1 above in your daily lessons, or you may decide to use shorter, light-touch ways in which to undertake the formative assessment of your pupils. As above, you need to decide *what* it is that you want to assess, as this will help you to decide on an appropriate way to do this.

Table 8.3 details some formative assessment techniques commonly used in MFL classrooms. The last four in particular are great for obtaining quick feedback on learning from the pupils.

Table 8.3 Formative assessment techniques for the modern foreign languages classroom

Assessment technique	Examples
Questioning strategies	These can range from simple recall of factual information to higher-order questions, such as 'how' and 'why'.
Quizzes	These are a competitive way to check understanding of factual information or vocabulary. They can also be created digitally using Blooket, Quizlet or Kahoot.
Whiteboards	The teacher asks a question and pupils write the answer on a whiteboard, which they then hold up for the teacher to see. This can also be done digitally on a tablet and held up, or the answers displayed on the main screen in the classroom.

Table 8.3 (cont.)

Assessment technique	Examples
Think-Pair-Share	The teacher asks a question, or sets a topic for pupils to think about. Pupils discuss this in pairs and then share their answers or thoughts with the class.
Four corner game	The teacher asks a question with four possible answers written on card clearly posted at each of the four corners of the classroom. Pupils choose the answer they think is correct by going to the corner. Those who get it wrong need to sit down. This can be made more active, if space allows, by having pupils run in a circular direction round the class to music (while hopping, skipping, etc.) and when the music stops, the pupils run to the corner to choose an answer. (It need not be question and answer, the teacher can ask 'Which of these four words am I thinking about?')
Sequence cards	Pupils work in groups and are each given a sentence cut up on paper. Together they have to lay out the sentences in the correct order. This can also be done with one group in front of the class with large text on card and the rest of the class direct them to the correct sequence.
Snowball fight	Each pupil writes a question or an action statement to do with the current topic or lesson content on a piece of paper, scrunches it into a ball and throws it across the classroom. Other pupils pick these up and have to answer the question or demonstrate the action statement.
Musical whiteboards	Pupils sit in a circle with their mini whiteboard with music playing in the background. When the music stops, pupils must write the correct answer on the board and hold it up. The last person to hold up the correct answer (or anyone who writes an incorrect answer) loses their spot in the circle, which slowly shrinks until only one pupil is left.
Thumbs up/thumbs down	Pupils can show how confident they feel in what they have learned in the lesson by giving a thumbs up, thumbs down or in between.
Exit passes	Pupils write their answers to a question or write a piece of vocabulary/topic word on a sticky note which they stick to the board on leaving class. Instead of answering a question, teachers can use this technique to ask pupils for feedback on the lesson, i.e., what they found easy or difficult, what they found interesting or boring. They can also write something they would like the teacher to go over again with them in the next lesson.
Traffic lights	The teacher can check comprehension by asking pupils to hold up a card with different coloured dots, green to show fully understood, orange to show partially understood and red to show having difficulty understanding.
Stop/Go cards	Each pupil has a card with 'Stop' on one side and 'Go' on the other side. Pupils signal whether they understand an explanation/new concept or whether they need further explanation by the side they show the teacher.

FOOD FOR THOUGHT

Can you think of other formative assessment strategies to add to Table 8.3?

8.2.2.3   Making Formative Assessment Work

To ensure that formative assessment is as effective as you would like it to be, there are a number of things that you can do.

1. Share the learning intentions and success criteria for your lessons with your learners.
2. Help your learners identify the success criteria, so that they know when they have achieved them.
3. Negotiate learning intentions with your learners, so that they feel part of the process.
4. Ensure that any targets are realistic and achievable and that they relate to learners' progression in the language.
5. Do not set too many targets, as this will overburden learners and make them lose focus.
6. Be precise in your target setting to keep your learners focused.
7. Help your learner to self-assess.
8. Look at data coming from assessment with your learners and reflect on what this means for their language learning.
9. Provide guidance as to how learners might achieve their targets.
10. Provide targeted feedback so that learners know their next steps to improve their language learning and make further progress.

8.2.2.4   Self-Assessment Strategies

An important part of formative assessment is getting your learners to develop the ability to self-assess. By helping learners to develop skills in self-assessment, you enable them to monitor their learning and think about future behaviours (Andrade & Cizek, 2010; Brown & Harris, 2013).

There are numerous ways in which this can be integrated with classwork, examples of which are given in Table 8.4.

Table 8.4 Self-assessment strategies for pupils

Self-assessment strategy	Example
Self-test	During or after a lesson, see how much you can recall of the lesson (i.e., vocabulary, structures, phrases) by making a list without looking at your exercise book or worksheets. Check afterwards with your notes.
Presentation	Record a 1-minute presentation (audio or video) incorporating as much as you can from today's lesson or this topic.
Portfolio	Create a collection of things associated with the topic or lesson – words, images, audio, video – as a collage, poster or digital file.
Exit pass	Write down two areas (e.g., food items, drinks) you feel you have learnt well and one area where you are less confident (e.g., ordering food) and hand to the teacher at the end of the lesson.

Table 8.5 Peer-assessment strategies

Peer-assessment strategy	Example
Quiz your partner	Devise a short quiz on the day's lesson and test your partner. Give advice on how your partner can improve.
Dragon's Den	Listen to your partner's 1-minute presentation (audio or video) on today's lesson or this topic. Write or tell your partner how well they did. Use 'Two stars and a wish' approach.
Swap work	Regularly stop and look at your partner's work and give them encouragement and feedback on how well you think they are doing.
Think-Pair-Share	Use Think-Pair-Share as an opportunity to self-assess, but also to give feedback to your partner on responses to the question or topic from the teacher.
Poster praise	Read wall displays or posters on current topics prepared by your classmates. Give advice or comments on any aspects of the display by sticking Post-it notes on the displays or posters. (A variation of this can also be done online using one of the resources already given.)

8.2.2.5   Peer-Assessment Strategies

Peer assessment can be very useful in giving immediate feedback and indicating future directions for learning (Topping, 2009). It is important that pupils are encouraged to participate in peer assessment. Not only do they obtain valuable feedback from their classmates, but it also helps to develop their own ability in interpreting success criteria. Some examples of peer-assessment are included in Table 8.5.

Involving and encouraging your learners to use peer assessment is an excellent way of introducing them to the principles and mechanics of assessment. For each of the peer-assessment strategies above, you could ask your pupils to make a list of features or content they would look for in their partner's work. Through prompts and examples, the pupils should be encouraged to think about how they will rate their partner's work by coming up with short statements that describe performance or desired elements. Through this process, the pupils learn how to co-construct assessment rubrics with you and the formative assessment grows dynamically in an organic way. Taking time to carry out this process with your learners will help to show the value of assessment to your learners, demystifying it and removing the anxiety usually related to assessments and tests.

 TRY THIS OUT

Devise two peer-assessment strategies to add to the list above.

Situate these in a topic area.

List some prompts that you could use with your pupils to help them devise the assessment rubrics for the two strategies.

This section has evaluated the use of summative and formative assessment in the MFL class and provided examples of how to do this.

8.3   Relationship between Assessment *of, for* and *as* Learning in Modern Foreign Languages

Having looked at two of the most widely known forms of assessment – summative assessment and formative assessment – I will try to clarify three terms used in education and explain their role and also how they interrelate. These are assessment *of* learning, assessment *for* learning and assessment *as* learning.

8.3.1   Assessment *of* Learning

Assessment *of* learning is designed to produce evidence of what pupils have learned or achieved and it is used by teachers and national bodies as a measurement of knowledge and skills. This kind of assessment is often summative, but can also be formative. As assessment *of* learning contributes to results that often become public, that is, national examinations, then the assessment instruments have to be constructed in such a way that the results are credible and can stand up to scrutiny. This is because the results obtained in assessment *of* learning will very often contribute to pivotal decisions affecting the future of learners. For classes you teach which may be preparing learners for a national examination, it is important that the pedagogy and assessment that you use align with the curriculum in which these examinations are set. One way of ensuring this is to use the same learning objectives as are used in the curriculum framework in question and in any endorsed textbooks. One example of this is the Cambridge curriculum coherence model (Jackson, 2021).

8.3.2   Assessment *for* Learning

Here the emphasis is on finding out what pupils have learned and where there are still difficulties or gaps in their learning. Using formative assessment strategies (see Section 8.2) during pupil learning and at multiple points within a lesson, a series of lessons, or a unit of work provides teachers with a wide range of information which helps teachers to inform future planning and to decide on the next steps for individual learners, or groups of learners, in terms of selecting or adapting learning and teaching strategies, resources and groupings. It is an interactive process where the teachers use the information gathered and feed this back to their pupils, working together with them on the best way forward to advance their learning. In so doing, teachers motivate their pupils in their learning and create a culture of commitment and success.

8.3.3   Assessment *as* Learning

In assessment *as* learning pupils are learning about themselves and how they learn, which may vary from one learner to another. They develop metacognitive strategies, that is, they become aware of how they learn. In doing so, they reflect regularly on their work, often through self- and peer assessment and with help from their teacher. As they move forward, they gradually take more responsibility for their own learning and review the learning techniques they have been using. This is crucial to learners' development and needs to be supported. Within this process, the learner and the teacher have different roles.

8.4   Developing Metacognitive Strategies in Assessment

Related to assessment *as* learning above, it is very important that pupils learn how to develop metacognitive strategies in assessment to help them identify how they learn best. This section explores the role for both the learner and the teacher in this.

8.4.1   Role of the Learner in Developing Metacognitive Strategies

As a teacher, encourage your pupils to ask themselves the following questions:

- What is the purpose of this particular learning?
- In terms of prior learning, what do I already know about this area of language, concept, etc?
- Do I already have strategies that will help me in this? What are they?
- Do I understand what this topic, concept, language area is all about?
- What success criteria have I set myself for improvement?
- Have I reached my goals and how will I recognise when I have?

8.4.2   Role of the Teacher in Developing Metacognitive Strategies in Learners

There are a number of ways that you can help your language learners develop the necessary metacognitive strategies in assessment, namely:

- Teach and model self-assessment strategies to help learners in self-assessment.
- Help learners to set appropriate goals and monitor their progress towards achieving these.
- Provide learners with examples of good practice and work.
- Help learners to set appropriate success criteria.
- Provide learners with frequent opportunities to practise developing these strategies.
- Encourage learners to take risks in their learning.
- Create an atmosphere where learners feel supported and their achievements valued.

8.5   Providing Learners with Feedback on Their Learning and Recording Their Progress

This section will examine why it is important to provide learners with regular feedback on their learning and how to record their progress.

8.5.1   Giving Feedback on Learning

As stated above, it is important to offer advice and guidance as to what learners need to do to improve. The way in which you provide feedback must always be supportive. Avoid deficit models of focusing on what learners *do not know* and *cannot do* and instead focus on helping them to *improve*. Constructive feedback should mention what learners are doing well, but should also highlight where learners are not doing so well and offer advice on how to improve. Positive comments on work could be along the lines of:

> *I really like how well you have completed this piece of work/can talk about x.*
> *You seem to have difficulty in y or z. Why not try ...?*
> *You should consider doing a or b to get better in this/working with a partner to be able to ...*

Ultimately, you want your learners to review their learning routinely and regulate how they do this. This happens when feedback challenges ideas, introduces new information and creates a culture of self-reflection. It should not merely be focused on how to get the right answer, or the learners will constantly be asking you what you want them to do. Rather, effective feedback should focus learners' attention on the task and help them to adjust their thinking and look at different ways to improve their learning and understanding.

Feedback can be given in a variety of ways and some of these ways have been outlined above, that is, giving comments on individual pieces of work that pupils have handed in, clarifying difficult concepts and suggesting alternative ways of doing things. Sometimes it may be useful to do this with a whole class, where you can outline and give examples of parts of classwork that have been done well, but also indicate what has not been done so well and why this is so. It could be as simple as drawing attention to a misconception or some interlingual interference that learners should watch out for. You should offer strategies and examples of successful learning and talk through the criteria that illustrate these. At other times you will be giving individual feedback. This may be on work you have corrected (in exercise books, on worksheets or on digital files) or work or performance observed in class. As work in schools is often digital or computer-based, pupils may not always be handing in paper versions of work. Often these will be digital text files, images, audio or video. These can present challenges, but also opportunities for the teacher. One challenge for teachers will be to stay abreast of the increasing number of apps and technologies used in education. Another challenge will be to keep a record of the progress of classes and individuals and some thought needs to go into storage and retrieval of work and assessments. An opportunity that presents itself is the ability to use digital tools to put notes and comments on pupils' work, being able to highlight areas to improve and to be able to provide links to advice and exemplars of best practice. A particular advantage of digital tools is being able to send audio feedback to pupils, which can often save teachers time, but allows teachers to personalise feedback and even to use tone of voice and informal language to encourage and motivate learners. (For more advice and examples in using digital tools, please see Chapters 9 and 10.)

The feedback should not be overwhelming, however. Resist the temptation to comment on every single aspect of a piece of work, as a long list of areas to improve will demotivate learners and may even lead learners to drop language learning if they have the opportunity to do so. Instead, you should give encouragement and praise for a few areas and mention an area that individuals should focus on. This approach is often referred to as 'two stars and a wish' and can be very effective.

8.5.2   Record Keeping

In order to ensure that assessment and feedback contribute to effective learning, assessment and feedback should be accessible and transparent, so that pupils and other users (parents and support staff) can routinely review progress and see what next steps may be necessary. It is, therefore, essential that teachers keep comprehensive records of attainment and progress that are informative, relevant and show the development of pupils' learning across the duration of the year or course.

Table 8.6 is an example of a pupil record sheet where performance in formative (and summative) assessments can be recorded showing chronological progress across the duration of a year or course. Qualitative comments can be recorded in the third column with advice on next steps.

Table 8.6 provides a simple way to record pupil progress and can be adapted for different skill areas and to contain different activities. Indeed, the activities used for assessment may not be known in advance, in which case the second column can be

Table 8.6 An example of a Pupil Record Sheet

Pupil Name:			
Skill: Speaking			

Topic	Activity	Comments on performance	Date
Family	Role Play		
School	Report		

Table 8.6 (cont.)			
Topic	Activity	Comments on performance	Date
Hobbies	Prepared talk		
Town and country	Interview		
Pets	Survey		
Holidays	Storytelling		

You can view and download this table at www.cambridge.org/lynch.

left blank and filled in when the assessment has taken place. It is important that each pupil has access to their records and profiles so that they can track their progress and know what it is they need to do to improve and how to go about it. If a paper version is being used, it can be kept in a self-access ring binder in the classroom. Increasingly, pupils and teachers are using digital solutions, where pupil record sheets can be accessed online with the appropriate privacy and access settings enabled.

SUMMARY

In this chapter, we have analysed the relationship between learning and assessment and looked at various approaches to assessment. The features of formative and summative assessment have been evaluated and examples given, as well as the use of self- and peer-assessment. The inter-relationship between assessment *of* learning, assessment *for* learning and assessment *as* learning has been explored and their place in supporting pupil learning, including how to develop the necessary meta-cognitive strategies in assessment. The importance of giving regular feedback to pupils on their learning has also been examined. Many of the techniques and suggestions detailed in this chapter can be adapted for different classes and year groups. The important point is to look at these assessment strategies and determine which is suitable for a particular task and appropriate in terms of age and stage or level of difficulty. I encourage you to use as wide a range of strategies contained in this chapter as possible, experimenting particularly with those with which you are less familiar.

REFLECTIVE QUESTIONS

1. In your experience of teaching languages so far, do you predominantly use summative or formative assessment strategies in class? Does this vary from class to class? If so, why?
2. Consider your repertoire of assessment strategies. Are there any particular assessment strategies outlined in this chapter that you currently do not use and which you would like to incorporate into your language lessons, or learn more about?

FURTHER READING

For more information on formative assessment, please read:

Black, P. & D. Wiliam, 1998. Inside the black box: Raising standards through classroom assessment. *Phi Delta Kappan*, 80(2): 139–48.

Black, Paul, Chris Harrison, Clare Lee, Bethan Marshall & Dylan Wiliam, 2003. *Assessment for Learning: Putting it into practice* Buckingham: Open University Press.

For a comprehensive look at formative assessment, you should consult:

Andrade, H.L. & G.J. Cizek, 2010. *Handbook of Formative Assessment*. New York: Routledge.

For a more critical review of formative assessment, read:

Bennett, R.E., 2011. Formative assessment: A critical review. *Assessment in Education: Principles, Policy & Practice*, 18(1): 5–25. doi: 10.1080/0969594X.2010.513678.

For information on an international project examining formative dynamic assessment and drama-based pedagogies within CLIL, please visit:

Playing Beyond CLIL, no date. eLearning Platform. Online. www.playingbeyondclil.eu

A discussion of the relationship between learning objectives and curriculum frameworks can be found at:

Jackson, F., 2021. Describing coherence of curriculum, pedagogy and assessment. Cambridge University Press and Assessment. International Education Blog. Online. https://bit.ly/3Ch8Oh4

9 Digital Literacy

Introduction

Chapter 8 looked at assessment *of, for* and *as* learning in modern foreign languages. In Chapter 9, we shall be examining issues surrounding digital literacy. The learning objectives for Chapter 9 are, therefore, as follows:

1. Understand the importance of digital literacy to learners and learn about types of digital content.
2. Demonstrate how to keep your learners safe online.
3. Understand what the issues are for teachers of modern languages in terms of digital literacy, including artificial intelligence.
4. Present how to develop knowledge and skills in digital literacy.
5. Determine what is useful and how and when to use it.

Overview

Technology has become part of the personal and social aspects of our lives. In the classroom, digital literacy is the pupils' ability to discern quality sources and evaluate the appropriateness of online content as it relates to the task or activity they are undertaking, as well as respecting the rights of the owner of content. In addition, pupils need to be aware of steps necessary to keep themselves and others safe online as well as how to use social media in a considerate and respectful manner. This chapter examines what these issues mean for the student teacher in a modern foreign language classroom and how the student teacher can best develop their knowledge and skills in this area. In addition, it looks at the benefits of technology in modern foreign language learning and teaching, *what* is useful, *when* to use it and *how* to use it, as well as containing important caveats and highlighting common pitfalls.

9.1 Importance of Digital Literacy

This section will look at the definition of digital literacy and why it is important, and examine issues surrounding the rights of owners of content. It will also consider issues relating to keeping safe online, the use of social media and how to use it in a respectful and considerate manner.

9.1.1   Digital Literacy: A Definition

Digital literacy is the ability to access, manage, understand, integrate, communicate, evaluate and create information safely and appropriately through digital technologies for employment, decent jobs and entrepreneurship. It includes competences that are variously referred to as computer literacy, ICT literacy, information literacy and media literacy. (UNESCO, 2018b: 6)

In terms of the pupils in your class, it is important that you help them to learn how to identify quality sources and how to make an informed judgement as to the appropriateness of any online content that they may access, use or create in the course of their learning. As we will see, there are a variety of types of online sources.

9.1.2   Types of Online Sources

There is an ever-increasing range of online content that learners can access online, and it is not the purpose of this section to examine all of these. However, this section will look at the most commonly available types of digital content frequently used by learners and what purpose(s) they can serve.

Web page

Web pages are the most common form of online content learners will come across. It is not surprising, therefore, that the World Wide Web (WWW) is used as a source of information, text, video and audio content in the modern languages classroom. As well as finding authentic resources in the foreign language to be taught, there are a multitude of websites that host interactive games and activities that can be used in class (see Section 7.2.7).

Blogs

Blogs have been used as a resource for learning in schools, higher education and teacher training. The variety of ways in which blogs can be used is not limited to these purposes; you may have ideas about another use for blogs. Blogs are part of what is known as 'Web 2.0 technologies' (Wankel & Blessinger, 2013), a label given to online platforms where it is possible to respond rather than simply read and take in information. Blogging is a good way of recording reflections on studies. Most computer operating systems and devices offer a range of blogging apps where comments and reflections can be published.

Wikis

A wiki is a website or database developed collaboratively by a community of users, allowing any user to add and edit content, of which Wikipedia (www.wikipedia.org) is the best-known and most commonly used example.

Wikis are very similar to blogs, but have the added collaboration feature, where other users can edit the content. Like blogs, they are easy to set up, are often free to use, and are popular with teachers creating online lessons and courses. You may already be familiar with some other wikis that are interesting to language teachers.

9.1.2.1   Creating Blogs and Wikis

Blogs and wikis are quite common and are used by individuals, organisations and also commercial companies. You may see popular television chefs giving advice on cooking dishes on a blog, or an organisation using a blog to give information on a service. Commercial companies will often use blogs to talk about their products or use wikis as a user-centred forum to discuss issues with, or features of, their products. You will probably have used or seen many of these in your daily life. Learners are, then, very familiar with these tools. Given how useful blogs and wikis are in not only disseminating content, but also in providing a place for interaction, it makes sense to use these in the teaching of modern languages. This could be a way of publishing or discussing ideas or questions you may have related to learning and teaching with other teachers. Or, you may want to use blogs and wikis with the learners in your classes to present information, promote discussion or canvass views from your learners on topics studied in class.

Many people who use blogs have more than one. To create a blog you have to create an account with a company that hosts the page and provides the framework. Many of these are free to set up and use.

 TRY THIS OUT

Task

The instructions here are for creating a WordPress blog; instructions will be very similar for other blog providers.

1. Go to https://wordpress.com
   You will have to give your email address and create a password (and remember it).
2. Follow the instructions to create your blog and guidelines for your first post on it.
3. Make a note of the URL for your blog and save this in a Word document and bookmark it in your web browser.
4. With your new blog, you should now *write your first post*. This could be a short introduction – who you are and why you are writing the blog. The post does not have to be long, but as you write it, consider that others will be reading it, so make it interesting.
5. Send the address to a fellow student teacher or your mentor for feedback.
6. Do a search for blogs on topics that interest you to get an idea of what different blog posts look like. You will find many blogs on language learning and teaching.

9.1.2.2   Evaluating Blogs

Having explored a little what blogs are, the kinds of blog people can write, the sorts of subject that are in posts, what blog creation is like, and so on, the next step is to consider the potential for using blogs in language learning. There are several ways in which you can review your own understanding of issues related to using blogs.

FOOD FOR THOUGHT

Consider the following in relation to using a blog for language learning and teaching:

- One of the most common paradigms is the 'language as skills': in what ways could blogs contribute to the development of the skills (reading, writing, speaking, listening)?
- Review common teaching methodologies: what would blogs offer for communicative language teaching?
- Consider features you know from second language acquisition (SLA) theories: how would blogs help learners develop communication strategies?
- Would blogs offer potential for learner differences: what kinds of motivation could blogs stimulate?

You may find this website useful in listing a number of blogs that are used for language learning:
https://blog.feedspot.com/language_learning_blogs

This section has looked at the importance of digital literacy and introduced the most common forms of online content that pupils and teachers are likely to come across. Section 9.2 examines the issues of choosing appropriate content online, safety and respect.

9.2   Safety Online

It is important to make sure that the school in which you are teaching has measures in place to protect users online, both pupils and staff. This may include requirements such as firewalls, antivirus software, content filters and encrypted, password-protected networks. It is crucial that you have regular, open conversations with your learners about the benefits, but also the dangers of the internet. Do not rely on this being the job of someone else in your school or institution, as it is the responsibility of all educators to keep learners safe. Typical areas to cover in your discussions with learners should include:

- identifying whether a website or online resource is genuine or fake;
- what cookies do and what information they may be collecting;
- whether a person or organisation is actually genuine;

- why a person might want to see, send or believe something;
- why a person may want their personal information;
- the reason why something has been posted online (e.g., has something been designed to influence you in a particular way?);
- whether something they see online is fact or opinion.

9.2.1   Use of Social Media

Social media has become ever more prevalent in society and it is no different for young people. The availability of smartphones means that children and young people have the potential to access and use social media from anywhere and at any time of the day. Although social media provides opportunities for children and young people to explore the world and to communicate with others, this can come with risks. As a teacher, it is important that you have regular conversations with your pupils on the use of the internet. In particular, you should discuss the effects and risks that may come with use of social media, including cyberbullying, online grooming, and emotional and online abuse.

If your school uses social media to enhance its relationship with its learners and the community, care should be taken to protect children and young people. This includes obtaining appropriate consent before posting any identifiable information or images of learners and only using authorised social media accounts with effective privacy and security controls.

As a member of staff, you should follow your institution's social media policy for staff. The UK National Society for the Prevention of Cruelty to Children (NSPCC) offers clear advice in this area. The NSPCC state that staff should:

- not engage or communicate with children or children's families via personal or non-school-authorised accounts;
- be aware of their digital footprint – the information about a person that exists on the internet as a result of their online activity;
- only use authorised school accounts to send school communications;
- use staff accounts for professional purposes only, including email, website and social media accounts;
- take steps to avoid being found by children on social media, by selecting strict privacy settings, using a different display name and choosing an appropriate display picture;
- not use social media in a way that would breach other school policies.

(NSPCC Learning, 2024)

9.3   Digital Literacy Issues for Modern Foreign Languages Teachers

This section will consider issues for modern foreign languages teachers in terms of digital literacy and offer advice.

Teachers have a responsibility for pupil safety online and they play a role in helping pupils develop a considerate and respectful approach in their use of social media. Another important aspect is respecting the rights of the owner of content. Not only is this an issue for the teacher, but pupils must also be made aware of what they can find and use online without violating the rights of the owner of the content.

9.3.1 Respecting Owners' Rights

As there are so many resources online, it can seem like a treasure trove of ready-made materials that a teacher can use in class. Many resources can be easily copied or downloaded and integrated with lessons, either in their original form or amended to suit the level or needs of a particular class. However, before you use any resources that you find online, you should make sure that you respect the rights of the owner of this resource. If the owner has not given permission for use of their resource, you may be infringing copyright (ISTE, 2016), which is not something that may be ignored. The owner or creator of the resource will have put a lot of creative effort into producing their resource. Using it without permission can lead to loss of revenue and recognition for the owner of the resource, which may make it difficult to earn a living from their work. This may also discourage them from producing resources in the future, thereby stifling creativity and leading to an impoverished pool of resources. There is also the potential danger that the copyright holder may take legal action and sue you for unauthorised use of their material, resulting in financial penalties for you and your institution, or even criminal charges. These are important factors not only for you as a teacher to consider as you search for suitable content for your lessons, but also for learners whom you may task in a lesson to produce information or resources as part of an educational project or research. You should therefore ensure that your learners are fully aware of these issues (see ISTE, 2016). If in doubt, contact the owner of the materials or check statements they may have provided regarding the use of their material.

9.3.2 Appropriateness of Content

An important skill for teachers to develop is not only being able to find online content for the language area or topic to be taught, but also to be able to evaluate the appropriateness of the online content as it relates to the task or activity they are undertaking. While there are a lot of free and commercial resources available to download online, as a teacher you need to check if what you find is suitable for your learners. A prime concern will be to consider whether the resource relates to the learning task or activity you are planning. Web resources can often seem attractive, but it is important that the resource is in line with effective modern foreign languages pedagogy (see Chapter 2).

Pedagogy

Is the proposed resource in line with effective communicative approaches to L2 learning and teaching? There is a risk of choosing something that looks attractive, that you think your learners will like, but which does not help them learn anything new or develop their communication skills. Vocabulary or grammar resources found online can seem helpful, but it depends on how they will be used. It is important that their use does not become simply Grammar–Translation.

Age

Is the content age-appropriate? Does it relate to the interests and terms of reference of the target age group? What is suitable for younger learners will not appeal to older learners. The content must be relatable to the learners in terms of interest, but also in terms of their cognitive ability.

Level of language

Is the L2 used at the level of the target group of learners? It is sometimes easy to find an online resource in the foreign language for the topic that is being taught, but it is vital to check that the language presented in the resource corresponds to your curriculum or course, that is, that the language satisfies the language areas, grammar and lexicon as specified in the unit of work (see Chapter 5). If the language is too simple, then learners may get bored. If the language is too difficult, then it will impede comprehension and progress. Often you will find a resource that will work well for your learners with some additional help, such as providing learners with a glossary of unusual or unfamiliar language.

Accessibility

It is important that any websites, tools or technologies that you choose or create are designed so that any of your learners who have disabilities can use and interact with them. This means paying attention to issues such as the 'alt text' image alternatives (see Chapter 7), headings, contrast, options for resizing text, keyboard access and visual focus, moving, flashing and blinking content, and multimedia alternatives.

Inclusiveness

Inclusivity is often discussed alongside accessibility. What is important is to make sure that learners are not excluded due to technical constraints, language and geographic barriers, demographic, race, religion, gender, sexuality or socioeconomic differences.

Universal Design for Learning (UDL)

Accessibility and inclusivity can be promoted if one respects the principles of UDL:

> Universal Design means the design of products, environments, programmes and services to be usable by all people, to the greatest extent possible, without the need for adaptation or specialized design. Universal Design for Learning (UDL) is a process in which curricula (goals, methods, materials and assessments) are intentionally designed to offer flexible and inclusive approaches that can be customized and adjusted for individual needs. UDL offers a framework for guiding educational practice that aims to achieve flexibility and

accessibility in the ways information is presented, the ways students respond or demonstrate knowledge and skills, and the ways they are engaged in the learning process (e.g. with the course content, and interactions with peers and instructors), while reducing barriers in instruction. (UNESCO, 2018a: 16)

Artificial Intelligence (AI)

Perhaps the most exciting and also the most discussed development in the digital world is artificial intelligence. Artificial intelligence (AI) is a field of technology where computers perform advanced functions normally produced by humans. The attraction of AI for teachers is strong, as it can potentially free up time for teachers to spend more time supporting learners by carrying out routine, bureaucratic or time-consuming tasks. This can range from creating materials and lesson plans suitable for different stages of learning to providing tailored feedback to learners. Large Language Models (LLM), such as ChatGPT, have drawn a lot of attention for their ability to answer questions, create text, and seemingly interact with learners. Popular AI applications used in modern language teaching include:

LingoTeach, which creates texts and exercises;
Magic Padlet, which is used to generate classroom resources at different levels;
Turboscribe, which converts audio and video to text;
Tts.mp3.com, which converts text to speech in a variety of languages that can then be downloaded as a sound file.
Image Accessibility Creator, which generates alt text from images;
I can't draw, which adds AI-generated art to padlets;
Mizou, which provides feedback on pupil work.

These applications and others, which sometimes offer free versions, can be easily found by a quick internet search. More applications are being regularly added online to the already vast range currently available and it is a teacher's job to keep abreast of what is on offer.

One can see that such applications can provide teachers with a wide array of useful tools which can be used to aid learning, teaching and assessment. Through experience of using these, teachers will be able to select applications and tools suited to the needs of their learners. Teachers must also, however, as with selecting any content or tools, maintain a critical and analytical stance and assure themselves of the suitability and accuracy of content and exercises created by AI applications. ChatGPT, for example, has been known to produce convincing texts, but they may not always be accurate. The classroom teacher is ultimately responsible for the selection and creation of appropriate materials, tasks and activities to enhance pupil learning.

Artificial intelligence, big data and social networks are areas that need careful consideration. These areas have often been shown to replicate racial, gender, cultural and other biases that lead to unconscious discrimination, usually through bias embedded in the data or the algorithm, or both. While I would not discourage the use of AI, it is the duty of teachers to be aware of the dangers and not just the benefits of AI-assisted learning. Teachers must make sure that their learners are equipped with the appropriate knowledge and skills to make informed and relevant use of artificial intelligence tools (Krumsvik, 2023). Advances in artificial intelligence are happening at an exponential rate and it is fair to assume that it will become an inevitable aspect of our lives, including its use in education. As such, teachers should ensure that they remain aware of new developments and use these appropriately in their teaching.

Section 9.3 has examined digital literacy issues for modern foreign languages teachers and offered guidance on specific areas.

9.4　Developing Knowledge and Skills in Digital Literacy

This section will present ways in which modern foreign languages teachers can develop their knowledge and skills in digital literacy further. This is intended as initial guidance in digital literacy and teachers should look for opportunities on a regular basis to maintain and improve their knowledge and skills in this area.

We live in a world where online and digital technologies abound. In almost every aspect of our lives, we interact with digital technologies, very often completing many of our daily tasks online. This can range from checking our diaries, looking up public transport timetables, ordering shopping and take-away meals to banking, filling in forms for local services to keeping in touch with friends and family and streaming music, television and films. It is daunting to consider such a list and imagine being expert in using all the digital tools involved. Thankfully, most tools that we use every day have similar interfaces and we are generally the end-user, often carrying out transactional processes. In education, however, we often expect a bit more from our learners. This can involve asking learners to research topics, to evaluate sources and to create content. As already indicated, it is important to be discerning in terms of pedagogy, age-appropriateness, level of language, accessibility and inclusiveness, among other aspects. This development of knowledge and skills can be done in a number of ways, for example by taking online courses and webinars to learn or enhance your digital skills, by experimenting with new digital tools and platforms, or by peer learning from colleagues and friends. No single person will have a monopoly of all knowledge and skills and, in return for helping a colleague or friend to learn new skills or knowledge, they may be able to help you with an area which is new or difficult for you. It is a question of embracing technology and digital literacy and making it work for us where it best suits our needs as language teachers. As a teacher you are not only responsible for developing your own skills and knowledge in digital literacy, but you are also responsible for supporting your learners to do this as well.

There are numerous ways in which you can help your learners develop their knowledge and skills in digital literacy. As part of learning about new topics, or learning about the culture or geography of countries where the L2 is spoken, you could encourage your learners to write blogs and wikis, perhaps as part of project work or research. Learners could record videos and upload them to the web or send them to partner classes in an exchange school. This exposure to digital resources and being able to read and write across a wide variety of media formats is a way for learners to demonstrate how **transliterate** they are. Of course, in most classes it will be rare to use only digital resources and in most classrooms what is to be seen is **layered literacy**, where print and digital resources overlap.

9.5 What Is Useful and How and When to Use It

As with any learning and teaching opportunity, technology and digital tools and platforms should have a purpose or function. As has been stated above, although technology is a major part of pupils' lives, you should not be using it just for the sake of it. If it does not enhance learning, then another learning and teaching approach may be more appropriate. There is often an assumption that the mere presence of technology is enough to motivate pupils and to hold their attention. As it is now already a large part of learners' everyday lives, however, it seems less likely that this assumption would automatically follow. Teachers have often cited their use of presentation applications, such as PowerPoint, as constituting digital literacy, but in many classrooms the overuse of such apps has made them another version of 'chalk and talk', only this time via the computer, in an example of a very teacher-centred Direct Teaching approach.

Digital tools and platforms should only be used in language classes if they bring tangible benefits to the learning and teaching of modern languages. Teachers should ask themselves a number of questions before deciding on their use, namely:

- Do the technologies, digital tools or platforms help render the language content communicative?
- Do they develop language skills?
- Do they help revise or recycle previously learned language?
- Do they contribute to formative assessment?
- Is their use compatible with learning for sustainability (i.e., helping learners to build a socially just, sustainable and equitable society)? (see UNESCO, 2024)

Asking oneself these questions will help to ensure that you primarily use technology, digital tools and platforms to motivate your learners and help them make progress in their foreign language learning. This learning may well focus on language development (structures, vocabulary), but technology can also open windows to learn about and appreciate the culture of the countries in which the L2 is spoken. This may often be through accessing the websites of the national television stations or newspapers of those countries, or listening to their music, podcasts and webcasts. Similarly, digital technology may allow learners to access literature and entertainment in L2. There are many ways in which digital technology can enhance the learning and teaching of modern languages – you just need to give free rein to your imagination and be creative.

....

SUMMARY

This chapter has considered the importance of digital literacy to learners and explored types of digital content. It has looked at ways to keep your learners safe online, as well as issues of relevance for modern foreign languages teachers. The next chapter will look at remote learning, teaching and assessment, including looking at the benefits and drawbacks of remote and hybrid learning.

REFLECTIVE QUESTIONS

1. Consider your normal use of technology, digital tools and platforms in your classes. Does their use enhance pupil learning and progress in L2? If so, how do you know? If not, what changes are necessary?
2. When choosing content for your classes, what guides your choice of content and activities?

KEY TERMS

layered literacy The ability to understand a cross-section of overlapping print and digital resources.
transliteracy The ability to read and write across a wide variety of media formats.

FURTHER READING

If you would like to know more about internet accessibility, refer to the following online resources.

World Wide Web Consortium, 2025. Web Accessibility Initiative (WAI). Online. www.w3.org/WAI

Global Initiative for Inclusive ICTs (G3ict), 2022. Global Report on Assistive Technology (GReAT). Online. https://bit.ly/4g7Sg9j

For information about online safety:

Department for Education, 2023. Teaching online safety in schools. Online. https://bit.ly/3E1DnId

An interesting look at the use of artificial intelligence in schools can be found at:

Krumsvik, R.J., 2023. Adaptive learning tools and artificial intelligence in schools – some trends. *Nordic Journal of Digital Literacy*. 18(1): 4–7.

Remote Learning, Teaching and Assessment

Introduction

Chapter 9 examined the importance of digital literacy and considered the issues for modern foreign languages teachers and their pupils. Chapter 10 will examine issues surrounding remote learning, teaching and assessment and offer advice on appropriate methods. This chapter, thus, sets out to consider remote learning, teaching and assessment and the practical implications of these approaches as they relate to modern language learning and teaching.

The learning objectives for this chapter are as follows:

1. Examine different models of remote delivery – synchronous, asynchronous or hybrid – in terms of pedagogical principles, including the benefits and drawbacks of each approach in the learning, teaching and assessment of modern languages.
2. Consider practical steps and advice on how to prepare for remote learning, teaching and assessment, including how to make the most of the digital tools and platforms currently available to teachers and learners.
3. Determine when and where it is appropriate to use a live synchronous approach and where an asynchronous approach is better.
4. Examine hybrid approaches, where a mixture of in-school teaching takes place, but also incorporating the remote approach.
5. Support teachers with practical advice for planning and preparing learning, and the use and deployment of equipment and resources for remote and hybrid learning and teaching.

Overview

This chapter should be read in conjunction with Chapter 9 on digital literacy in terms of being able to access, manage, understand, integrate, communicate, evaluate and create information safely and appropriately.

In recent years remote and hybrid approaches to learning, teaching and assessment have risen in prominence. The reason for this dramatic rise can be easily traced to the Covid-19 pandemic when countries implemented strict lockdown measures to try to restrict the spread of the virus. As public buildings and workplaces closed, schools, colleges and universities looked for alternative ways to provide learning, teaching and assessment. The result was an exponential expansion of online teaching. Online learning, teaching and assessment is not new. It has been used as a way of educating learners in many countries over many years. However, the major difference is that these existing online courses were previously a niche area designed to accommodate work and lifestyles. An online course, for example, would offer learning opportunities for learners who could not travel to educational institutions due to excessive travel distances and times, or to help those already in work to access learning at a time when they were free and which did not clash with work or caring commitments in the way normally scheduled day-time classes and courses would (Globokar, 2010). As such, the pedagogical approach was usually customised to suit the needs of the user. This chapter looks at how and when teachers can incorporate remote learning, teaching and assessment approaches in a modern languages class and the practical implications related to doing so.

10.1   Models of Remote Delivery

We will look at three different models of delivering learning and teaching remotely – synchronous, asynchronous and hybrid. The features of each model will be explored along with the benefits and any drawbacks.

10.1.1   Synchronous Learning and Teaching

Teaching in synchronous mode means that your pupils will access your live class in real time, using a computer, laptop or other device to join the class (Ng, 2020). Teachers may use a proprietary platform such as Microsoft 365 or Google Workspace for Education, which are two of the most popular online productivity suites available. Schools, colleges and universities may also use Zoom to deliver classes synchronously, although Zoom is more an online collaboration tool than an online productivity suite.

In a live online class you can chat 'face to face' using webcam and microphone. If you wish to display materials, for example a PowerPoint presentation, a whiteboard, an image or a video, you can use the share screen feature on these platforms to do so, which essentially allows Direct Teaching. You can use the break-out rooms features in Zoom or Microsoft Teams or in Google Workspace to allow group work. A useful feature on all of these platforms is the ability to record the teaching session. This is useful for pupils who may be absent, or to allow participants to look back at what they have learned and revise, or simply to have a second look at difficult content.

The advantage of this form of delivery is that learners can join from anywhere with internet access and it may save them time and money travelling to the place of learning. It does depend, however, on having a strong and stable internet connection with enough bandwidth and enough data on the user's internet plan. Problems that can affect synchronous teaching are slow or weak internet connections, which can cause audio and video to be choppy, lag or drop completely. Access to a computer or device can also be problematic if many users in a household need to connect remotely for education or work purposes simultaneously, or if the household does not possess enough devices. This was often a problem during the Covid-19 pandemic lockdowns and was felt particularly acutely in poorer households. Limited data plans can also be an issue, as live online teaching requires a lot of data.

10.1.2   Asynchronous Learning and Teaching

Part of your teaching will no doubt involve preparing work for your classes which they can do at their own pace to a specified deadline. This type of approach is referred to as asynchronous (Kumar & Eisenberg, 2023). This will require careful thought as to what you prepare, how skills are practised, how work is submitted and how you give feedback. For example, how do I give listening and speaking practice, and how do I monitor work and progress? Advice is provided in Section 10.2.

In asynchronous teaching, you will essentially be creating virtual classrooms and the main tools that you will be likely to use are Google Classroom, Microsoft Teams with OneNote Class Notebook, or Zoom.

Each of these companies provides guides or tutorials to show you how to use their products. For OneNote, go to the Microsoft website and search for the page 'Getting Started with the OneNote Class Notebook: A Walkthrough for Educators'.

A useful feature of OneNote is the Class Notebook, which allows you to create an online space for your classes. Using this with Teams is a useful way of working with a remote class. For full details, search for 'Use OneNote Class Notebook in Teams' on the Microsoft website.

Google Classroom is a comprehensive and user-friendly alternative used by a number of schools providing similar functionality to Microsoft OneNote and Teams. For full details, look for 'Getting started with Google Classroom' on Google's website.

10.1.3   Hybrid Learning and Teaching

Hybrid learning is an approach which offers a range of benefits to both the learners and the teacher. It offers the choice of learning in class with the teacher or through online access to lessons, or if the learner wants, a bit of both. The benefit to the learner is having the flexibility to access learning when it suits their individual timetable. It also helps to reduce costs, if getting to the learning institution is expensive. Hybrid learning is often confused with blended learning, which is different (Dziuban et al., 2018). Blended learning is, as the term indicates, a blend of both traditional teaching, where the learner is sometimes in the classroom with the teacher, and online learning, where parts of the class are delivered online. This allows learners to learn at their own pace, as well as giving them the flexibility to suit work or lifestyle needs, although it still requires some attendance at in-person classes.

10.1.4   Virtual Learning Environments (VLEs)

The solutions offered above in terms of providing online delivery possibilities for learning and teaching via online productivity suites such as Microsoft 365 and Google Classroom are often termed Virtual Learning Environments (VLEs). In education, virtual learning environments tend to be thought of, however, as primarily web-based solutions, rather than as productivity suites with online tools. They are usually used as a supplement, or a support, for largely traditional in-class teaching and are predominantly used in higher education, such as in colleges and universities. There are several common VLEs used in many countries, the two most widely used being Blackboard's VLE 'Learn' and the open source platform 'Moodle' (https://moodle.org). A relatively new VLE or LMS (Learning Management system) which is becoming increasingly popular is Cloud School (www.cloudschool.org) from the not-for-profit charitable organisation of the same name, whose vision is to support disadvantaged young people through online educational programmes. Like many companies which offer hosting, Cloud School offers templates that can be used to create web pages.

Figure 10.1 is a screenshot of a course skeleton created with Cloud School. It shows the tools that you can add to your pages.

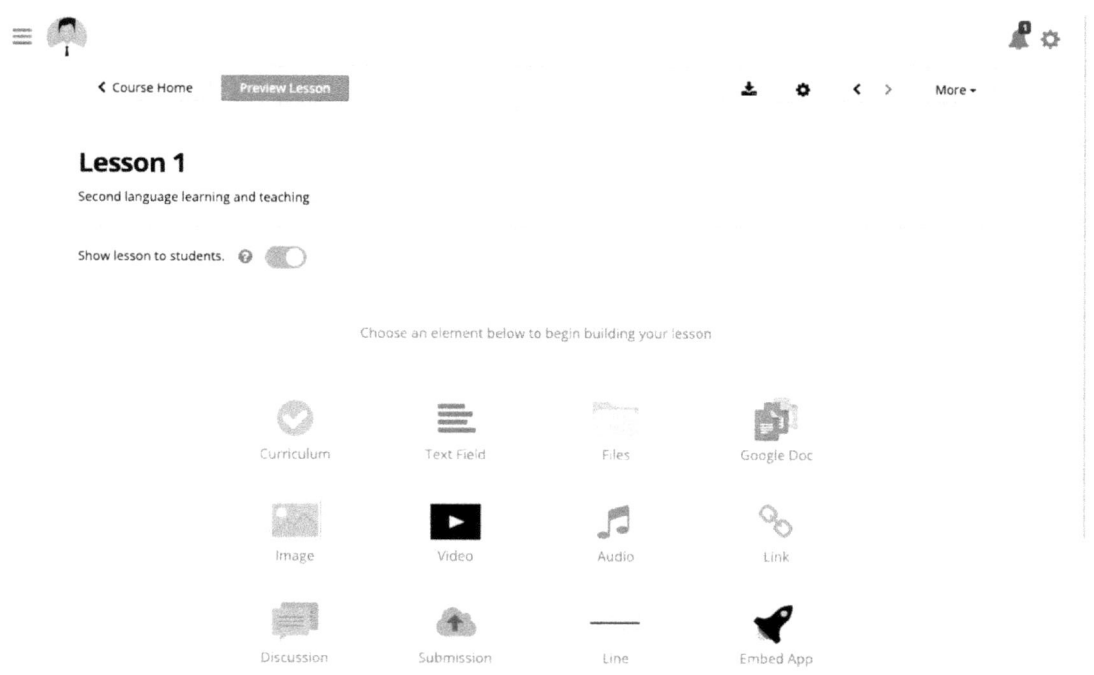

Figure 10.1 An example of a launch page for an online language learning course

If your school does not have access to any of the VLEs mentioned, you can make your own online classroom with Google Sites. For advice on how to do this, search for 'How to use Google Sites' on Google's website.

Like Cloud School, Google Sites allows teachers to create a website very quickly and to add a variety of learning and communication tools. Cloud School and Google Sites are viable alternatives for schools and communities suffering financial hardship that cannot afford to purchase commercial productivity suites.

 TRY THIS OUT

Create a free Google or Cloud School account for yourself.

Follow the guidance on the site to create a web page.

Add some tools (e.g., communication, whiteboard, folders).

Send the URL for your web page to another student teacher or your mentor for feedback.

10.2 Advice for Remote Learning, Teaching and Assessment

As this book is principally concerned with teacher education in mainstream settings, the advice that follows in this section is framed within the parameters of how remote learning, teaching and assessment practices can complement normal classroom teaching and its more widespread use in the event of school closures and is based on experience of responding to the needs of pandemic-induced lockdowns. This advice is not intended as a guide to writing bespoke online courses, which would require more guidance than can be offered in this chapter (see Further Reading).

10.2.1 Advice for Synchronous Teaching

When planning a lesson which will be delivered live and accessed by learners on their computers and devices, there are a number of considerations for effective learning, teaching and assessment.

Pedagogy

It is important that your lesson does not compromise on sound pedagogical principles and practices for language learning and teaching. There is a danger that lessons may become viewing-only with the teacher presenting for the majority of the lesson and learners becoming passive viewers. In a real live classroom, this would not be the case, so you need to decide how much Direct Teaching is necessary and what its purpose is. As introduced in Chapter 6, having decided what you want to teach, it is important to decide how you are going to do it. You should try to recreate the real communicative classroom as far as possible. This may mean, among other things:

- teaching in groups;
- use of pair work;
- individual learning;
- whole-class teaching;
- skills practice;
- multi-skill activities;
- multi-task activities.

A typical lesson, then, may involve you in presenting activities or new language structures to the class and then setting tasks that involve pupils working individually. As pupils work on tasks, they can ask the teacher for help by use of the hands-up function on their online platform. If pupils wish others not to be part of this, they can use the 'message individual' option. Where teachers wish pupils to work in pairs and groups, they can set up break-out rooms. The teacher can still be messaged by pupils who require help and the teacher can join the different break-out rooms as required, or simply drop in to break-out rooms to monitor pupil progress.

Flipped learning

The concept of flipped learning (Kavanagh et al., 2017) has been around for a number of years and is very useful in online learning. In a flipped learning environment, pupils can be set readings, research or tasks to complete before the scheduled class and use the time in class for discussion and group work. For any work being completed in advance of the class, instructions should be clear and unambiguous. Resources should be easy to access and suited to the age and stage of the learners. When learners are participating in the online class, instructions should be clear and resources easy to find. Most of the popular online activity suites have folders where learners can view or download resources.

Skills practice

As you would in a normal face-to-face classroom, there should be opportunities for skills practice. This is most effective when set up to take place in break-out rooms, where pupils may be working in groups, perhaps on role-play scenarios, in discussion groups or giving prepared talks or presentations. A useful tool that learners (and the teacher) can use in discussions is the virtual whiteboard, on which ideas and plans can be shared.

Assistive technology

Of vital importance to many learners when working online is the ability to take advantage of accessibility features and assistive technology. As mentioned in Chapter 7, pupils with visual or hearing impairment should be made aware of the tools available in operating systems and platforms, such as filters enhancing text display, screen readers, subtitles or closed captioning. A number of operating systems, platforms and software have automatic closed captioning built in, which appears in real time and is fairly accurate. If you are preparing work for your pupils, you can generate subtitles in advance and correct any mistakes that software programmes may generate. If you use YouTube, it too has automatic closed captioning. You may decide to use some websites or resources where there is no automatic closed captioning. For those sites, you may consider installing one of the many browser extensions that exist, since they are capable of automatically generating closed captions for web pages.

Differentiation

Just as you would do in normal classroom settings, you should ensure that you cater for learners' needs in your online lessons too. This can be done by providing a variety of resources differentiated by task, text and outcome and making learners aware of this. Sometimes you may decide to direct certain pupils to certain tasks and materials, at other times you may decide to offer them a choice of tasks and materials that vary according to complexity or difficulty of text or task. It is important that you let learners know how and where to access these resources and that they are labelled or have a description that details level of difficulty and any other useful information, especially if work is self-access.

Assessment

Whether you have been able to teach synchronously or asynchronously, your pupils will complete work for you and will require feedback on it. Depending on the school you are in and the applications, tools, platforms and devices available in school, you may be sent work by pupils in various forms. If this is sent as a Microsoft Word document or similar, it is quite easy to correct work, write feedback on it and return it to them. Another option is to provide access to answer keys to allow for self-assessment. It is less easy to give pupils feedback when the work you are sent is in PDF format or an image file, perhaps taken on a smartphone, but there are nonetheless ways to do this, as illustrated in Table 10.1.

If you wish to give oral feedback on pupil work, there are a number of possibilities, as indicated in Table 10.2.

10.2.2   Advice for Asynchronous Teaching

This type of approach may be the preferred mode of online teaching in your school in the event of a closure such as the Covid-19 pandemic lockdowns that began in 2020. Or, it may be an approach used regularly as an alternative or supplement to in-class teaching. This may be a way of offering flexibility for study arrangements, or during exam leave for senior pupils, or a way of providing teaching during short-term illness of individual pupils. As this approach requires learners to work on their own in advance of lessons, careful thought must be given as to what you prepare, how skills are to be practised, how work is submitted and how you give feedback. For example, how do pupils send you examples of speaking work or assessments they have carried out?

Table 10.1 Giving feedback on image files or PDFs

Editing PDFs	
Microsoft Windows	Adobe Reader has basic annotation tools built in: https://get.adobe.com/uk/reader
	Alternatively, PDFelement is free software from Wondershare, which gives you lots of possibilities: https://pdf.wondershare.net. This also works on Macs.
Apple Macs	Adobe Reader has basic annotation tools built in: https://get.adobe.com/uk/reader (also works on iPhones)
	Alternatively, there is GraphicConverter, a graphics application by Lemke software, which is very powerful and edits not only image files, but also PDFs: www.lemkesoft.de/en/products/graphicconverter
Android tablets and phones	Xodo is a PDF reader with lots of annotation tools that are easy to use: www.xodo.com. It also has a version for Windows phones and tablets and iPhones and iPads.
Editing image files	
Microsoft Windows	Windows still provides Microsoft Paint, which is very easy to use to edit or annotate image files and is available from the Microsoft Store.
Apple Mac	GraphicConverter, a graphics/image programme by Lemke software, is very powerful. It is very easy to use to edit/annotate image files. You can find it at: www.lemkesoft.de/en/products/graphicconverter/
Android tablets and phones	A free and easy to use programme from the Play Store is iMarkup, which allows you to use and edit or annotate image files.

Note: On tablets (all platforms), Word's Ink function allows you to write freehand on documents using your finger or stylus.

Table 10.2 Giving oral feedback to pupils

Type of OS used	Commonly used app
Giving oral feedback on Windows computers	Use the Voice Recorder app. Search the Microsoft website for 'How to use Voice Recorder'.
Giving oral feedback on Mac computers	Use Quicktime Player. Search the Apple website for 'Record audio in QuickTime Player on Mac'.
Giving oral feedback on Android tablets and phones	On most tablets and smartphones (all platforms), there is a voice recorder either built in or available to download from the appropriate app store.

Approaches to asynchronous learning and teaching

Many of the points considered above in terms of synchronous learning and teaching apply to asynchronous learning and teaching. In asynchronous teaching, flipped learning is often the preferred approach and the same rigour as detailed above for synchronous teaching is necessary. Due attention must be paid to using the most effective and communicative pedagogy and encouraging different modes of learning and teaching. Resources should be easy to access, at the ability levels of the learners, and allow for the development of all skill areas. Pupils should be made aware of assistive technology that can help them in their learning. Where there is the need for pupils to demonstrate oral proficiency or to provide evidence of work they have done, you should ensure they know how to submit this, whether this is uploading audio recordings through a command on the VLE or platform being used, or by emailing an audio or video file to you.

10.3 Choosing between Synchronous and Asynchronous Modes of Learning and Teaching

Section 10.3 will present some views on the roles of the teacher and the learner. This may help you to determine when and where it is appropriate to use a live synchronous approach and when an asynchronous approach with your classes may be more appropriate.

Faced with different approaches, the teacher must decide which option is the most appropriate for their classes. The choice a teacher makes will often be determined by how they see the role of the teacher and the learner. As a teacher, it may be useful to ask yourself what you see as your role as the teacher in the classroom. Do you see yourself as the person who controls what is happening and is responsible for ensuring learning takes place? Some possible views on the role of the teacher, though not mutually exclusive, are:

- The teacher is central to the learning.
- The teacher should provide models for the learners.
- The teacher should direct activities.
- The teacher is a facilitator.
- The teacher is a participant in the learning process.
- The teacher is a guide for activities.
- The teacher is also a learner (and researcher).
- The teacher is an adviser.
- The teacher decides what to teach.
- The teacher is responsible for creating an environment that encourages risk-taking.

Some possible views of the role of the learner, again not necessarily mutually exclusive, are:

- The learner is responsible for their learning.
- Learners should interact and learn from each other.
- Learning is personal growth.
- The learner should become more and more aware of the learning process.
- The learner brings preconceptions and previous knowledge to the classroom, and needs to learn how to accommodate these and work with these (as well as being aware of them).
- Learners can be directed by skilled teachers.
- If a learner does not understand fully this is not necessarily a drawback – by continuing to trust the teacher they will be able to perform the appropriate tasks.

FOOD FOR THOUGHT

Consider the views on the role of the teacher above. Where do you stand in terms of each of these statements?

What do you think of the roles of the learner presented above?

Are there any other roles for the teacher or for the learner that you would like to add to either of the lists above?

Do these lists help in determining whether to use a synchronous or asynchronous approach in terms of remote learning, teaching and assessment?

10.4   Practical Considerations for Schools on Remote Learning, Teaching and Assessment

Section 10.4 considers practical consideration to help teachers to decide which model of remote learning, teaching and assessment to use.

Schools wishing to bring in an element of remote learning, teaching and assessment may often do so to suit local needs or because of potential pedagogical benefits. Table 10.3 lays out reasons why schools may opt for a synchronous, asynchronous or hybrid approach.

Sometimes the choice of what form of remote learning, teaching and assessment schools use is determined by practical considerations and external factors and not by what is considered to be the most effective pedagogy by teachers. This was the case during the worldwide pandemic between 2020 and 2023 when schools, colleges and universities were forced to close for extended periods of time and pupils had no option but to learn from home.

As Table 10.4 shows, there are a number of factors that can influence a school's choice of remote learning, teaching and assessment. It is also clear that these factors may overlap and that schools may go back and forth between synchronous, asynchronous and hybrid models of remote delivery of lessons, depending on changing circumstances. The information presented in Tables 10.3 and 10.4 may help schools and teachers to reflect on the provision they would prefer to adopt. It must be recognised, however, that financial and physical resource factors and public health policies may play a large part in determining what schools actually undertake.

10.5   Points to Note in Planning Lessons Involving Remote Learning, Teaching and Assessment

The steps you undertake to use remote learning, teaching and assessment with your learners will ultimately depend on the purpose. If the reason for its inclusion is

Table 10.3 Potential benefits of different models of remote learning, teaching and assessment (LTA)

Remote model of LTA	Potential benefit of approach
Synchronous	• Teacher can teach directly. • Teacher can give explanations. • Teacher can answer questions. • Teacher can help pupils who have difficulty. • Teacher can facilitate discussions. • Teacher can participate in discussions (whole class and groups). • Teacher can decide what is taught. • Teacher can motivate and encourage pupils.
Asynchronous	• Learner is responsible for their learning. • Learner can decide what to learn and what to leave out. • Learner becomes more aware how they learn. • Learner develops more autonomy. • Learner develops enquiry and research skills. • Learner brings questions, ideas, reflections to the next class. • Reduces travel costs to school.
Hybrid	• Learner has all the benefits of synchronous approach. • Learner has the flexibility of attending classes in person or accessing the classes broadcast online. • If the teacher decides to use an asynchronous approach to the online lessons, the learner has the additional benefit of flipped learning and all other benefits of an asynchronous approach.

Table 10.4 Factors influencing choice of different models of remote learning, teaching and assessment (LTA)

Remote model of LTA	Factors influencing choice of approach
Synchronous	• Teachers want to deliver lessons as close to class conditions as possible. • School wants to keep to timetabled hours of provision. • No time to adapt resources and make them asynchronous. • No VLE/LMS to host resources and architecture of courses. • Not confident that pupils will access resources and work on their own. • Parental pressure to deliver lessons by webcam. • Public transport or travel and socialising in general may be restricted.
Asynchronous	• Pedagogical decision not to film class teaching. • Flipped learning model preferred. • Recognition that pupils may not be able to get online at scheduled class times. • Not enough bandwidth or poor internet connectivity in school or at home.

Table 10.4 (cont.)

Remote model of LTA	Factors influencing choice of approach
Hybrid	• No access or restricted access to internet at home. • Not enough laptops or devices at home for all who need it. • Laptops or devices lack the software, processing power or memory to run the applications needed for live sessions. • Public transport or travel and socialising in general may be restricted. • Caring responsibilities restrict attendance at school or for 'live' lessons. • Need to keep school open and provide classes for children of key workers. • Need to provide free school meals to families on low incomes. • Intermittent access to laptops and internet at home due to sharing amongst family members. • Desire for variety in approach. • Reduces travel costs to school. • Public transport or travel and socialising in general may be restricted. • Caring responsibilities restrict attendance at school.

pedagogical and has not been forced on schools by external factors, then you need to be confident that you can justify the reasons for this remote delivery, even if it is only partial inclusion of a remote element. If remote learning has been forced on schools due to external factors, such as a pandemic-induced lockdown, then you have to make sure that you respond as best you can, albeit in difficult circumstances, to the needs of your learners. Advice for both scenarios is given in the following subsections.

10.5.1   Inclusion of Remote Learning, Teaching and Assessment for Pedagogical Reasons

You need to be sure that this remote or online element will enhance pupils' progress and is not simply technology for technology's sake. In addition, you must convince colleagues, pupils and parents. A possible way to approach this is as follows:

• Examine your scheme of work or syllabus for the academic year for the class in question.
• Identify any parts of the course where remote or online delivery may be beneficial. This may be because the work involves lots of individual effort or research, which can be completed just as effectively on one's own as working individually in the classroom.
• Decide whether the remote element is to be of a synchronous, asynchronous, or hybrid nature.
• Once you have decided the nature of the element, you need to adapt the task so that learners know what to do. A task you want pupils to complete on their own, for example, must contain clear instructions, details of where to access resources and advice on where and how to submit work.

- For live teaching and general teleconferencing, invest in a good-quality directional microphone. Wireless microphones with headsets allow more versatility.
- If you are teaching a synchronous lesson (or recording a lesson to be viewed later), invest in an auto-tracking camera, so that you can move around the class(room) and do not have to stay at the front of the class all the time.
- Set up a system for monitoring engagement of learners in class, for example when and for how long they access resources, how long to they spend on different parts of learning.
- Design a system of support for learners when working on their own.

10.5.2 Inclusion of Remote Learning, Teaching and Assessment Due to External Factors

When the Covid-19 pandemic occurred in early 2020 and schools were forced to shut down overnight, teachers and pupils had to come to terms with new ways of working very quickly. There were a number of immediate problems:

1. Poor interconnectivity in many schools.
2. A lack of suitable software and hardware in schools to deliver remote lessons.
3. Many teachers had very little experience of using online productivity suites and platforms. Some teachers had never used Microsoft Teams, OneNote, Google Classroom or Zoom before.
4. There were problems of access at home. Some homes had only one computer for the whole family, yet the parents needed it to work remotely, all children in the family needed a computer to access lessons, so access was difficult and sometimes impossible.
5. Many homes had poor internet connectivity, or had limited data, which remote working consumed very quickly.
6. Looking at screens for too long was not good for pupils' eyes. Some pupils with disabilities found watching or using a screen all the time (or at all) detrimental to their health.

Although schools, teachers and pupils experienced a steep learning curve, experience gained during the Covid-19 pandemic has now better equipped them in terms of skills, resources and ways of working for any future lockdowns or closures. However, regardless of the useful experience acquired from previous lockdowns, a number of the problems would still remain, notably points 4–6 above.

So, what could teachers do? Well, this would largely depend upon local situations, as well as individual factors, but planning and preparing for such events is strongly recommended. To build up the competence and confidence in remote learning and teaching for both pupils and staff, teachers should regularly incorporate elements of remote delivery into their classes. This could be, for example:

- Posting some work (or homework) from time to time online on the school's VLE or LMS, which pupils have to complete by a given date, upload to a folder, or email to the teacher. This should not be restricted to reading and writing, but include practice of all skill areas (although not all work need focus on all skills).

- Recording small segments of teaching, particularly when introducing new language structures, which pupils can quickly replay and practise.
- Lobby your school management or school board to buy laptops or tablets for use in school. This has happened in many schools since the pandemic.
- To mitigate the effects of restricted access to laptops, devices or the internet, ensure that as much of the work posted as possible is asynchronous, so that learners can complete it when they do have access to everything they need.
- To prevent eye strain and other ailments caused by excessive use of computers, include tasks where pupils are not required to work on devices, using textbooks, instruments or portfolios instead.
- For live teaching and general teleconferencing, see advice in Section 10.5.1.
- If you are teaching a synchronous lesson (or recording a lesson to be viewed later), see advice in Section 10.5.1.
- Set up a system for monitoring engagement of learners in class, as per advice in Section 10.5.1.
- Design a system of support for learners when working on their own.

SUMMARY

This chapter has sought to examine different models of remote learning, teaching and assessment, looking at benefits and drawbacks, to help teachers make an informed decision of what to use, how to use it and when to use it. Chapter 11 will look at the use of drama, music and games in modern languages teaching and how skills and competences necessary for successful language learning can be developed in the language classroom through the use of drama, music and games.

REFLECTIVE QUESTIONS

1. How do you rate your skill level in managing remote learning, teaching and assessment?
2. If you were to audit your skills in this area, where would you need professional development?

FURTHER READING

For advice on writing online courses on language learning, see:
Son, J.-B. (2018) *Teacher Development in Technology-Enhanced Language Teaching.* Cham: Springer International Publishing.

11 Drama, Music and Games

Introduction

Chapter 10 examined different models of remote learning, teaching and assessment, looking at benefits and drawbacks, to help teachers make an informed decision of what to use, how to use it and when to use it. Chapter 11 will discuss how to include drama, music and games in L2 classrooms and how to use these to enhance student learning. This will start with a look at why drama, music and games are useful in class, followed by an examination of ways in which to do this.

The learning objectives for this chapter are, therefore, as follows:

1. Analyse why drama is such a useful tool in the learning and teaching of L2.
2. Explore ways in which drama can contribute to language learning.
3. Examine why integrating music and song with L2 learning and teaching is so important.
4. Explore the ways in which music and song can contribute to L2 learning and what aspects of language learning they aid.
5. Examine why using games in L2 learning is useful.
6. Explore different types of games and activities and points to be aware of when using games.

Overview

The importance of drama in language teaching cannot be underestimated, whether this is simple role-play or more complex drama techniques. Drama has the potential to encourage adaptability in learners, their fluency, and their level of communicative competence in an immersive way. It puts language into context and gives learners experience of success in real-life situations in a safe environment, as well as giving them confidence to deal with those situations in the real world (Hulse & Owens, 2019; Maley & Duff, 2005). This chapter looks at how skills and competences necessary for successful language learning can be developed in the language classroom through the use of drama, music and games. Developing an understanding of the culture and literature of countries where the foreign language is spoken and what is appropriate at different ages and stages of learning is also examined in this chapter. The use of music and rhyme helps to embed the foreign language in learners' minds, which promotes pedagogical diversity and consolidates learning, particularly with regards to pronunciation, fluency, listening comprehension, memorisation of vocabulary and grammatical structures, and cultural awareness (Degrave, 2019). Games can motivate learners and create a relaxed atmosphere where language skills can develop, thus promoting learner interaction, improving skills and consolidating knowledge.

11.1   Drama as a Tool in L2 Learning and Teaching

Drama in modern languages learning and teaching is not a new thing; it has been used by teachers for years in a variety of ways. Often this may be a role-play or improvisation or perhaps in a scripted way. There are many ways in which drama can enhance the learning and teaching of modern languages, but often the use of drama is neglected due to perceived pressures of getting pupils ready for exams. This often leads to a focus on practising set language phrases deemed as useful to pass tests. Another concern that teachers often have is that the pupils do not have enough knowledge of the foreign language (vocabulary, structures) to use the language meaningfully in drama activities, so these activities are often avoided. This is unfortunate, as drama can be beneficial in L2 learning and often sophisticated thought processes can be achieved with quite a basic range of vocabulary and language structures.

11.1.1   Why Drama Is Useful in L2 Learning

The old adage of 'Tell me and I forget, teach me and I remember, involve me and I learn' could have been written with drama in mind. Often explanations given by teachers are forgotten by pupils as there is no hook or involvement that makes the learning particularly memorable. However, when we connect this learning to something that seems real, even though this may be 'pretend' or acting, the learning tends to stay. As social creatures we interact with others, we communicate and interact with our body and our senses. Dramatic play often involves movement and the use of multiple senses (hearing, seeing, feeling) which can set off other thoughts and learning episodes. These can help to embed learning in pupils, sometimes through sensory experiences evoked by these drama techniques and sometimes due to emotional reactions to the situated learning.

Through the use of drama techniques, we encourage adaptability in learners and an ability to see or imagine other perspectives, creating more empathetic learners. In the safe and familiar environment of the classroom, we offer pupils the opportunity to evoke their imagination and experience real-life situations, preparing them for future occasions when they might experience similar situations (Hulse & Owen, 2019). We train them to be adaptable in a contextualised scenario, again another life skill, yet within the safe confines of the classroom working with fellow pupils and their teacher.

11.1.2   Drama Techniques for the L2 Classroom

There are a multitude of drama techniques that teachers can use in teaching and it would be impossible to examine them all in this chapter; however, we shall look at a number of those that are often found in L2 classrooms.

11.1.2.1   Role-Play

Perhaps the most common drama techniques found in L2 classrooms is the use of **role-play**. Role-play typically involves learners in a dialogue where they and their fellow pupils have to imagine themselves in a situation where they have to play a specific part. This is often part of a topic to allow learners to practise new vocabulary and language structures. This allows the learners to develop fluency in the L2, most often giving skills practice in listening and speaking. developing their communicative competence in an authentic situation. This may take the form, for example, of asking pupils to assume the parts of young people meeting for the first time and getting to know the other person. A more complex role-play may be where the learners are playing the roles of employees in leisure facilities responding to questions about opening times and availability of facilities.

11.1.2.2   Simulation

A more structured form of role play, simulations are scenarios which are more complex and more akin to real-life situations. When using simulations, pupils might assume other characters' identities, or simply play themselves in a given situation. There may be set rules to follow and decisions left for them to make.

11.1.2.3   Mime

By using mime, characters, modes, ideas and actions can be portrayed using this non-verbal technique. This technique is very popular with teachers as it can be used to present or practise new vocabulary and structures, to convey ideas and moods, and allows pupils to interpret and practise their L2 in a relaxed and often fun way.

11.1.2.4   Improvisation

A more spontaneous drama technique is improvisation where pupils adopt roles and are thrown into situations where they must produce speech for that context in a realistic way. Here they must think on their feet and produce language, as well as react to the language of others in a real-life scenario. The learners are taking risks with the language and produce authentic language. much in the same way as they would in their L1.

11.1.2.5   Scripted Plays

Scripted plays are a very good way to help learners experiment with the foreign language they are learning. They can vary the pitch and tone of their voice and have fun taking on another persona. This all helps lower the affective filter, i.e., reduces anxiety and the fear of making mistakes, builds confidence and gives learners the opportunity to acquire and practise language in a comfortable and creative environment (Dolean, 2016).

11.1.2.6   Process Drama

Process drama is a way of learning through drama. Mainly used in educational contexts, it is a coming together of the learners and the teacher to create drama and to experience situations through acting them out in the here and now, rather than rehearsing a script to perform later. This allows learners to be spontaneous and creative within meaningful contexts. The motivation and desire to participate in a free and often fun way can remove the fear factor associated with using the L2 in public and lead learners, even with a very limited language resource, to try out their language.

11.1.2.7   Process Drama and CLIL

A good example of how process drama can contribute to effective L2 learning and teaching can be found in the ERASMUS+ multinational project Playing Beyond CLIL, which is available to view on the European Union's ERASMUS+ website (the EU programme that funds and supports education, training, youth and sport in Europe). The Playing Beyond CLIL (PbC) project provides a locus for integrating drama techniques with subject disciplines through a process drama approach. As opposed to one-off learning episodes, PbC offers a way to develop an entire learning cycle, using drama techniques as a pedagogical strategy to develop learners' literacy skills across subject disciplines and languages. This is achieved by basing the learning around learning events that replicate interactive formats found on popular media, such as panel shows, documentaries or film trailers. The learning takes place over a number of lessons where the learners work towards production of one of the chosen formats, which are termed 'Show What You Know' (SWYK) learning events. This process involves learners in planning, designing and enacting the learning event and reflecting upon how it went. One of the products of the project was an eLearning Platform, available at the Playing Beyond CLIL website (no date), which provides teachers with a toolkit that includes assessment rubrics connecting the SWYK learning events to pedagogical principles and learning cycles, and helpful tools to implement PbC in the classroom. The PbC platform also provides planning templates, examples via videos, recorded webinars and a network where teachers can exchange and discuss ideas and materials.

TRY THIS OUT

Choose one of the drama techniques above in Sections 11.1.2.1–11.1.2.6.

Plan a short activity for an L2 class using this technique in a topic of your choice.

Show your plan to your mentor or a peer.

Amend your plan in the light of the feedback you receive from your mentor or peer.

11.2   Music and Song in L2 Learning and Teaching

As with learning any subject, anything that can make the task of learning seem easier or more accessible is a positive aid for the classroom teacher. This section will examine ways in which music and song can be integrated with L2 learning and teaching and why this is an effective strategy.

11.2.1   Ways in Which Music and Song Can Aid L2 Learning

Music and songs have been used for many years in modern language teaching and their benefits are widely recognised. Often the use of music and song in class can reduce anxiety by lowering the affective filter and pupils feel less inhibited about using the foreign language. This is particularly noticeable when pupils join in singing with the rest of the class or group where they do not feel that all eyes are on them. Pupils often do not regard music and songs in the L2 classroom as work, tending to regard it as a fun, recreational activity and, therefore, happily join in without realising that they are learning at the same time (Salcedo, 2010). The use of music and songs plays to the strengths of pupils who may have well-developed musical intelligence and is thus catering for one of the many different learning styles that may exist in your classroom. Using music and songs in class can increase learner attentiveness and motivation, as learners become interested in what the song is about. Using original songs from countries in which the L2 is spoken can also be a good vehicle to present and discuss cultural aspects of the L2 countries.

11.2.2   Contribution of Music and Song to Aspects of L2 Learning

Music and song are powerful tools at a L2 teacher's disposal. As a teacher, you may not be particularly musical yourself. You may not play an instrument or have a good singing voice. You may just not feel comfortable singing or playing an instrument in front of a class of pupils. However, these things should not deter you from using music and song in class. It is perfectly acceptable to stream audio or video files to present and practise music and there is an abundance of these that you can buy or download from the internet, many of them copyright-free (though you should always ensure you comply with copyright laws when streaming or playing audiovisual files in class).

So, what can music and song do in terms of helping your learners with L2? Here are a number of benefits that music and song can bring to the L2 classroom.

11.2.2.1   Pronunciation

When pupils sing in L2, they very often mimic the pronunciation of the person singing the song without realising it. This helps them acquire the natural flow and rhythm of the language, which may be quite different from their mother tongue. Italian, for instance, is a melodic language with rises and falls in the sentence, whereas English and French are less so. Through repeatedly listening to a song and frequent practice in singing it, learners' pronunciation and accent in the L2 can improve noticeably.

11.2.2.2   Fluency

As an alternative to frequent practice and repetition of phrases in class, singing along to music in the L2 naturally helps learners' fluency as they match their words to the notes. Often this happens without conscious effort from the learners, who are caught up in the atmosphere or mood of the song.

11.2.2.3   Listening Skills

As pupils listen attentively to try to make out the words of a song, sometimes trying to decipher where one word stops and another begins, they are fine-tuning their ear and developing their listening skills further.

11.2.2.4   Memory of Vocabulary and Language Structures

Music and rhyme are just as effective in helping learners learn and remember words in L2 as they are in L1. Our brains latch onto the rhythm of a song and this helps learners retain what they hear. People often talk about not being able to get a song or a tune out of their head and we can use this 'ear worm' technique to help our learners remember new words and phrases in L2.

11.2.2.5   Cultural Awareness

In listening to and analysing the texts of songs in L2, we often get an insight into the culture of the country or countries where the L2 is spoken. These aspects of culture may be quite different from our own and it offers the L2 teacher a way into presenting and discussing the culture and sometimes the history of the foreign countries. This may be linked to a variety of topics, for instance food, clothes, dance, music or their attitude to the environment, amongst other things.

Above all, music and song can make languages fun and add an element of relaxation and enjoyment to the L2 learning. With a little thought and preparation in advance, you can use music and song to reinforce vocabulary and grammar, as well as hone listening and speaking skills.

⇨ TRY THIS OUT

Think of a song or a piece of music that you consider will help your pupils in their L2 learning.

Explain why you think this music or song is suitable.

Devise a lesson, or part of a lesson, where you incorporate this song or music.

11.3   Place of Games in L2 Learning and Teaching

This section will examine the use of games in L2 learning and teaching and why it is useful. I will explore different types of games and how to use them and highlight points to be aware of when using them in class. In my many years of teaching languages, I have always found games to be an invaluable part of my language toolbox. You only need to see the multitude of games on our television channels, or observe how many people commuting to school and work are playing games on their devices, to appreciate what a large part games play in our lives.

11.3.1   Why Games Are Useful in L2 Learning

The reasons why using games in class is so effective are very simple. First and foremost, games provide a way to learn the L2 in a fun and enjoyable context. This in itself lowers the affective filter and motivates pupils to use the language they have been learning, especially if there is an element of competition. Second, games promote interaction and collaboration between pupils in the classroom, as well as encouraging pupils to complete tasks. Third, games help pupils to develop self-confidence and take ownership of their learning. Fourth, games can generate a lot of enthusiasm and energy, be this physical, mental or emotional energy, contributing to motivation. Lastly, games help to build emotional maturity and the skills to deal with success or failure in a safe space.

11.3.2   Games and Activities for the L2 Classroom

It is not my intention to provide a long list of different games in this chapter. Indeed, the chapter would need to be a lot longer to do this. Instead, I would like to present the features of a few different types of games and look at how and with whom they might be used. I will provide some examples of this and point you to sources where you can find games that you can use straight away or adapt for your classes.

11.3.2.1   Games for Vocabulary Building

These games focus on vocabulary building and quite often are introduced by the teacher to recycle or practise new vocabulary that has recently been presented. These games can be quite simple or more elaborate, requiring more resources. A typically simple game, requiring no resources, would be the Guessing Game. In this game, one pupil mimes or thinks of an activity, or an object, and the other pupils must work out what it is. This is also good practice of asking questions as the person miming and thinking can only respond with 'yes' or 'no'. A game requiring a bit more preparation would be the Corners Game. For this game, each corner or area of the room is labelled (e.g., colours, places in town, animals) and pupils must choose where to go when the music stops. The teacher chooses from a pile of cards the card which eliminates all pupils who went to that corner or area. Those left are brought into the centre of the room and given a forfeit, for example some aerobic actions or singing a song. Be aware of issues of mobility and inclusion.

11.3.2.2   Games to Build Memory

Games which can help build memory are useful in class, especially if you are not certain whether your pupils have the time or opportunity to revise at home. One such game is Matching Pairs. In this game, pupils flip over cards to find matching pairs. If they find a matching pair, they keep it. The winner is the pupil with the most matching pairs at the end of the game. Variations of this game include matching a picture to a word or phrase and matching the L1 to the L2. It can be played by pairs of pupils or by splitting the class into two teams. There are also online tools that can be used to create matching games, such as Kahoot and Quizlet. The matching game can be adapted to whichever topic or language item or structure is being taught. This is another game which requires few resources, yet is very effective, and can be used with beginners and lower intermediate learners.

11.3.2.3   Games to Develop Skills

There are lots of games which can be used to develop or practise the different L2 skill areas. Some of these games may focus on one skill, while other games may involve two or more skills. A simple game, which also allows pupils to move about the classroom, is called the Circle Game. For this game, pupils are seated on the floor and 'labelled' according to five colours, five days of the week or whatever language is being practised. When the item is called, all those pupils with that 'label' must stand up and run round the outside of the circle. The winner is the one who gets back to their original place first. This game needs no resources and is a good game to use with beginners. As with the Corners Game, be aware of issues of mobility and inclusion.

If you are looking for a game to practise writing skills, then Consequences is a good game which does not need any more resources than a sheet of paper. In Consequences the pupils work in groups of eight. Certain categories are chosen, for example: name of first person, name of second person, where they meet, at what time, what the weather is like, what each says, and what the result is. Each pupil in the group has a sheet of paper. After writing down an item corresponding to the category, they fold it over and pass it on to the next person, at the same time receiving a piece of folded over paper from someone else. The pupil receiving the paper last reads it out and illustrates the story with cartoon captions. Another version of this is to draw a body with the teacher reading out the instructions as the drawing gets done, for example, big green eyes, a little nose. It can even be drawn in two halves. The person at the end must describe the person that they have received.

11.3.2.4   Games to Practise Question Forms

Pupils are frequently asked questions in class, but we must not forget to provide opportunities for them to ask questions as well. A game which promotes active use of questioning by the pupils is Alibi. In Alibi, one pupil must leave the room and the others decide who the culprit in a recently committed misdemeanour is. The returning pupil must ask questions – physical description, what the person was wearing, interests, and so on – to find out who the person is. A certain amount of time is allocated for guessing the culprit. A variation of this game is where two pupils are sent out of the room as 'suspects' in a crime. They have a few minutes outside the room to get their stories straight (their alibi) before returning to the room, where the other pupils question each of the suspects as 'detectives' to try to find out who the culprit is. This is a fun activity which can allow pupils to use a variety of tenses in their questions. As such, this game is suited to pupils at intermediate or more advanced levels.

11.3.3   Issues to Consider When Using Games in Class

When using games in your L2 class, there are a number of issues that you must consider in order for these to go well in class – purpose, preparation and appropriacy. Like all of your lessons, those involving games need to be carefully thought through to get the maximum value out of them for your learners.

11.3.3.1   Purpose

Sometimes you may use games as a reward, or even a time filler, where the class may have finished everything you had prepared for them quicker than you had anticipated and you have five or ten minutes left before the end of the lesson. If this happens, you should make sure that your game practises the language of the lesson. It is far more effective, however, if you have planned to use a game in class and are using it for a reason. It is important to decide on the purpose of the game. Is it to build and retain vocabulary? Is it to practise a particular skill or skills? Is it related to a certain new language structure or point of grammar? As your time is often limited with your class each week, it is imperative that what you do has a purpose and is not playing games purely for the sake of playing games.

11.3.3.2   Preparation and Planning

To make sure that your game works well, it is essential that you plan in advance. Chapter 6 looks at lesson planning in great detail, but a few issues need particular consideration when using games in your lesson. If you are using specific materials and equipment, you must ensure that you have obtained or prepared these in advance. The layout of the classroom may not be suitable for the game you have chosen, especially if the game requires pupils to move around. This means that you may need access to the room in advance to set it up. Another alternative would be to have the pupils set the classroom up, giving you an opportunity to use more target language input while instructing pupils how to do it.

11.3.3.3   Appropriacy

In terms of appropriacy, there are a number of points to consider. Have you considered the level of maturity of the learners and whether the game may seem too childish to them. This may be the case when using the same game you have used with younger learners with older pupils or adult learners. That said, I have often found that even adults sometimes like childish games and can be quite willing to participate in seemingly silly games.

It is important also to consider fairness. Does the game give some learners a particular advantage? If so, your pupils will certainly spot this and air their grievances. Have you considered whether certain pupils will be disadvantaged, perhaps because of a disability, for example hearing impairment, visual impairment or mobility issues. If your game requires pupils to run around, then this will almost certainly create problems for pupils with mobility issues or visual impairment.

A game where pupils move about the class can present other issues. The most important of these is safety. You must ensure that you take every precaution to prevent any of your pupils from accidentally hurting themselves or others. If the game requires pupils to lie on the floor, then is the floor clean enough? Could the lying down part of the game be done just as well standing up? If the game involves touching other people, are you sure that all your pupils are okay with this? Some pupils, for example pupils who have autism, may not be comfortable with this. Other pupils may also find it unacceptable due to religious or cultural beliefs.

However, if you have considered these points and you are sure they are not an issue, and you have thought about the purpose of the game and planned your game well, then I would advise you to incorporate games as often as you can into your classroom teaching. If you do so, I am sure you will reap the rewards of successful learning for your pupils and a happy class.

 TRY THIS OUT

Consider the types of games outlined in Sections 11.3.2.1–11.3.2.4 above.

Choose one of these types of game and devise a lesson, or part of a lesson, where you use this game in class.

Explain the purpose of the game, the planning implications and for whom the game would be appropriate.

Show your plan and rationale to your mentor or a peer and ask for feedback.

SUMMARY

This chapter has explored the value of drama, music and games in the L2 classroom. Each section has considered the rationale for their use in a structured approach. Section 11.1 examined the role of drama in L2 classrooms and how this can be used before providing guidance on a number of popular drama techniques and how they can be used in class, including a discussion of process drama and CLIL. In Section 11.2 the focus was on the role of music and song, exploring their use in the L2 classroom and how they contribute to different features of L2 learning. Section 11.3 explained why it is important to incorporate games into L2 learning and teaching and looked at the benefits of different types of games and what parts of language learning they can support. Examples were provided and guidance given on the stage of class(es) at which these games could be used. Finally, issues to consider when using games in class were considered and advice given.

It is important to emphasise that this chapter has only explored some of the considerations of using drama, music and games in class, although hopefully this has given you some guidance and confidence to use these in your own teaching. More detailed guidance and sources are given in the Further Reading section below.

REFLECTIVE QUESTIONS

1. Do you have any concerns about using drama, music or games in class? If so, what are these and why do you think you have these concerns?
2. How might you go about addressing these concerns? Think about how and where you may find guidance and support.

KEY TERMS

process drama Unscripted drama where participants are assigned roles and are asked to improvise scenarios.

role-play Imitating the character, traits or behaviour of someone else.

FURTHER READING

If you are interested in finding out more about using process drama in modern languages, read Hulse and Owen's article:

Hulse, B. & A. Owens, 2019. Process drama as a tool for teaching modern languages: Supporting the development of creativity and innovation in early professional practice. *Innovation in Language Learning and Teaching*, 13(1): 17–30.

A very useful resource book for drama techniques and activities is:

Maley, A. & A. Duff, (2005. *Drama Techniques: A resource book of communication activities for language teachers.* Third edition. Cambridge: Cambridge University Press.

For detailed advice and guidance on integrating process drama and formative dynamic assessment with CLIL, visit the Playing Beyond CLIL ERASMUS+ website, to which I was a contributor, at:

Erasmus+, 2021. EU programme for education, training, youth and sport. Playing beyond CLIL. Online. https://bit.ly/42LS58n

See also the following article by some of the Playing Beyond CLIL participants:

Arnaiz Castro, P. et al., 2022. Deeper learning and assessment in drama-based CLIL learning spaces. *Language Education and Multilingualism – The Langscape Journal.* doi:10.18452/ 25444

A very useful and practical resource looking at drama and games with CLIL is the eBook *playingCLIL*:

Playing CLIL, 2015. Playing CLIL ebook. Content and Language Integrated Learning inspired by drama pedagogy. Online. www.playingclil.eu/this-is-the-playingclil-ebook

The following article examines the use of music in the L2 classroom:

Degrave, P., 2019. Music in the foreign language classroom: How and why? *Journal of Language Teaching and Research*, 10(3): 412–20.

A comprehensive examination of digital games in second and foreign language teaching and learning is provided by:

Reinhardt, J., 2019. *Gameful Second and Foreign Language Teaching and Learning: Theory, research, and practice*. Cham: Springer International Publishing.

Organisation and Management

Introduction

Chapter 11 looked at how the skills and competences necessary for successful language learning can be developed in the language classroom through the use of drama, music and games.

Chapter 12 will examine the importance of organisation and management to successful learning and how to achieve this in the L2 classroom. It will also consider the benefits of working collaboratively with other education professionals. Potential causes of disruption to classes will be examined and strategies proposed to prevent it occurring as well as what to do if it does happen. This chapter will also look at ways in which to create and maintain a restorative approach to behaviour management.

The learning objectives for this chapter are, therefore, as follows:

1. Examine the importance of effective organisation and management and how to achieve a productive, interactive and positive learning atmosphere in class.
2. Explore the benefits of carousel group work.
3. Explore how to work collaboratively with colleagues.
4. Examine behaviour management, including causes of disruption and how to prevent them.
5. Consider how to create and maintain a restorative approach to behaviour management.

Overview

In order to deliver effective lessons, teachers must choose appropriate resources, materials and equipment to suit the pedagogical aims of each lesson. This chapter looks at the importance of organisation and management and how to achieve a productive interactive and positive learning atmosphere in class. I make the distinction between classroom management and behaviour management. Classroom management for me encompasses how teachers organise their physical classroom, the materials and equipment they use in a lesson and how they manage the transitions between activities. Behaviour management is how teachers try to prevent disruption to lessons and how they deal with it when it occurs. The chapter will discuss planning ahead and walking through your lesson in advance, and why teachers ignore these at their peril. Resources can also be human resources, such as other colleagues, or specialists in additional support needs. This chapter looks at how to involve colleagues in planning and the benefits of collaborative working with colleagues.

This chapter also examines behaviour management and how to maintain a safe and orderly environment in the modern foreign languages class that is conducive to successful learning. Potential causes of disruption and strategies to prevent them are examined, as well as what to do when, in spite of all the efforts of the teacher, disruption still occurs. There are many reasons why disruption may occur and this chapter considers a wide range of potential causes and specific strategies to minimise them in the modern foreign languages classroom. The chapter also considers how to create and maintain a restorative approach to behaviour management in the classroom, as well as how to promote successful teacher–student relationships and foster academic engagement.

12.1   Effective Classroom Organisation and Management

This section will examine how effective classroom organisation and management strategies can produce a productive, interactive and positive learning atmosphere in class.

12.1.1   Creating Effective Learning Opportunities

For lessons to run smoothly a number of factors need to be considered. To optimise effective learning opportunities in class requires good organisational skills and forward planning. This means deciding a number of key things in advance: the class layout, the materials to be used, the equipment that will be needed, and the management of activities (Kelly, 2018). Let's consider these one at a time.

12.1.1.1   The Class Layout

The physical layout of the classroom is important for a number of reasons. The aims of the lesson and the activities you have chosen may require a specific layout of desks and chairs. If you require the pupils mainly to work individually, then an arrangement of the desks and chairs in rows may be suitable. However, if you want your pupils to interact, either in pairs or in groups, then sitting in rows may not be conducive to the task(s). You may decide that arranging the desks and chairs into groups may be more suitable. If you have not been allocated a room solely reserved for the teaching of your classes (and the likelihood is that you will be using classrooms used by many different teachers), then you need to give thought in advance as to how you will manage the layout of the class. It may be that the classroom is free before your class, though that is not always the case. This may mean that you need to go to the classroom(s) before school begins to adjust the layout of the room, or during an interval or lunchbreak. You may have some non-contact time before the lesson in which to arrange the room, but there may be someone teaching in that classroom when you are free. If you cannot gain access to the classroom before your lesson, do not despair: at the beginning of the lesson, you can instruct your pupils to rearrange the desks and chairs how you want them. This also provides a good opportunity to give input in the target language as you give instructions in the TL to the class. Most of your instructions will be in the command form and already familiar to your pupils. You are not wasting time rearranging the classroom with the pupils, rather you are providing regular and valuable TL input which is easily acquired by the pupils. This set-up time should be built into the timings on your lesson plan. Do not forget to rearrange the classroom at the end of the lesson, which provides yet another opportunity to give your pupils valuable TL input.

12.1.1.2 The Materials

When preparing your lesson, you will decide on materials that are suitable for the various tasks and activities in the lesson. Are these materials attractive? Are they well laid out? Are they suitable in terms of the known ability levels of the class and their terms of reference? If materials are difficult to read or the work is pitched at the wrong level, then this may affect the smooth running of your lesson; for example, some pupils may need more or less time than you thought to complete a task, which may have a knock-on effect on the pace of the lesson or the transition between activities. For more advice on responding to the needs of your pupils, review Chapter 7 on differentiation.

12.1.1.3 The Equipment

Depending on the activities that you have planned for your pupils, you and the pupils may be using different types of equipment. These may be computers, laptops, tablets, screens, interactive whiteboards (IWBs), audio equipment, televisions or specialist equipment for pupils with additional support needs. If you are not familiar with any of the equipment that you plan to use in your lesson, it is very important that you find an opportunity to try these out in advance. Often a more experienced colleague will be happy to show you how to use equipment. Even if you are familiar with the equipment you will be using, it is a good idea to check it in advance to ensure it is not defective in any way and working as you expect. IWBs can be useful in class, but remember these are made by different manufacturers, so your previous experience of using them may have been with a different make and model. Does the IWB need to be calibrated? Do you know how to do that for this particular make and model? Will you be using the internet? Do you have a back-up plan if the internet goes down? For peace of mind, but more importantly to ensure your pupils receive quality lessons, check any equipment in advance. If you find any faults, then you will still have time to come up with an alternative solution.

It must be recognised, however, that the availability of equipment will vary greatly between and within countries, or even between schools within the same local authority. Often financial restraints mean that schools may have very little, or no, technology or resources at their disposal. As with any teaching scenario, teachers need to be aware of the equipment and resources available and adapt advice to their situation. The most important resource is the teacher, who is also the crucial factor in determining whether effective learning takes place or not.

12.1.1.4   The Management of Activities

In terms of classroom organisation and management, there are a number of factors to be aware of to ensure the smooth running of the class and transition between activities, namely:

a.   Pupils should be familiar with working in pairs, in groups or individually.
b.   Learner autonomy should be encouraged, especially if pupils have been set tasks to work on.
c.   Instructions to pupils on tasks and activities should be clear and unambiguous (these could be displayed on the board or screen, on worksheets or on instruction cards at group desks).
d.   Teachers should share the lesson objectives with pupils so that they know what to do and when.
e.   Help sheets, dictionaries and answer cards should be readily available to allow pupils to access help and correct their own work, if required.
f.   Extra work for each group or level should be made available for those who finish early (this is particularly important if groups are rotating around 'bases').
g.   Pupils should be encouraged to use technology appropriately, e.g., internet and applications, but it should also be made clear when smartphone usage is inappropriate or prohibited.
h.   Pupils should be proficient in the use of equipment (laptops, tablets, any specialist equipment).
i.   Functional posters relating to the topic being studied as well as useful vocabulary, structures and grammar should be displayed on the walls of classrooms as reminders and prompts for pupils.
j.   All members of staff participating in the lesson should have a copy of the lesson plan.

 TRY THIS OUT

Review a lesson you have taught recently.

Examine your lesson plan and compare it with the list of features a.–j. in Section 12.1.1.4.

Make notes on your lesson plan of anything you feel that it lacked and anything you would add to the lesson if you were to teach it again.

12.2   Benefits of Carousel GroupWork

This section will explore the benefits of using carousel group work in class and techniques and strategies to support it. Carousel arrangements are an excellent way of achieving a number of different goals. They can be theme-based or focus on a specific skill or skills, and can be used to differentiate learning or facilitate assessment (Buck & Wightwick, 2013).

There are many types of group work, but the two most common forms are:

- *Collaborative learning*, in which members of the group work together to collectively solve a problem.
- *Cooperative learning*, where members of the group divide tasks between them to achieve a common goal.

Both of these types of group work can be integrated into a carousel arrangement.

The form of group work you choose will depend on the aims of your lesson(s), but whichever one you choose there are benefits in adopting a group work approach since it facilitates a number of things, namely:

1. skills practice
2. differentiation
3. the teaching of grammar
4. assessment
5. classroom management
6. behaviour management

Let's now look at each of these in turn.

12.2.1   Skills Practice

As opposed to a Direct Teaching approach, group work allows learners to focus on skill areas in a concentrated way. This could be by working in groups organised by skill area, for example a speaking group, a listening group, a reading group and a writing group. These groups may also involve learners in multi-skill activities. Rotating to the next group after a given period of time in a carousel-like way, learners may experience concentrated time in three or more skill areas within a single lesson.

12.2.2   Differentiation

In different ability groups, learners may work on tasks at their ability levels according to their needs. If the teacher sets work for three of the groups to allow them to work autonomously and works intensively with a fourth group, the teacher can tailor any input, tasks or explanations to the ability level of the group with which they are working. When the groups rotate, the teacher can adjust the level of difficulty or complexity to the needs of the next group. This is an obvious advantage over giving input or explanations in a whole-class setting where the teacher needs to choose the level at which to pitch everything they want to say. This is a good way of differentiating the input for different sections of the class, rather than providing homogenous core input to the whole class, then setting tasks at different levels. It is advisable to create a bank of suitable and varied materials at different levels for the learning and teaching of topics. Having a bank or list of differentiated tasks and activities to cater for differing ability levels will also help.

12.2.3   Teaching of Grammar

Similar to differentiation above, in a carousel group work arrangement, the teacher can adjust how much of any language structure or grammar is presented, or the complexity of the explanation, depending on the ability level of each group.

12.2.4   Assessment

A benefit of working in groups is that it provides an opportunity to assess the learners in different ways and in different skill areas. If the groups are set up as different skill areas, then the work that is undertaken can fulfil the role of class work and also as evidence of assessment (formative or summative, depending on the purpose). The teacher can decide to gather evidence of pupils' progress in one or more skill areas by taking in the work of a particular group (or all groups) and assessing it to provide feedback to the learners later. If the teacher is working with the speaking group, they can listen in and monitor learners as they carry out speaking or multi-skill tasks and make an assessment. This use of group work for assessment has the advantage of using classwork as a means of assessment, allowing more time for learning and teaching, and avoids suspending the work of a class to assess them.

12.2.5   Classroom Management

In general classroom management terms, carousel group work provides a number of benefits. By working in groups, learners can be given a greater variety of tasks than perhaps would be possible in a whole-class setting. By moving round 'stations' in the class, learners' interest is kept fresh with a variety of short, achievable, time-limited tasks, which helps with motivation. If equipment, or other learning resources, is in short supply, then these can be allocated to a particular group. For instance, there may only be six or seven laptops available in class, but the class numbers twenty-eight pupils. In a whole-class setting where all pupils are working on the same task, this would be a problem. In a carousel group work setting, this problem is sidestepped, as the task involving the use of the laptops can be allocated to one of the group 'stations'. This is a benefit that I found very useful in schools where costly resources such as books or audio devices were not always available or rationed out to teachers in small quantities.

12.2.6   Behaviour Management

What appears to be very much the norm in lessons where behaviour management problems are prevalent is a greater reliance on whole-class teaching. This in itself brings many challenges. It is very difficult to hold the attention of a group of any individuals for long periods of time, even with adults. The problem is multiplied manyfold when the learners are children, who generally have shorter attention spans and need a variety of activities to engage their interest. This is compounded if children receive lecture-style teaching for much of the lesson, and sometimes for the entire lesson. In a group work setting, this becomes less of a problem. The sequence of short achievable tasks, the variety of activities, and the chance to be involved actively in their learning by collaborating with their peers in a group setting grabs learners' attention and motivates them to participate in the lesson fully. In addition, as a teacher you can decide the best composition of group membership to minimise disruption, especially where you know that certain group-ings of pupils may not be advisable.

A typical class in a carousel group work setting may look similar to Figure 12.1.

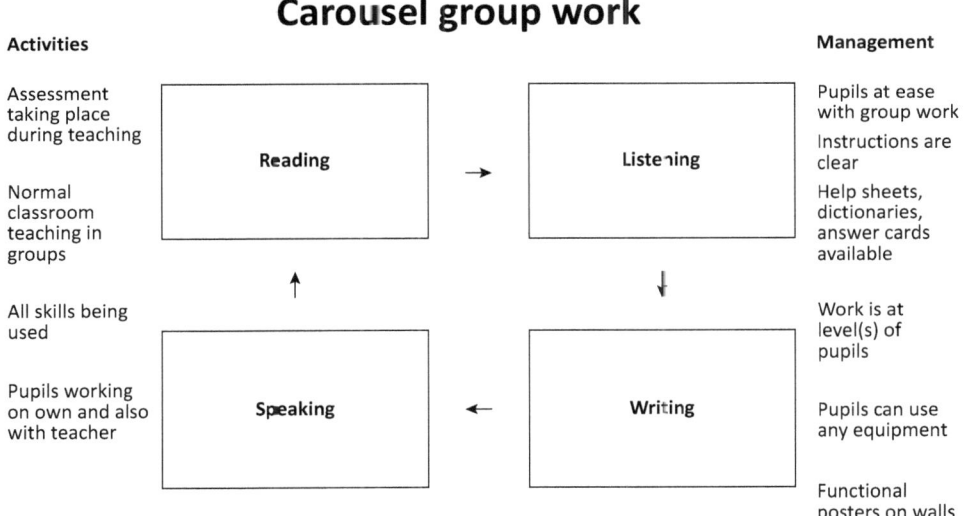

Figure 12.1 A graphical representation of what a carousel group work setting in an L2 class might look like

Section 12.2 has explored the use of carousel group work and how it can contribute to effective classroom organisation and management and enhance learning and teaching.

12.3   Working Collaboratively with Colleagues

Resources can also be human resources, such as other colleagues, or specialists in additional support needs. This section looks at how to involve colleagues in plan-ning and the benefits of collaborative working in the L2 classroom.

One of the greatest resources that you may have the good fortune to have is the help of other colleagues. These colleagues may be other teachers, learning support assistants, foreign language assistants, parents or even senior pupils helping with more junior classes. If you are fortunate enough to have other professionals or helpers in your class, then it is imperative that you make the most of this very valuable human resource. As mentioned in Chapter 6, you should involve these people in your planning and canvass them for their ideas. It is also important that you discuss the way in which you would like to organise the class and that you explain to your helpers your way of working, especially if it is not how they are used to working with other classes or teachers. You should explain to them what their role is at the different points in the lesson and what their responsibilities are.

If the other person is a foreign language assistant, another teacher of the target language or an adult or senior pupil who has proficiency in the TL, then it is a good idea to assign them to assist a particular group or skill area where you know the pupils will need help. Having two of you working together means you are more likely to be able to respond to a greater amount of needs in the class and support your pupils. This makes the management of differentiation easier, as you can support more learners at the same time. A second person can also contribute to assessment, either by carrying out assessments with the pupils, or by supporting groups while you undertake the assessments.

There is also the obvious benefit to general classroom management, where you have the assistance of another person in class with managing resources and equipment. Behaviour management is also less of an issue when another person is in the classroom supporting you and the pupils.

12.4   An Examination of Behaviour Management, What Causes Disruption and How to Prevent It

This section explores behaviour management and how to deal with disruption. Causes of disruption are examined and proposals for preventing it. This section also offers advice on what teachers can do if disruption occurs.

12.4.1   Causes of Disruption

There can be many causes of disruption in a class, especially in most schools where the pupils are only there compulsorily due to their age and the school's catchment area. No matter what the school, disruption can occur despite teachers' best efforts to plan relevant and interesting lessons. This may be due to factors beyond the teacher's control, such as an incident that has happened in the playground, tensions between groups of pupils, or a problem at home.

12.4.1.1 Disruption Caused by Inappropriate Learning and Teaching Strategies

A factor contributing to disruption that I have frequently witnessed is the use by the class teacher of inappropriate learning and teaching strategies. This is often characterised by an over-reliance on whole-class teaching, the lesson being too teacher-centred, or a mismatch between learning intentions and the pupils' needs. Indeed, sometimes more than one of these factors is evident. It is very difficult for young learners to concentrate for extended periods of time, so delivering a lesson in a lecture-style format will only ensure learners switch off, become tired, and seek alternative stimuli by chatting to classmates or checking their mobile phones, and so on.

12.4.2 Preventing Disruption

If we look at things that we do have control over, then we can take steps and develop strategies to prevent or minimise disruption. There are simple steps that you can take to prevent most forms of disruption. One obvious step is to make sure that you prepare your lessons thoroughly. For instance:

Lesson plan: Did all staff involved in the lesson have a copy of it?
Materials: Are they attractive? Are they at the level(s) of the pupils? Are they ready?
Equipment: Does it work? Is it set up?
Arriving at class: Did you insist on pupils entering class in an orderly fashion? Or did they drift into class at different times?
Moving rooms: If you need to take your pupils from your classroom to a specialist room, did you make pupils aware of how to behave when moving from one part of the school to another?

Asking yourself these basic questions will help you prepare for your lessons.

12.4.2.1 Choosing Appropriate Learning and Teaching Strategies

Do you stick to one form of lesson delivery or do you use a variety of strategies? Depending on what the aims of the lesson are, you should consider using a range of approaches. These may include the following:

- group work;
- paired work;
- whole-class teaching;
- pupils working in teams;
- teacher-led work;
- pupil-centred learning;
- skills-centred learning;
- multi-skill activities;
- multi-task activities.

Indeed, you may find yourself using a mix of different approaches within the same lesson. It is important to ask yourself why you have chosen a particular approach or approaches.

12.4.2.2   Making It Relevant

Making the lesson relevant to the learners is crucial. Does your lesson relate to their terms of reference or situation? How would you find this out? Often content and activities used in class may not reflect the context, interests or situation of the learners. If this happens, then the learners will stop paying attention to their tasks and this is sometimes when low-level disruption will occur.

12.4.2.3   Make a Class Contract

An approach that can help with behaviour management that is used in many schools is to make a class contract. A class contract will normally contain a set of entitlements and a set of responsibilities. It is important, however, that you make this workable and that you are consistent and fair. Do not be tempted to promise things that are unworkable, for example suggesting that if pupils behave they can listen to music during their lessons or play on their phones. This can often lead to distraction and inattention and set up conditions for more disruption. A reasonable set of entitlements may be that you promise to deliver well-prepared lessons that are interesting and relevant to them. In return, a set of responsibilities could include that the pupils will arrive at lessons prepared for the class and will participate in learning.

12.4.3   What to Do When Disruption Occurs

Whatever the planning, preparation and strategies you have undertaken to prevent disruption, there will inevitably still be occasions when disruption occurs in your class. The most important thing here is how you react and deal with it. So what can you do?

Keep calm

Try to keep calm. Breathe normally and be aware of the pitch and tone of your voice. When we are nervous, our voice will often rise in pitch and become quite squeaky or screechy. This nervousness will be sensed by and transmitted to the pupils. Your aim should be to keep yourself calm and also to keep your pupils calm.

Avoid confrontation

Although you may feel annoyed by a pupil's behaviour, do not get into a confrontation. This can often escalate very quickly and involve you and the pupil in a prolonged exchange and an initial form of low-level disruption becomes blown out of all proportion. An argument is a bit like a fire. If you keep feeding it, then it will keep going. A better strategy is to remain calm and ask the pupil to remain in class at the end of the lesson to have a chat about their behaviour.

Treat your pupils with respect

If you show pupils by your actions that you respect them, you are more likely to receive respect in return. Be careful not to say anything disrespectful or hurtful to a pupil and avoid sarcasm at all times.

Decide on strategies for dealing with disruption before teaching

Deciding what you will do in advance if disruption occurs will stop you from reacting in a knee-jerk fashion and saying or doing something that you will then regret. Make yourself aware of the modern languages department's behaviour management policy and guidelines and use these consistently. If there is a graded list of sanctions, then use them fairly and consistently. Do not go straight to the most serious sanction if the disruption does not merit it, as you then have nowhere to go afterwards if the pupil does not comply. Do not be tempted to make the pupil write out lines in the L2 or do extra exercises. This course of action is using the L2 as a punishment and is the quickest way to alienate a pupil from the subject.

Persistent misbehaviour

If a pupil persistently misbehaves, then the cause may lie outside the classroom. If this is the case, then consider consulting more senior or experienced colleagues, or colleagues in pastoral positions in your school. It may be that parents need to become involved. There are occasions where you cannot resolve a situation on your own. Remember that you have colleagues and work as part of a team. This will also benefit the pupil, who may need help in a variety of ways.

Be forgiving

Above all else do not take things personally and do not bear a grudge. Be forgiving and model the type of behaviour you would like to see so that your pupils have an example to follow. If you have taken steps to use a sanction for bad behaviour in your class, give your pupil(s) a chance to reduce its severity with good behaviour. For example, I have used a simple technique of writing a pupil's name on the board if they misbehaved in class, which was a signal to the pupil to wait and see me at the end of the lesson. However, if the pupil's behaviour improved, I would remove their name from the board and the need to chat with me after the lesson.

This section has focused on behaviour management, examining potential causes of disruption and strategies aimed at preventing disruption, and offered advice on what teachers can do if disruption nevertheless occurs.

12.5   A Restorative Approach to Behaviour Management

This section will look at restorative practice (McCluskey et al., 2008) and how this approach is used to help pupils improve their behaviour in school.

Restorative practice is an approach to behaviour management that has been gaining a lot of interest in many countries. Unlike more authoritarian approaches to behaviour management which focus on blame, guilt, adversarial processes and punishments, a restorative approach focuses on responsibility and problem-solving, on dialogue and negotiation, and on repair, apology and reparation. Originally derived from work done in restorative justice in criminal justice systems, which allows offenders to make amends for crimes, restorative approaches to behaviour management in schools share the ethos of restorative justice of looking to the future and helping individuals to change their behaviour in a positive way. Restorative practice thus helps pupils to understand the implications and effects of their actions and actively helps them to choose steps towards positive behavioural change. This improves pupil–teacher relationships in the classroom and can lead to better engagement in learning from pupils.

12.5.1   Features of Restorative Practice

Schools that adopt a restorative approach usually take a whole-school approach to it. For it to work well, restorative approaches require the consensus of all involved, staff and pupils (Short et al., 2018). Where this is most successful, staff and pupils are trained in how to reflect on actions and how to engage with each other in meaningful dialogue.

Although some schools may use different terminology to describe restorative practice, the approach adopted in most schools has the following features:

Respect: where everyone knows they will be listened to and their opinions valued.
Responsibility: encouraging everyone to take responsibility for their own actions.
Repair: developing the skills needed to identify solutions and make amends.
Re-integration: providing structured support to solve problems and allow young
    people to remain in mainstream education.

FOOD FOR THOUGHT

Consider the advice in Section 12.4.2 on preventing disruption. Are there any other strategies that you could add?

SUMMARY

This chapter has focused on the important areas of organisation and management and how teachers can achieve a positive interactive ethos in class. The value of choosing both appropriate resources and pedagogy has been considered and a major focus has been an examination of the benefits of using a carousel group work approach in the L2 classroom. These benefits included skills practice, differentiation, the teaching of grammar, assessment, classroom management and behaviour management. How to work collaboratively with colleagues in class was discussed and highlighted the benefits for both the learners and the teacher. Behaviour management was examined and Section 12.4 focused on causes of disruption, how to prevent disruption and what to do when disruption occurs. The chapter concluded by looking at restorative practice as a way of addressing behaviour management problems in schools.

REFLECTIVE QUESTIONS

1. Think back to your time as a pupil in school. Did your school adopt a restorative approach to behaviour management, an authoritarian approach, or a different model of behaviour management? Has your experience as a pupil affected your choice of approach now and, if so, in what way(s)?
2. Do you consider yourself to be more teacher-centred or learner-centred in your teaching? Reflect on your recent teaching opportunities and look for features of your lessons which may help you answer this question.

FURTHER READING

If you are interested in finding out more about approaches to behaviour management, refer to Paul Dix's book:

Dix, P., 2017. *When the Adults Change, Everything Changes: Seismic shifts in school behaviour.* Carmarthen: Independent Thinking Press.

The Education Endowment Foundation offers advice on improving behaviour:

Rhodes, I. & M. Long, 2019. *Improving Behaviour in Schools: Guidance report.* London: Education Endowment Foundation. Online. https://bit.ly/4gweiDL

The two publications below are very clear and give a good overview of restorative practice in schools.

McCluskey, G. et al., 2008. Can restorative practices in schools make a difference? *Educational Review*, 60(4): 405–17.

Short, R., G. Case & K. McKenzie, 2018. The long-term impact of a whole school approach of restorative practice: The views of secondary school teachers *Pastoral Care in Education*, 36(4): 313–24.

Collaboration and Professional Development

Introduction

Chapter 12 looked at the areas of organisation and classroom management as well as behaviour management, and how student teachers can develop skills in those areas.

This final chapter will look at ways in which teachers, and all involved in education, can maintain their knowledge and skills, continue to develop their professional learning, and maintain links with other education professionals. Attention will also be given to how teachers can look after their own well-being and mental health.

The learning objectives for this chapter are, therefore, as follows:

1. Evaluate the importance of continuing professional development (CPD), research and curriculum development.
2. Analyse and categorise ways in which teachers can maintain their skills and knowledge and build on them further.
3. Determine the scope for collaborative working and opportunities for networking.
4. Evaluate the importance of teacher well-being and of looking after one's physical, emotional and mental health and to provide advice on support available.

Overview

Continuing professional development is discussed, emphasising the importance of maintaining skills and keeping abreast of current research and **curriculum developments** in the teaching of modern foreign languages. Examples of **professional learning** are given, as well as advice on how collaborative working with colleagues locally, nationally and internationally can enhance learning and teaching. In addition, links are given to sources of further information and advice on a range of opportunities available to teachers to help them with their career-long professional learning (CLPL). Indeed, CLPL is a very apt way to conceive of your professional learning as it underlines that you will be involved in developing your knowledge and skills throughout your career. This chapter will also examine the important area of **teacher well-being** and give guidance and advice on how student teachers can build their own **emotional resilience**, preparing them for a career in the classroom, and show them how and where to find support in terms of their own well-being and mental health.

13.1   The Importance of Continuing Professional Development

At the end of your initial teacher education or training, as a student teacher you will have studied and gained knowledge, skills and experience in a wide range of areas necessary to become an effective teacher. This will range from pedagogical approaches to language teaching, skills development, unit planning and lesson planning to differentiation, classroom management and assessment, among other areas. You will be at the start of your career as a teacher and eager to use the knowledge, skills and methods you have learned in your first post as a qualified teacher. Like many newly qualified teachers (NQTs), you may be required to undergo a period of induction or probation in your initial months or year(s) of teaching. Wherever you find yourself and whichever education system you will work in, it is important to recognise that, while you may have gained expertise and confidence in many aspects of teaching, you are at the beginning of your journey as a teacher. In order to maintain your knowledge and skills as a modern languages teacher, and indeed to build further on them, means that you must engage continually in your professional development (Kennedy, 2011). This is an integral part of your work as a teacher to help you to continue to provide high-quality and effective learning experiences for your pupils that will inspire them and contribute to successful language learning.

13.2   Maintaining Knowledge and Skills

To maintain and build your knowledge and skills, you have to be aware of the current stage of your professional development. This means reviewing your current knowledge and skills, identifying particular learning and training needs and planning how you will address these. You may often find this out through collaborative research with other colleagues. Sometimes your development needs will be obvious; indeed they may have already been pointed out to you by your mentor, line manager or a peer during teaching or other collaborative work. However, you should not wait for others to bring such needs to your attention. Effective teachers will engage in a regular and systematic process of self-reflection that integrates this with their professional lives (Farrell, 2020;

Table 13.1 Steps in the professional learning process	
Step	Action required
Step 1	Audit your current knowledge and identify your current stage with particular areas.
Step 2	From this audit, identify your most pressing need or needs.
Step 3	Plan how you will begin to address each need.
Step 4	Reflect on your progress.
Step 5	Build this new learning or skill into your practice.

Zeichner & Liston, 2013). One way of doing this is to break down the process into a series of steps, as outlined in Table 13.1.

Let's now look at these in detail.

Step 1: Auditing your knowledge

If you are keeping up to date with your reflections on your lessons, it will be easy to locate where you are in a particular area or areas. Look over your self-evaluations of lessons or evaluations received from mentors and peers and create a table where you can see at a glance your status in each area. This could involve colour coding, for example green for 'doing well', orange for 'developing' and red for 'cause for concern'. Or you may prefer to use number ranking or emojis as indicators, as is used in Table 13.2.

Step 2: Identifying development need(s)

From the audit of your areas of teaching, you may find yourself with quite a number of areas where you would like to improve or refresh your teaching. It is important to realise, however, that you cannot address all of these issues at the same time. A more effective strategy is to prioritise which area(s) to work on first and which can wait for another day. The selection of which area(s) to tackle first should be obvious if you have carried out an audit of your progress as in Step 1 above. Choose the area with which you are experiencing the most difficulty and set that as your first target. It can be tempting to choose an area that may seem easier to address, but if it is easier, then you can most likely address that area at a later time, finding it easier to work on and most likely quicker to address.

Step 3: Planning to address need(s)

Having decided on which area(s) or need(s) to address, plan how to go about addressing this. If you are not sure where to start, consult a more experienced colleague or mentor.

There are a number of ways in which you may decide, or be advised, to go about addressing these needs. One source of help may be reading or re-reading guidance or literature dealing with this area. You may decide to watch colleagues and learn from what they do. If there is a training course you can attend that focuses on this area, try to book a place on it.

Table 13.2 An at-a-glance audit of areas of strength and areas of concern*

Areas	Progress 👍 🙂 🙁	Particular strength	Particular concern
Lesson planning	👍	Can plan most lessons satisfactorily; achieve desired learning outcomes	
Mode of teaching	🙂	Generally use a mix of teaching modes, although would like to develop ability to use group work more.	
Assessment	🙁		I rely too much on assessing writing skills. Find it difficult to assess speaking skills in class.
Other area Other area			

*Appendix 13.1 is a template of this form.

Step 4: Reflection

You will want to know if the actions you have taken to address a particular need or needs are having an effect, so be systematic in your reflections. This may involve keeping a diary or devising a tracking sheet where you note the actions you have taken and analyse the success or otherwise of your actions. Or you may ask a mentor or peer to observe you undertaking these actions with your class(es) and seek their advice on how well they think you are doing in this area. You could also video yourself teaching and analyse this later, but be aware that you may need to seek permission before recording any of your classes. Set a realistic timeframe for reviewing your progress in this area(s) – or a series of review points – and look at any evidence you have gathered, for example observations from colleagues, self-evaluations of lessons or video evidence.

Step 5: Building into teaching

As you gain more competence and confidence in this new strategy, technique or skill, integrate it with your teaching as appropriate and try to build upon it further. Remember to keep this under review, which you can do in the same ways described

Table 13.3 An example of a planning and review sheet to record professional learning*

Area	Reason or concern	Proposed action	Reflection on action taken
Mode of teaching	Most lesson evaluations show a predominance of teacher-led activity. Need to build in more group work.	1. Read more on how to use group work in class. 2. Observe colleagues using this with their classes and discuss how to do this. 3. Try this out with one or two of my classes over the next four weeks.	1. Reading gave me greater understanding of when and how to use group work. 2. Observation of colleagues using group work was very useful in terms of the practice of using group work. 3. Have experienced success with two classes where I have used group work. 4. Will extend to my other classes.
Assessment	I rely too much on assessing writing skills. Find it difficult to assess speaking skills in class.	1. Access literature on formative assessment. 2. Discuss with colleagues and ask for advice on assessment strategies. 3. Book place on upcoming regional training seminar on formative assessment strategies. 4. Try out strategies for speaking assessment learned in points 2 and 3 above.	1. Literature made me reflect on why I mainly used writing assessment. 2. Discussion with colleagues and training seminar showed me examples of how to assess speaking skills as part of my teaching. 3. Have tried this out with one class and had some success. Will continue to try out strategies with class and extend to all my classes.

*Appendix 13.2 is a template of this table.

in Step 4. Table 13.3 is an example of a planning and review sheet to record professional learning.

13.2.1 Keeping Abreast of Current Research

A very important part of your professional learning is making sure that you keep abreast of current research, not only in modern language teaching and learning, but also in other wider areas of education. There are many ways of doing this, for example:

- joining professional associations for language teaching;
- subscribing to magazines and journals of professional associations;
- accessing peer-reviewed academic journals;
- reading national policy and curriculum documents;
- attending training workshops or conferences at local, regional or national level.

These are common ways in which to learn about research and developments in language teaching and in education more generally and you may find yourself using a mix of the suggestions above. Some of the recommendations have financial implications – you may have to pay an annual subscription to a professional association or for a magazine or journal subscription. Workshops and conferences may require a fee to be paid, but if there is a staff development fund in your school, you may be able to get your institution to cover or contribute towards the costs involved.

13.2.2 Keeping Abreast of Curriculum Developments

When there are developments in a national curriculum, these are often accompanied by workshops and events organised by the local authority or regional or national bodies, or even individual schools. You may be invited to attend one or more of these, or benefit from the learning shared by a colleague or your line manager who has attended such an event. In many countries, the national bodies or agencies tasked with supporting education will post new developments and support materials on their website or virtual learning environments (VLEs). It is important that you regularly access these online sources to make sure that your teaching reflects any changes to curriculum arrangements.

FOOD FOR THOUGHT

How do you currently maintain your knowledge and skills as a teacher?
Do you engage in particular staff development activities and, if so, what are these?
Which activities have you found particularly helpful and which less so?

13.2.3 Examples of Professional Learning

Having analysed why continuing professional development is so important to your work as a language teacher and explored ways in which you can determine your development needs, let's look at some other examples of professional learning not mentioned above.

Practitioner enquiry

As the name suggests, **practitioner enquiry** is where you may investigate an aspect of your teaching in an experiential way with a view to gathering information or data, which you then analyse with the aim of developing or improving a specific area in your teaching, whether this is knowledge gained, methods, or a particular skill or skills. This is often called action research.

Professional reading

Not dissimilar to practitioner enquiry, this will involve you in critical analysis of reading around aspects of your professional practice in the classroom. As with practitioner enquiry, you may find yourself, as a consequence of your reading, interrogating an aspect of your practice and making changes to your teaching as a result.

Online learning and blogs

There are countless web pages and blogs from teachers and other educational professionals on the internet offering advice and resources, often for free. This is a very community-minded endeavour on the part of individuals and groups of teachers who are willing to share their knowledge, expertise and resources. By looking online you will often find useful advice, tips and guidance on aspects of professional learning. However, as with anything you find online, you need to assure yourself of the appropriacy of the advice or materials offered. In terms of your professional learning, you should ask yourself:

- Does the advice or approach encountered online contradict the teacher education you have received from your tutors or mentors?
- Is this web page or blog a reputable source, or does it cite verifiable sources?
- Is there a hidden agenda?

If you are satisfied that the online advice or resources you have encountered are in line with best practice and research in modern language learning and teaching, then they may be good sources of professional learning.

Co-operative or team teaching

Through working collaboratively with colleagues in class, you may learn a lot that will help you with your professional learning. From joint planning of lessons, you will learn how and why to choose a particular approach. While teaching classes together, you have the chance both to observe your colleague in action and to try out things for yourself without having to assume full responsibility for the learning and teaching. This allows you more headspace to concentrate on developing skills and approaches in a safe and supported environment.

Leading or participating in a working party or task group

Another opportunity for professional learning may come from participation in school working parties or task groups. Often these are short-life working groups (SLWGs) set up to find solutions to specific problems, or to look at how to integrate a new local or national initiative or requirement with classroom teaching. Working with others to discuss these issues is a great way to develop problem-solving skills as well as allowing you to derive benefit from the co-construction of new knowledge that working with others brings. As you gain experience in your teaching, you may be asked to lead a working group, which allows you to develop organisational and leadership skills, while at the same time developing knowledge and experience of the issue you are tasked with investigating.

Participation in activities relating to assessment and moderation

A regular part of your teaching will involve assessing the work of your learners. To ensure that assessments are valid and reliable, schools will carry out standardisation and moderation activities, which may be local to the school or institution, or part of a regional or national scheme. Standardisation usually involves blind marking a sample of work or scripts across the grade range and then comparing your assessment with colleagues teaching classes on the same course. Through discussion and with reference to the marking criteria, markers learn to identify the features of an 'A', a 'B' and an 'E' grade (if that is your system) and everything in between, and are then able to mark the rest of the assessments confidently. As an extra layer of quality assurance, markers will moderate each other's assessments by exchanging a sample of work they have marked at different levels when they are near the end of their marking, or after they have finished marking. Each marker will mark some of their colleagues' scripts. Where there are discrepancies or disagreements, discussion will take place to agree on a final mark for the work. A third marker will be brought in if the first two markers cannot reach agreement.

The processes of standardisation, the application of that standardisation to your marking and the subsequent moderation of that marking are very good staff development activities and contribute to your professional knowledge and skills as a teacher.

TRY THIS OUT

Choose one or two of the examples of professional learning from Section 13.2.3 above.

Try this out over the course of twelve weeks.

Keep a diary of how this goes and what you learn.

At the end of the twelve weeks, reflect on what you have learned and how this has helped your professional development.

13.3 Collaborative Networks and Opportunities for Networking

In the field of modern language learning and teaching there are multiple ways in which teachers can, and should, seek to collaborate on a regular basis with other teachers and other educational professionals to extend their knowledge, enhance their skills and keep up to date with current thinking and practices in the field.

13.3.1 Local Networks

As mentioned earlier in this book when looking at social constructivism (Chapter 4), learning is an essentially social activity and learners make best progress when they interact with others. This is just as true for teachers as it is for your pupils and is why a number of the actions described above involve working with peers or mentors. As we go through our careers as teachers, we are fortunate to be in a profession where people are happy to help each other and share ideas. This is at the heart of teaching, a human activity where we share our knowledge and skills with a genuine desire to collaborate and support each other. In my first years as a language teacher, I was very fortunate that the head of languages at my school took me and another new modern languages teacher to a meeting of the local branch of the Modern Languages Association. At these meetings, languages teachers from across the region discussed areas of interest and local priorities and took action to address them. This action sometimes involved arranging upskilling activities for teachers or setting up short-life working groups (temporary task forces) to collaborate on areas of concern. In terms of responding to matters of local interest in language teaching, many schools and regions have established informal networks to share news, ideas and resources on social media platforms. Teachers can often find new ideas and resources they can use or adapt for their own classrooms, but as mentioned in Section 9.4 on online learning and blogs above, you need to assure yourself of the appropriacy of the advice and materials offered and decide if they are suitable for your purposes.

13.3.2   National Networks

At the same time as being part of a local network of languages teachers, you will almost certainly have the opportunity to join national networks. Some of these networks may be part of official national education bodies or agencies, whilst others may be professional subject associations, membership of which is voluntary. I would strongly recommend that you join any national networks or associations, even if that entails having to pay an annual subscription. Such national networks have the benefit of being able to pool the ideas, knowledge and intellect of a great number of teachers and education professionals and their members are usually enthusiastic and active in the field. As larger organisations, national networks and associations often provide downloadable resources for use in class, put on events specific to areas of learning and teaching, and organise national conferences. All of these are great sources of professional learning that will aid your development as a languages teacher. In the UK, the Modern Language Association and several individual language teacher associations amalgamated in 1990 to form the Association for Language Learning (ALL), which supports those involved in the teaching of foreign languages at all levels. In the USA, the Modern Languages Association of America (MLA) provides opportunities for its members to share their teaching experience and publish scholarly articles, and it arranges an annual convention. In Australia, the Australian Federation of Modern Language Teachers Associations (AFMLTA) represents teachers of all languages in Australia. Like ALL and MLA, AFMLTA promotes and provides professional learning, publications and conferences.

13.3.3   International Networks and Programmes

A number of national organisations and associations have forged links with similar associations in other countries. AFMLTA in Australia, for example, has links with

ALL in the UK. It also has links to the American Council on the Teaching of Foreign Languages (ACTFL). This allows even greater sharing and cross-fertilisation of ideas and work through publications, events and conferences. One of the largest and most internationally representative teaching associations in the world is the International Association of Teachers of English as a Foreign Language (IATEFL), which provides opportunities for its members to share and learn from each other, as well as organising international conferences.

Among the most active programmes internationally is the European Union's Erasmus+ programme, whose purpose is to support education, training, youth and sport in Europe. With an annual budget of billions of euros, Erasmus+, like its predecessor programme Erasmus, provides frameworks and funding for large and small collaborative projects and research, and mobility opportunities for teachers and lecturers, pupils, students and organisations. Its website has a searchable database of project reports and resources on a wealth of different subjects related to education and training (Erasmus+, no date). Within many of the reports, there are links to free downloadable resources, platforms and training on a variety of areas.

Figure 13.1 represents the many networks which exist to support your professional learning and development.

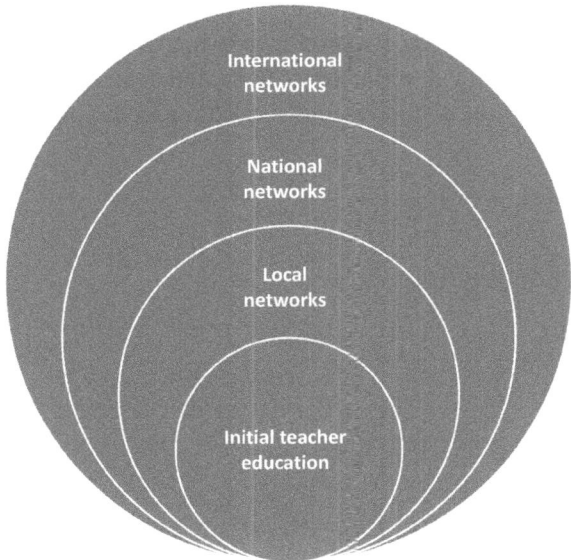

Figure 13.1 A graphical representation of how multiple support networks relate to each other

This section has examined why professional learning is so important to teacher development and presented strategies for maintaining one's skill as a teacher and keeping abreast of the latest developments in modern language teaching. It has also explored ways in which teachers can collaborate to improve their knowledge and skills at local, national and international level.

Section 13.4 will look at the importance of teacher well-being and provide guidance and strategies to help teachers with their physical, emotional and mental health.

13.4   The Importance of Teacher Well-Being

This section considers the importance of looking after one's own welfare as a teacher and how this can, in turn, benefit the learners in your class. It will examine factors that negatively impact on teacher well-being and provide guidance on how and where to seek support.

As teachers we always look out for the needs of our pupils. We make it a priority to attend to their needs and to go the extra mile for them. However, as teachers carry out their duties looking after the education and well-being of their pupils, they very often neglect their own well-being, putting others' needs before their own. When this continues over a period of time, teachers begin to feel exhausted and stressed, and can experience feelings of low self-worth and poor **self-efficacy**. This often leads to a general lack of self-confidence in their abilities as a teacher. Often feeling physically and mentally exhausted, many teachers experience burnout, which causes significant numbers to leave the profession early. These effects are not only devastating for the teaching profession, but also directly affect pupils. If a teacher does not feel they are in a good place (Figure 13.2), they will find it difficult to plan and teach lessons effectively, having a direct negative impact on their pupils' learning and progress.

Figure 13.2 A tired and stressed teacher at a desk

13.4.1   Factors That Contribute to Poor Self-Efficacy

These feelings of lack of control and stress can adversely affect the mental health of teachers, which can manifest itself as poor physical health as well. There are many contributing factors that can exacerbate these problems. Teachers will often have very heavy workloads, teaching large classes and working long hours. They can often feel overwhelmed with everything that is expected of them. In addition, teachers often do not set good personal or professional boundaries, taking a lot of work home and working very late in the evening and at the weekend. It is important for teachers to remember, however, that they are only human, and not machines. Working late into the night will lead to lack of energy, contribute to interrupted or restless sleep patterns and lead to teachers feeling permanently under pressure and stressed. If we look at personality traits, we find that quite a number of teachers are perfectionists. Psychologists describe this personality style as striving for flawlessness, often leading to being very self-critical (Eyre, 2016; Bergviken-Rensfeldt et al., 2018). In many cases, perfectionists will never be happy with their achievements, contributing to feelings of inadequacy.

13.4.2   Building Emotional Resilience

Having established why teacher well-being is so important and having examined factors that contribute to poor self-efficacy, what can teachers (and student teachers) do to manage their well-being?

As with any job, it is important to establish healthy boundaries between work and personal life. Teaching is a high-pressure job, where teachers are constantly on show in public view. In fact, there are very few other jobs where an employee is under such intense scrutiny.

The way that you think about things has an impact on your mood, anxiety and stress levels. This means that you must establish a realistic work–life balance and resist the urge or the feeling of pressure to work late into the night planning lessons and assessing work. Often teachers will spend a lot of time on preparing classes, but have made themselves so tired that they struggle to deliver these in the classroom the next day. Remember, you need time to eat, sleep, spend time with your family and friends and do non-work-related activities. A healthy and more efficient approach is as follows:

1. Look at your diary and identify the slots of time during the week when you will plan lessons.
2. Be strict with yourself and set a time limit for this planning. Do not go over this time limit. It is important to remember that good enough is enough. Spending another hour tweaking a lesson may have negligible observable results in class.
3. Try to plan for a series of lessons, so that you are not continually chasing yourself for the next day's lesson. That way, when you do have some non-contact time, either in school or out of school, you are not rushing to plan the next lesson for, say, that afternoon, but rather you are planning lessons for the next week. This in itself reduces pressure and will help prevent anxiety and stress.

Above all, try to stay positive and keep everything in perspective. We often worry about problems, are self-critical and think we are not up to the job, but remember these doubts may not necessarily be accurate assessments of what is happening.

When we are stressed or feeling low, such negative thoughts may pop into our heads, but they should be banished as they are quite often without any substance.

13.4.3   How and Where to Find Support

Despite your best efforts to stay on top of everything, there may be times when you experience setbacks, or when your plans do not work out as you had hoped. This may lead you to become anxious and question whether you can really do this job. It is important to remember, however, that you are not alone. You are part of a larger team who may have had similar experiences to what you may be undergoing and have already had help in developing strategies to deal with those experiences. Thus, there are a number of actions you can take, including:

1. Discuss your concerns or problems with a peer or colleague in the school. Often, we stay silent, perhaps thinking that 'everyone is coping, except me'. When you speak to peers you may find they are going through the same experience. Sharing your worries is often enough to start you thinking about how to address them and you can often work on them together, supporting each other.
2. Confide in your mentor or line manager and ask them for their support. Your mentor will be used to helping colleagues new to teaching and will be able to share strategies with you and advise how to cope with problems that are worrying you.
3. If there are specialist support services in your school or in the education authority, do not hesitate to make use of them. These services are set up to provide guidance and support.

Place2Think Support Service for Students

Since 2018, the University of Edinburgh has piloted a support service for student teachers. The service is provided by the charity Place2Be (no date), whose mission is to support children and young people's mental health.

Place2Be has been working in schools for the last twenty-five years and has initiated Place2Think at the University of Edinburgh, which provides a safe, reflective space for student teachers to make sense of their emotional responses to the children they teach and is supported by a full-time consultant clinical psychologist.

As well as delivering lectures for student teachers on a variety of topics related to supporting the mental health of pupils, Place2Think provides sessions for student teachers to consider their own mental health and to consider their own self-care.

The success of this initiative was so great that it was extended in 2024 to two other universities in Scotland with plans to extend this work into schools. These proposals, as with the pilot at the University of Edinburgh, have been supported by the Scottish Government.

It would be great to see such a service as Place2Think provided for all student teachers everywhere, but I hope that Section 13.4 of this chapter has underlined how very important teacher well-being is to successful learning and teaching and given you some strategies to ensure your own teacher well-being. It is vital that you look after your own physical, emotional and mental health to allow you to continue to enjoy this wonderful profession. This will help you be the best teacher you can be and help you support your learners, because your pupils deserve the best version of you and *you* deserve that too!

SUMMARY

Section 13.1 sought to make the case for continuing professional development and advocated strategies whereby teachers can maintain the skills and knowledge in modern language teaching gained in the areas presented in Chapters 2 to 12 of this book. This has been illustrated in Section 13.2 by a step-by-step guide to the professional learning process, where teachers audit their knowledge and skills, identify needs, plan how to address these needs and reflect on progress. How to keep abreast of current research and curriculum developments in modern language teaching was explored, with examples of professional learning given ranging from practitioner enquiry and online learning to how participating in working parties and taking part in assessment and moderation activities can assist in teachers' professional development. Section 13.3 recognised the value of cooperative working and promoted participation in a range of local, national and international networks and programmes. Section 13.4 evaluated the importance of teacher well-being and why it is crucial to consider one's self-care as a teacher. Factors contributing to poor self-efficacy were examined and practical advice given on how and where to find support and how to build emotional resilience. If teachers do not attach the necessary importance of looking after themselves physically, mentally and emotionally, then they will not be in a healthy enough position to put the advice contained in the chapters of this book into practice. For this reason, the importance of the concluding section of this book cannot be overstated.

REFLECTIVE QUESTIONS

1. Consider the wide range of areas that you have explored in your journey to becoming a modern languages teacher. How easy or difficult have you found maintaining your knowledge and skills? You may find it helpful to discuss this with a fellow colleague or your mentor.
2. Considering the issue of teacher well-being, how much importance have you attached in your professional learning to your own self-care? Is this something you do regularly? Or is this something that you promise yourself you will do when you have more time?

KEY TERMS

curriculum development The process by which an institution plans and designs content in an educational setting.

emotional resilience The ability to respond to a stressful or unexpected situation or crisis.

practitioner enquiry Class-based research to support learning needs and to enhance experiences in the classroom.

professional learning The process of stimulating thinking and professional knowledge to ensure practice is critically informed and relevant.

self-efficacy An individual's belief in their ability to carry out their roles and responsibilities effectively.

teacher well-being The status of teachers with regard to their physical, emotional and mental health.

FURTHER READING

Professional learning

If you are interested in a nationally organised approach to professional learning, then have a look at the website of the General Teaching Council for Scotland (GTCS).

General Teaching Council for Scotland (GTCS). Online. www.gtcs.org.uk/professional-upda te/professional-learning

At Cambridge International there is a range of professional development opportunities. Find out more at:

Cambridge International Education. Professional development. Online. https://bit.ly/ 40PkNMv

Professional associations

There are professional associations that support professional learning and networking in different countries.

In the UK:

Association for Language Learning (ALL). Online. www.all-languages.org.uk

In the USA:

Modern Language Association of America (MLA). Online. www.mla.org

In Australia:

Australian Federation of Modern Language Teachers Associations (AFMLTA). Online. https://afmlta.asn.au

Full details on support for education and training, youth and sport in Europe are available at:
Erasmus+, no date. Online. https://erasmus-plus.ec.europa.eu

Modern language journals

The two journals below publish articles on research into modern language teaching and learning:

Modern Language Journal. Online. https://onlinelibrary.wiley.com/journal/15404781
Modern Language Review. Online. www.mhra.org.uk/journals/MLR

Well-being

For advice on supporting the well-being of both pupils and teachers:

Murray, J., 2024. *100 Ideas for Primary Teachers: Wellbeing*. London: Bloomsbury.

To find out more about the work of Place2be and Place2think, please refer to:

Place2Be. Online. https://bit.ly/3EₑELaI

APPENDIX 13.1

Table A13.1 Template for At-a-Glance Audits of Areas of Strength and Areas of Concern

Areas	Progress 👍 ☺ ☹	Particular strength	Particular concern
Enter area		Evidence of strength	Describe concern

You can view and download this table at www.cambridge.org/lynch.

Table A13.2 Template for Planning and Review to Record Professional Learning

Area[*]	Reason or concern[†]	Proposed action	Reflection on action taken
Enter area		1. 2. 3. 4.	1. 2. 3. 4.
Enter area		1. 2. 3. 4.	1. 2. 3. 4.

[*] e.g. Assessment
[†] Description of the concern
You can view and download this table at www.cambridge.org/lynch.

References

Amineh, R.J. & H.D. Asl, 2015. Review of constructivism and social constructivism. *Journal of Social Sciences, Literature and Languages,* 1(1): 9–16.

Andrade, H.L. & G.J. Cizek, 2010. *Handbook of Formative Assessment.* New York: Routledge.

Armstrong, A.C., D. Armstrong & I. Spandagou, 2010. *International Education: International policy and practice.* London: Sage.

Arnaiz Castro, P., S. Breidbach, D. Coyle, J. de Vigne, K. Hahl & M. Lynch, 2022. Deeper learning and assessment in drama-based CLIL learning spaces. *Language Education and Multilingualism – The Langscape Journal,* 5(1): 124–39. doi:10.18452/25444.

Art of TEFL, 2021. Writing skills practice in the EFL classroom. Online. https://bit.ly/3CflPGY

Association for Language Learning (ALL). Online. www.all-languages.org.uk

Atkinson, D., 2011. A sociocognitive approach to second language acquisition, in D. Atkinson (ed.), *Alternative Approaches to Second Language Acquisition.* Abingdon: Routledge, 2011, 143–66.

Australian Federation of Modern Language Teachers Associations (AFMLTA). Online. https://afmlta.asn.au

Beckmann, T. & T. Ehmke, 2023. Informal and formal lesson planning in school internships: Practices among pre-service teachers. *Teaching and Teacher Education,* 132: 104249.

Bennett, R.E., 2011. Formative assessment: A critical review. *Assessment in Education: Principles, Policy & Practice,* 18(1): 5–25. doi: 10.1080/0969594X.2010.513678.

Bergviken-Rensfeldt, A., T. Hillman & N. Selwyn, 2018. Teachers 'liking' their work? Exploring the realities of teacher Facebook groups. *British Educational Research Journal,* 44(2): 230–50.

Biber, D., Stig Johansson, Geoffrey Leech, Susan Conrad & Edward Finegan, 1999. *The Longman Grammar of Spoken and Written English.* Harlow: Longman.

Black, P. & D. Wiliam, 1998. Inside the black box: Raising standards through classroom assessment. *Phi Delta Kappan,* 80(2): 139–48.

Black, P. & D. Wiliam, 2009. Developing the theory of formative assessment. *Educational Assessment, Evaluation and Accountability,* 21(1): 5–31.

Black, P., C. Harrison, C. Lee, B. Marshall & D. Wiliam, 2003. *Assessment for Learning: Putting it into practice.* Buckingham: Open University Press.

Borg, S., 2003. Teacher cognition in language teaching: A review of research on what language teachers think, know, believe, and do. *Language Teaching,* 36(2): 81–109. doi: 10.1017/s0261444803001903.

Braddon-Mitchell, D. & K. Miller, 2020. Conativism about personal identity, in A. Sauchelli (ed.), *Derek Parfit's Reasons and Persons: An introduction and critical inquiry.* New York: Routledge, 159–269.

British Dyslexia Association, 2023. About dyslexia. Online. www.bdadyslexia .org.uk/dyslexia/about-dyslexia/what-is-dyslexia

Brown, G.T. & L.R. Harris, 2013. Student self-assessment, in J.H. McMillan (ed.), *Sage Handbook of Research on Classroom Assessment.* Los Angeles: Sage, 367–93.

Bruner, J., 1996. *The Culture of Education.* Cambridge, MA: Harvard University Press.

Buck, J. & C. Wightwick, 2013. *Teaching and Learning Languages: A practical guide to learning by doing.* Abingdon: Routledge.

Burns, A. & J. Siegel, 2018. Teaching the four language skills: Themes and issues, in A. Burns & J. Siegel (eds.), *International Perspectives on Teaching the Four Skills in ELT: International perspectives on English language teaching.* Cham: Palgrave Macmillan.

Butler, M., 2012. Resource-based learning and course design: A brief theoretical overview and practical suggestions. *Law Library Journal,* 104: 219.

Butzkamm, W., 2003. We only learn language once: The role of the mother tongue in FL classrooms – death of a dogma. *Language Learning Journal* 28 29–39.

Cambridge English, 2024a. *B1 Preliminary for Schools: Developing listening skills for Cambridge English Qualifications: A guide for teachers.* Cambridge: Cambridge University Press and Assessment. https://bit.ly/42mFWyA

Cambridge English, 2024b. *B2 First for Schools: Developing reading skills for Cambridge English Qualifications: A guide for teachers.* Cambridge: Cambridge University Press and Assessment. https://bit.ly/4hmU0wr

Cambridge International Education. Professional development. Online. https://bit.ly/40PkNMv

Cauldwell, R., 2013. *Phonology for Listening: Teaching the stream of speech.* Birmingham: Speech in Action.

Center for Applied Special Technology (CAST), 2024. Universal design principles. Online. https://udlguidelines.cast.org

Chang, S.C., 2011. A contrastive study of grammar translation method and communicative approach in teaching English grammar. *Language Teaching,* 4(2): 13.

Clouder, L., M. Karakus, A. Cinotti, M. V. Ferreyra, G. Amador Fierros & P. Rojo, 2020. Neurodiversity in higher education: A narrative synthesis. *Higher Education,* 80(4): 757–78.

Collins, A., J.S. Brown & S.E. Newman, 2018. Cognitive apprenticeship: Teaching the crafts of reading, writing, and mathematics, in L. B. Resnick (ed.), 1989, *Knowing, Learning, and Instruction: Essays in honor of Robert Glaser.* New York: Routledge, 453–94. https://doi.org/10.4324/9781315044408

Convery, A. & D. Coyle, 1993. *Differentiation: Taking the initiative.* London: Centre for Information on

Language Teaching and Research (CILT).

Cook, V., 2001. Using the first language in the classroom. *Canadian Modern Language Review*, 57(3): 402–23.

Coyle, D. & Meyer, O., 2021. *Beyond CLIL: Pluriliteracies teaching for deeper learning.* Cambridge: Cambridge University Press.

Coyle, D., 2007. Content and language integrated learning: Towards a connected research agenda for CLIL pedagogies. *International Journal of Bilingual Education and Bilingualism*, 10(5): 543–62

Degrave, P., 2019. Music in the foreign language classroom: How and why? *Journal of Language Teaching and Research*, 10(3): 412–20. doi: http s://dx.doi.org/10.17507/ jltr.1003.02

Dennen, V.P., 2004. Cognitive apprenticeship in educational practice: Research on scaffolding, modeling, mentoring, and coaching as instructional strategies, in D. Jonassen & M. Driscoll (eds.), *Handbook of Research on Educational Communications and Technology*, 804–81. New York: Routledge.

Department for Education, 2023. Teaching online safety in schools. Online. https://bit.ly/3E1DnId

Didenko, A.V. & I.L. Pichugova, 2016. Post CLT or Post-Method: Major criticisms of the communicative approach and the definition of the current pedagogy. *SHS Web of Conferences*, 28. International Conference on Research Paradigms Transformation in Social Sciences, 2015. doi: https://doi.org/10.1051/s hsconf/20162801028

Dix, P., 2017. *When the Adults Change, Everything Changes: Seismic shifts in school behaviour.* Carmarthen: Independent Thinking Press.

Dolean, D.D., 2016. The effects of teaching songs during foreign language classes on students' foreign language anxiety. *Language Teaching Research* 20(5): 638–53. ht tps://doi.org/10.1177/ 1362168815606151.

Dörnyei, Z., 2020. *Innovations and Challenges in Language Learning Motivation.* London: Routledge.

Dziuban, C.D, C.R. Graham, P. D. Moskal, A. Norberg & N. Sicilia, 2018. Blended learning: The new normal and emerging technologies. *International Journal of Educational Technology in Higher Education*, 15: Article 3.

Education Scotland, 2017. Languages. Online. https://bit.ly/4fvOLZW

Ellis, N.C., 2009. Constructing a second language: Analyses and computational simulations of the emergence of linguistic constructions from usage. *Language Learning*, 59: 90–125.

Ellis, R., 2005. Principles of instructed language learning. *Asian EFL Journal* 7(3): Article 1

Ellis, R., P. Skehan, S. Li, N. Shintani & C. Lambert, 2019. The pedagogic background to task-based language teaching, in R. Ellis, P. Skehan, S. Li, N. Shintani & C. Lambert (eds.), *Task-Based Language Teaching: Theory and practice.* Cambridge: Cambridge University Press, 3–26.

Erasmus+, no date. Online. https://eras mus-plus.ec.europa.eu

Erasmus+, 2021. EU programme for education, training, youth and sport.

Playing beyond CLIL. Online. https://bit.ly/42LSb8n

Eyre, C., 2016. *The Elephant in the Staffroom: How to reduce stress and improve teacher wellbeing*. London: Routledge.

Fallace, T., 2023. The long origins of the visual, auditory, and kinesthetic learning style typology, 1921–2001. *History of Psychology*, 26(4), 334–54. https://doi.org/10.1037/hop0000240

Farrell, T.S.C., 2020. *Reflective Teaching*, Alexandria, VA: TESOL International Association.

Ferlazzo, L. & K.H. Sypnieski, 2018. Writing frames and writing structures, in *The ELL Teacher's Toolbox: Hundreds of practical ideas to support your students*. San Francisco: Wiley, 151–63.

Finocchiaro, M. & C. Brumfit, 1983. *The Functional–Notional Approach: From theory to practice*. Oxford: Oxford University Press.

Florian, L., K. Black-Hawkins & M. Rouse, 2017. Learning from others: Achievement and inclusion across the case-study schools, in L. Florian, K. Black-Hawkins & M. Rouse (eds.), *Achievement and Inclusion in Schools*. Second edition. London: Routledge, 131–45. https://doi.org/10.4324/9781315750279.

Franklin, C., 1990. The use of the target language in the French language classroom: Co-operative teaching as an aid to implementation. PhD thesis. University of Edinburgh.

Freebody, P. & A. Luke, 2003. Literacy as engaging with new forms of life: The four roles model, in G. Bull & M. Anstey (eds.), *The Literacy Lexicon*. Second edition. Sydney: Pearson, 51–66.

Gardner, H.E., 2006. *Multiple Intelligences: New horizons in theory and practice*. New York: Basic Books.

Gatbonton, E. & N. Segalowitz, 2005. Rethinking the communicative approach: A focus on accuracy and fluency. *Canadian Modern Language Review/La revue canadienne des langues vivantes*, 61(3): 325–53.

General Teaching Council for Scotland (GTCS). Professional learning. Online. www.gtcs.org.uk/professional-update/professional-learning

Ghefaili, A., 2003. Cognitive apprenticeship, technology, and the contextualization of learning environments. *Journal of Educational Computing, Design & Online Learning*, 4(1): 1–27.

Glazzard, J. & M. Green, 2022. *Learning to be a Primary Teacher: Core knowledge and understanding*. Second edition. St Albans: Critical Publishing.

Global Initiative for Inclusive ICTs (G3ict), 2022. Global Report on Assistive Technology (GReAT). Online. https://bit.ly/4g7Sg9j

Globokar, J.L., 2010. *Introduction to Online Learning: A guide for students*, London: Sage.

Hall, G., 2011. Exploring English Language Teaching: Language in action, Abingdon: Taylor & Francis.

Hodkinson, A. & P. Vickerman, 2012. *Key Issues in Special Educational Needs and Inclusion*. London: Sage..

Honey, P. & A. Mumford, 1989. *The Learning Styles Questionnaire*, Maidenhead: Peter Honey.

Hulse, B. & A. Owens, 2019. Process drama as a tool for teaching modern languages: Supporting the development of creativity and innovation in early professional practice. *Innovation in Language Learning and Teaching*, 13(1): 17–30. doi: 10.1080/17501229.2017.1281928.

Hyslop-Margison, E.J. & J. Strobel, 2007. Constructivism and education: Misunderstandings and pedagogical implications. *The Teacher Educator*, 43(1): 72–86.

International Society for Technology in Education (ISTE), 2016. ISTE Standards: Education technology standards to transform learning and teaching. Online. https://iste.org/standards/students#1-2-digital-citizen

Irfani, B., 2017. Syllabus design for English courses. *English Education: Jurnal Tadris Bahasa Inggris*, 6(1): 21–41.

Jackson, F., 2021. Describing coherence of curriculum, pedagogy and assessment. Cambridge University Press and Assessment. International Education Blog. Online. https://bit.ly/3Ch8Oh4

Kamińska, P.M., 2014. *Learning Styles and Second Language Education*. Newcastle upon Tyne: Cambridge Scholars Publishing.

Kavanagh, L., C. Reidsema, J. McCredden, N. Smith, 2017. Design considerations, in C. Reidsema, L. Kavanagh, R. Hadgraft & N. Smith (eds.), *The Flipped Classroom*. Singapore: Springer, 15–35.

Kelly, P., 2018. Organising your classroom for learning, in T. Cremin & C. Burnett (eds.), *Learning to Teach in the Primary School*. Fourth edition. London: Routledge, 162–73.

Kennedy, A., 2011. Collaborative continuing professional development (CPD) for teachers in Scotland: Aspirations, opportunities and barriers. *European Journal of Teacher Education*, 34(1): 25–41.

Kim, Y., 2012. Task complexity, learning opportunities, and Korean EFL learners' question development. *Studies in Second Language Acquisition*, 34(4): 627–58.

Kolb, D.A., 1984. *Experiential learning: Experience as the source of learning and development*. Englewood Cliffs, NJ: Prentice-Hall.

Kormos, J. & A.M. Smith, 2012. *Teaching Languages to Learners with Specific Learning Difficulties*. Clevedon: Multilingual Matters.

Korthagen, F., 2010. Situated learning theory and the pedagogy of teacher education: Towards an integrative view of teacher behavior and teacher learning. *Teaching and Teacher Education*, 26(1): 98–106. doi: 10.1016/j.tate.2009.05.001

Korthagen, F. & Lagerwerf, B., 2001. Teachers' professional learning: How does it work? in F.A.J. Korthagen, J. Kessels, B. Koster, B. Lagerwerf & T. Wubbels (eds.), *Linking Practice and Theory: The pedagogy of realistic teacher education*. Mahwah, NJ: Lawrence Erlbaum Associates, 175–206.

Krashen, S. & T. Terrell, 1988. *The Natural Approach*. Hemel Hempstead: Prentice Hall.

Krashen, S.D., 1985. *The Input Hypothesis: Issues and implications*. Harlow: Longman.

Krashen, S., 1989. We acquire vocabulary and spelling by reading: Additional evidence for the input hypothesis. *The Modern Language Journal*, 73(4): 440–64.

Krumsvik, R.J., 2023. Adaptive learning tools and artificial intelligence in schools – some trends. *Nordic Journal of Digital Literacy*, 18(1): 4–7.

Kukla, A., 2013. *Social Constructivism and the Philosophy of Science*. Abingdon: Routledge.

Kumar, P. & J. Eisenberg, 2023. *Synchronous and Asynchronous Approaches to Teaching Higher Education Lessons in Post-Pandemic Times*. Cham: Springer International Publishing.

Kumaravadivelu, B., 2006. *Understanding Language Teaching: From method to postmethod*. New York: Routledge.

Leung, C. & A. Scarino, 2016. Reconceptualizing the nature of goals and outcomes in language/s education. *The Modern Language Journal*, 100(1): 81–95. https://doi.o rg/10.1111/modl.12300

Lightbown, P. & N. Spada, 2006. *How Languages Are Learned*. Oxford: Oxford University Press.

Long, M., 1991. Focus on form: A design feature in language teaching methodology, in K. de Bot, R. Ginsberg & C. Kramsch (eds.), *Foreign Language Research in Cross-Cultural Perspective*. Amsterdam: John Benjamins, 39–52.

Long, M., 2001. Focus on form: A design feature in language teaching methodology, in C. Candlin & N. Mercer (eds.), *English Language Teaching in Its Social Context: A reader*. Abingdon: Routledge, 180–90.

Long, M., 2014. *Second Language Acquisition and Task-Based Language Teaching*. Hoboken, NJ: John Wiley & Sons.

Long, R. & Y. Hatcho, 2018. The first language's impact on L2: Investigating intralingual and interlingual errors. *English Language Teaching*, 11(11): 115–21.

Lou, N.M. & K.A. Noels, 2016. Changing language mindsets: Implications for goal orientations and responses to failure in and outside the second language classroom. *Contemporary Educational Psychology*, 46: 22–33.

Lynch, M., 2015. Target language use in modern language classrooms: Perception and change among newly qualified teachers in Scotland. PhD thesis. University of Edinburgh.

Lynch, M., 2020. Problematising early career teacher cognition and its impact on pedagogic positioning in the teaching and learning of modern foreign languages in secondary schools. *Pädagogische Horizonte*. 4(2), 1–24. https://peda gogical-horizons.org/index.php/p h/article/view/103/65

Lynch, M. & N. Wang, 2022. Creating effective goals in TBLT for online collaborative English (as a foreign language) writing tasks. *Pädagogische Horizonte*, 6(2): 85–105. https://paedagogische-hori zonte.at/index.php/ph/article/view/ 179

Macaro, E, 2001. Analysing student teachers' codeswitching in foreign language classrooms: Theories and decision making. *The Modern Language Journal*, 85: 531–48.

Macaro, E., 2005. Codeswitching in the L2 classroom: A communication and learning strategy, in E. Llurda (ed.), *Non-Native Language Teachers: Perceptions, challenges and contributions to the profession.* New York: Springer, 63–84.

Mackay, C., 2019. Learning to Plan Modern Languages Lessons: Understanding the basic ingredients. London: Routledge.

Maley, A. & A. Duff, 2005. *Drama Techniques: A resource book of communication activities for language teachers.* Third edition. Cambridge: Cambridge University Press.

Malovrh, P.A. & A.G. Benati, 2018. *The Handbook of Advanced Proficiency in Second Language Acquisition.* Hoboken, NJ: Wiley Blackwell.

Marsh, D., 2002. *CLIL/EMILE – The European Dimension: Actions, trends and foresight.* Potential Public Services Contract DG EAC. Strasbourg: European Commission.

Marsh, D., 2012. *Content and Language Integrated Learning (CLIL): A development trajectory.* Córdoba: Servicio de Publicaciones de la Universidad de Córdoba. https://core.ac.uk/download/pdf/60884824.pdf

Maslow, A.H., 1943. A theory of human motivation. *Psychological Review*, 50(4): 370–96.

Matamoros-González, J.A., M. Asunción Rojas, J. Pizarro Romero, S. Vera-Quiñonez & S.T. Soto, 2017. English language teaching approaches: A comparison of the grammar-translation, audiolingual, communicative, and natural approaches. *Theory and Practice in Language Studies*, 7(11): 965–73. https://core.ac.uk/download/pdf/266995905.pdf

McCarthy, M. & R. Carter, 1994. *Language as Discourse: Perspectives for language teaching.* Cambridge: Cambridge University Press.

McCluskey, G., G. Lloyd, J. Kane, S. Riddell, J. Stead & E. Weedon, 2008. Can restorative practices in schools make a difference? *Educational Review*, 60(4): 405–17.

Meiring, L. & N. Norman, 2002. Back on target: Repositioning the status of target language in MFL teaching and learning. *The Language Learning Journal*, 26(1): 27–35.

Mickan, P., 2012. *Language Curriculum Design and Socialisation.* Bristol: Multilingual Matters.

Mignolo, W.D. & C.E. Walsh, 2018. *On Decoloniality: Concepts, analytics, praxis.* Durham, NC: Duke University Press.

Modern Language Journal. Online. https://onlinelibrary.wiley.com/journal/15404781

Modern Language Review. Online. www.mhra.org.uk/journals/MLR

Modern Language Association of America (MLA). Online. www.mla.org

Moore, A., 2001. *Teaching and Learning: Pedagogy, curriculum, and culture.* Abingdon: Routledge.

Murray, J., 2024. *100 Ideas for Primary Teachers: Wellbeing.* London: Bloomsbury.

Nation, I.S.P., 2009. *Teaching ESL/EFL Reading and Writing.* New York: Routledge.

Natsir, M. & D. Sanjaya, 2014. Grammar translation method (GTM) versus communicative language teaching (CLT): A review of literature. *International Journal of Education and Literacy Studies*, 2(1): 58–62.

Neil, P., 1997. *Reflections on the Target Language.* London: CILT.

Ng, C.H., 2020. Communicative language teaching (CLT) through synchronous online teaching in English language preservice teacher education. *International Journal of TESOL Studies*, 2(2): 62–73.

Nijakowska, J., 2008. An experiment with direct multisensory instruction in teaching word reading and spelling to Polish dyslexic learners of English, in J. Kormos & E.H. Kontra (eds.), *Language Learners with Special Needs: An international perspective.* Bristol: Multilingual Matters, 130–57.

Nijakowska, J., 2010. *Dyslexia in the Foreign Language Classroom.* Bristol: Multilingual Matters.

Norton, B. & C. McKinney, 2011. An identity approach to second language acquisition, in D. Atkinson (ed.), *Alternative Approaches to Second Language Acquisition.* Abingdon: Routledge, 73–94.

Norton, B. & K. Toohey, 2011. Identity, language learning, and social change. *Language Teaching,* 44(4): 412–46.

NSPCC Learning, 2024. Online safety and schools. Online. https://learning .nspcc.org.uk/online-safety/online-s afety-for-schools

Nunan, D., 2004. *Task-Based Language Teaching.* Cambridge: Cambridge University Press.

Omaggio, A.C., 1990. *Teaching Language in Context: Proficiency oriented instruction.* Fourth edition. New York: McGraw-Hill.

Ortega, L., 2011. SLA after the social turn, in D. Atkinson (ed.), *Alternative Approaches to Second Language Acquisition.* Abingdon: Routledge, 167–80.

Pachler, N. & K. Field, 2001. *Learning to Teach Modern Foreign Languages in the Secondary School.* London: RoutledgeFalmer.

Piaget, J., 1928. *Judgment and Reasoning in the Child.* London: Routledge & Kegan Paul.

Place2Be. Online. https://bit.ly/3EeELaI

Playing Beyond CLIL, no date. eLearning Platform. Online. www.playing beyondclil.eu

Playing CLIL, 2015. Playing CLIL ebook. Content and Language Integrated Learning inspired by drama pedagogy. Online. www.playingclil .eu/this-is-the-playingclil-ebook

Rahimpour, M., 2010. Current trends on syllabus design in foreign language instruction. *Procedia-Social and Behavioral Sciences*, 2(2): 1660–4.

Reinhardt, J., 2019. *Gameful Second and Foreign Language Teaching and Learning: Theory, research, and practice.* Cham: Springer International Publishing.

Research in Primary Languages. 2020. Online. https://ripl.uk

Rhodes, I. & M. Long, 2019. *Improving Behaviour in Schools: Guidance report.* London: Education Endowment Foundation. https://bit .ly/4gweiDL

Richards, J.C. & M. Pennington, 1998. The first year of teaching, in J.C. Richards (ed.), *Beyond Training.* Cambridge: Cambridge University Press, 173–90.

Richards, J.C. & T.S. Rodgers, 2001. *Approaches and Methods in*

Language Teaching. Cambridge: Cambridge University Press.

Robinson, P. & P.J. Robinson, 2001. *Cognition and Second Language Instruction*. Cambridge: Cambridge University Press.

Salcedo, C.S., 2010. The effects of songs in the foreign language classroom on text recall, delayed text recall and involuntary mental rehearsal. *Journal of College Teaching and Learning*, 7(6): 19–30.

Schmidt, R., 2001. Attention, in P. Robinson (ed.), *Cognition and Second Language Instruction*. Cambridge: Cambridge University Press, 3–32.

Schön, D.A., 2017. *The Reflective Practitioner: How professionals think in action*. Abingdon: Taylor & Francis.

Scottish Sensory Centre, 2023. Language and accessibility issues in curriculum and assessment plus workshops in art & design, modern languages, environmental studies. Online. www.ssc.education.ed.ac.uk/courses/deaf/dnov05c.html

Sharwood Smith, M., 1986. Comprehension versus acquisition: Two ways of processing input. *Applied Linguistics*, 7: 239–56.

Short, R., G. Case & K. McKenzie, 2018. The long-term impact of a whole school approach of restorative practice: The views of secondary school teachers. *Pastoral Care in Education*, 36(4): 313–24.

Sinor, J. & M. Kaplan, 2012. Creating your syllabus, in *GSI Guidebook*. Ann Arbor, MI: Center for Research on Learning and Teaching, University of Michigan. Online. https://bit.ly/40byViz

Skinner, B.F., 1957. *Verbal Behavior*. New York: Appleton-Century-Crofts.

Son, J.-B., 2018. *Teacher Development in Technology-Enhanced Language Teaching*. Cham: Springer International Publishing.

Sun, Y.A., 2008. Input processing in second language acquisition: A discussion of four input processing models: Working papers, *TESOL and Applied Linguistics*, 8(1): 1–10.

Swann, M., A. Peacock, S. Hart & M. J. Drummond, 2012. *Creating Learning without Limits*. Maidenhead: Open University Press and McGraw-Hill Education.

Taber, K.S., 2019. Constructivism in education: Interpretations and criticisms from science education, in Information Resources Management Association (ed.), *Early Childhood Development: Concepts, methodologies, tools, and applications*. Hershey, PA: IGI Global, 312–42.

Teoh, L.J., A.L. Solebo & J.S. Rahi, 2021. Visual impairment, severe visual impairment, and blindness in children in Britain (BCVIS2): A national observational study. *The Lancet Child & Adolescent Health*, 5(3): 190–200. doi:10.1016/S2352-4642(20)30366-7.

Thornbury, S., 2012. Speaking instruction, in A. Burns & J. C. Richards (eds.), *The Cambridge Guide to Pedagogy and Practice in Second Language Teaching*. New York: Cambridge University Press, 198–206.

Tomlinson, C.A., 2014. *The Differentiated Classroom: Responding to the needs of all learners.* Alexandria, VA: Association for Supervision & Curriculum Development.

Topping, K.J., 2009. Peer assessment. *Theory into Practice*, 48(1): 20–7.

UNESCO, 1994. The Salamanca Statement and Framework for Action on Special Needs Education. Adopted by the world conference on Special Needs Education: Access and Quality. Salamanca, Spain, 7–10 June. Online. https://unesdoc.unesco.org/ark:/48223/pf0000093427

UNESCO, 2018a. ICT Competency Framework for Teachers. Online. https://unesdoc.unesco.org/ark:/48223/pf0000265721.locale=en https://www.unesco.org/en/digital-competencies-skills/ict-cft

UNESCO, 2018b. A Global Framework of Reference on Digital Literacy Skills for Indicator 4.4.2. Online. https://bit.ly/41RBM1l

UNESCO, 2024. What you need to know about education for sustainable development. Online. www.unesco.org/en/sustainable-development/education/need-know

United Nations, 2006. Convention on the Rights of Persons with Disabilities. Adopted by the United Nations General Assembly, 13 December. Online. https://bit.ly/4gz24dn

van Vijfeijken, M., T. van Schilt-Mol, R.H. J. Scholte, E. Denessen, 2023. A quantitative study of teachers' beliefs and practices regarding fair classroom differentiation. *SN Social Sciences*, 3: 13.

von Glasersfeld, E., 1984. An introduction to radical constructivism, in

P. Watzlawick (ed.), *The Invented Reality.* New York: Norton, 17–40.

Vygotsky, L.S., 1978. *Mind in Society: Development of higher psychological processes.* Edited by M. Cole, V. John-Steiner, S. Scribner & E. Souberman. Cambridge, MA: Harvard University Press.

Wang, D., 2024. Translanguaging as a decolonising approach: Students' perspectives towards integrating indigenous epistemology in language teaching. *Applied Linguistics Review*, 15(4): 1385–406.

Wankel, C. & P. Blessinger, 2013. *Increasing Student Engagement and Retention in e-Learning Environments: Web 2.0 and blended learning technologies.* Bradford: Emerald Group Publishing Limited.

Watzke, J., 2007. Foreign language pedagogical knowledge: Toward a develop-mental theory of beginning teacher practices. *The Modern Language Journal*, 91(1): 63–82.

Wiliam, D., 2018. *Embedded Formative Assessment.* Second edition. Bloomington, IN: Solution Tree Press.

Wiliam, D. & M. Thompson, 2008. Integrating assessment with learning: What will it take to make it work? in C.A. Dwyer (ed.), *The Future of Assessment: Shaping teaching and learning*, New York: Routledge, 53–82

Willis, D. & J. Willis, 2007. *Doing Task-Based Teaching.* Oxford: Oxford University Press.

Willis, J., 1996. A flexible framework for task-based learning. *Challenge and Change in Language Teaching*, 52: 62.

Willy's ELT Corner, 2021. Engaging speaking activities for L2 learners.

Online. https://willyrenandya.com/engaging-speaking-activities-for-l2-learners

Woodrow, L., 2006. Anxiety and speaking English as a second language. *RELC journal*, 37(3): 308–28.

World Wide Web Consortium, 2025. Web Accessibility Initiative (WAI). Online. www.w3.org/WAI

Wray, D. & M. Lewis, 1997. Teaching factual writing: Purpose and structure. *The Australian Journal of Language and Literacy*, 20(2): 131–39.

Yana, D., 2016. A needs analysis for English speaking syllabus development. *ANGLO-SAXON: Jurnal Ilmiah Program Studi Pendidikan Bahasa Inggris*, 7(2): 122–30.

Zeichner, K.M. & D.P. Liston, 2013. *Reflective Teaching: An introduction.* Second edition. Hoboken, NJ: Taylor & Francis.

Zhao, A.H.Q. & C. Morgan, 2004. Consideration of age in L2 attainment – children, adolescents and adults. *The Asian EFL Journal*, 6(4). Online. www.asian-efl-journal.com/Dec_04_ahqz.pdf

Index

Additional Support Needs (ASN), 125
analytical and synthetic phonics, 49
application of L1 reading strategies to developing reading skills in L2, 51
approaches to the learning and teaching of foreign languages, 11
approaches to the learning and teaching of L2 that promote communication, 71
artificial intelligence (AI), 159
assessment *as* learning, 146
assessment *for* learning, 146
assessment in the modern foreign languages class, 135
assessment *of* learning, 146
assessment, choosing between summative and formative, 136
assistive technology, advice for OS types, 134
asynchronous learning and teaching, 165
asynchronous teaching, advice, 169
audio-lingual and audiovisual methods, 12
audio-lingualism, 12

behaviour management, 195
a restorative approach, 199
behaviourism, 60
blended learning, 165
building on prior knowledge, 97
building up reading proficiency, 51

carousel group work, benefits of, 193
classroom organisation and management, 190
code-switching, 29

cognitive apprenticeship, 61
cognitivism and other socially oriented approaches to second language acquisition, 19
collaborative networks and opportunities for networking, 209
collaborative networks
international, 210
local, 209
national, 210
collaborative working, 202
Common European Framework of Reference for Languages (CEFR), 19
communicative approach, 12, 25
Communicative Language Teaching (CLT), 12, 56
comparison of two different approaches to the teaching of grammar, 24
connection between learning and assessment, 136
constructivism, 60
Content and Language Integrated Learning (CLIL), 17
creating blogs and wikis, 154

decolonial approach to teaching, 20
developing a unit of work, 79
developing listening skills, 39
developing metacognitive strategies in assessment, 147
developing reading skills, 47
in l2, 37
in listening and viewing, 37
in reading, 37
in speaking, 38
in writing, 39
developing speaking skills, 42
developing writing skills, 45
development of reading strategies in L1, 49

differentiation
by length, presentation and density of text, 120
by outcome, 121
by questioning, 122
by support, 120
by task, 121
strategies, 119
digital literacy, 152
appropriateness of content, 157
developing knowledge and skills, 160
issues for modern foreign languages teachers, 156
respecting owners' rights, 157
what is useful and how and when to use it, 161
disruption, causes of, 196
prevention of, 197
what to do when it occurs, 198
drama as a tool in L2 learning and teaching, 178
drama techniques for the L2 classroom, 179
drama, music and games, 177
drama, use in L2 learning, 178
dyscalculia, 126
dyslexia, 126

emotional issues, 129
evaluating blogs and wikis, 155
evaluative feedback and support, 106
explaining approach, 11

factors that help develop reading skills, 51
features and use of formative assessment strategies, 140
features and use of summative assessment strategies, 139
feedforward, 7, 106
focus on form, 12
'formative assessment,' during individual lessons, 142
during unit of work, 140

'formative assessment' (cont.)
  techniques for the languages
    classroom, xvi, 142

games and activities for the L2
    classroom, 183
games in class, issues to
    consider, 185
games, in L2 learning and
    teaching, 182
  why they are useful in L2
    learning, 183
giving feedback on learning,
    148
Grammar–Translation
    Approach, 11

hearing impairment, 128
hearing, digital tools, 131
how to plan your lesson, 100
hybrid learning and teaching,
    165

inclusive approach, additional
    support needs, 130
inclusiveness, 158
information and
    communications
    technology and digital
    tools to support learners
    with additional support
    needs, 130

language acquisition, xvi, 13,
    14, 16, 17
layered literacy, 162
learning intentions, 97
learning styles, 123
lesson planning, 96
linguistic competence, 22
long-term planning, 77

management of activities, 192
materials, 104
mental health, digital tools,
    131
mobility issues, 128
mobility, digital tools, 131
models of remote delivery,
    164
modes of teaching, 61, 67
multi-skill and multi-task
    activities, 56
'music and song,' as aid to L2
    learning, 181

in L2 learning and teaching,
    181

needs analysis, 80
neurodiversity, 127
  digital tools, 131

online sites and digital tools,
    124
overarching teacher skills for
    effective differentiation,
    132
overuse of a mode of teaching,
    65

peer-assessment strategies,
    145
phonemic awareness, 51
phonological awareness, 51
planning checklist for writing
    draft lesson plans, xvi,
    110
planning for mixed ability and
    mixed needs, 98
pluriliteracies approach to
    teaching for learning, 18
Post-Method Condition, 20
pragmatic competence, 22
Presentation, Practice,
    Production (PPP), 23
professional development, 203
  portfolio, 7
  maintaining knowledge and
    skills, 203
professional learning, example
    of a planning and review
    sheet, xvii, 206
  examples of, 207
  keeping abreast of current
    research, 206
  keeping abreast of
    curriculum developments,
    207
progression and coherence in
    planning, 91
promoting self-esteem, 96
pupil code-switching, 30
purposes of learning foreign
    languages, 21

reading schemes, 51
record keeping, 149
remote learning, teaching and
    assessment, 163
  advice, 167

points to note, 172
practical considerations,
    172
Resource-Based Learning, 71

safety online, 155
self-assessment strategies,
    144
short-term planning, 87
social constructivism, 60
sociolinguistic competence, 22
sound–symbol relationship, 48
sources of evaluation, 108
success criteria, 98
supporting learning, 97
synchronous and
    asynchronous modes of
    learning and teaching,
    choosing between, 171
synchronous learning and
    teaching, 164
synchronous teaching, advice,
    167

Target Language (TL), 22
Task-Based Language
    Teaching (TBLT), 17, 35,
    56, 59, 71
TBLT framework, 72
teacher code-switching, 30
teacher cognition, 21, 34, 35
teacher well-being, 212
  factors that contribute to
    poor self-efficacy, 212
  building emotional
    resilience, 213
  how and where to find
    support, 214
teaching file, 7
teaching grammar, 32
translanguaging, 30
transliteracy, 162
types of online sources, 153
types of task, 72

Universal Design for Learning
    (UDL), 158

Virtual Learning
    Environments (VLEs), 166
vision, digital tools, 131
visual impairment, 127

working collaboratively with
    colleagues, 195

For EU product safety concerns, contact us at Calle de José Abascal, 56–1°, 28003 Madrid, Spain or eugpsr@cambridge.org.

www.ingramcontent.com/pod-product-compliance
Ingram Content Group UK Ltd.
Pitfield, Milton Keynes, MK11 3LW, UK
UKHW052126280426
470499UK00019B/504

9 781009 385169